A STUDY IN ETHICAL THEORY

A STUDY IN
ETHICAL THEORY

BY

D. M. MACKINNON

REGIUS PROFESSOR OF MORAL PHILOSOPHY
UNIVERSITY OF ABERDEEN

ADAM & CHARLES BLACK
LONDON

FIRST PUBLISHED 1957

A. AND C. BLACK LIMITED
4, 5 AND 6 SOHO SQUARE LONDON W.1

PRINTED IN GREAT BRITAIN
BY ROBERT MACLEHOSE AND CO. LTD
THE UNIVERSITY PRESS, GLASGOW

PREFACE

THIS book is sadly inconclusive. It is a study in ethical theory as its title suggests; it is not an 'ethics', but an attempt to study different styles of argument concerning the foundations of morality, by methods sometimes analytic and sometimes historical. It is informed by a desire to bring out some of the ways in which the problem (or problems) of the possibility of metaphysics impinges on moral reflection, the way we think we should live, choose, act. This impact is a much more complex and awkward thing than is sometimes allowed, and it is reciprocal. If the book has any value, it may be in the way it enables readers to see in a different context, and from an altered perspective, much with which they will be already familiar in books of greater scholarship and analytic power.

My debts are many and various: to my teachers, especially the late H. W. B. Joseph, and to Mr. Isaiah Berlin; to Prof. H. H. Price; to my colleagues here, and especially to Dr. R. W. Hepburn and (in the sections bearing on Kant's *Religions-philosophie*) Professor David Cairns; and to many others, like Professor and Mrs. R. B. Braithwaite to whom I owe some of the things that seem to me most important in the discussion of the utilitarians, even though they may very properly reject my own interpretation of what certainly came to my mind as a result of conversation with them in Cambridge.

Where Hegel is concerned, I am greatly in the debt of such French scholars as MM. Jean Wohl and Jean Hyppolite, from whose writings I have learnt a great deal. I have further been encouraged to treat Hegel boldly by things said to me by Principal T. M. Knox of St. Andrews; I hope he will not think me too bold!

But the extent of my indebtedness is too large to be

recorded here. My greatest and principal debt of thanks is, of course, due to my wife, without whose encouragement, persistent and devoted, the book would never have been begun, or, when begun, completed. To her alone therefore it is properly dedicated as a most imperfect token of gratitude and love.

OLD ABERDEEN   D. M. M.

CONTENTS

CHAPTER   PAGE

I. INTRODUCTION   1

II. UTILITARIANISM   22

    A. UNSOPHISTICATED UTILITARIANISM; B. THE APPROACH TO THOROUGH-GOING UTILITARIANISM; C. THE STRESSES AND STRAINS OF THOROUGH-GOING UTILITARIANISM; D. UTILITARIANISM AS AN 'ERFOLGSETHIK'; E. UTILITARIANISM AND METAPHYSICS

III. KANT   61

    A. INTRODUCTORY; B. KANT'S ETHICS AND HIS THEORY OF KNOWLEDGE; C. THE RATIONALISM OF KANT'S ETHICS; D. KANT'S CONTRIBUTION TO THE ENLIGHTENMENT OF WORKADAY, PRACTICAL PERPLEXITY; E. KANT ON THE RELATIONS OF ETHICAL TO NON-ETHICAL DISCOURSE; F. CONCLUSIONS

IV. THE NOTION OF MORAL FREEDOM   121

V. BUTLER   174

    A. BUTLER'S EMPIRICISM: INTRODUCTORY; B. BUTLER AND PRACTICAL PERPLEXITY; C. BUTLER AND THEORETICAL PERPLEXITY; D. THE RÔLE OF GOD IN BUTLER'S ETHICS; E. CONCLUSIONS

VI. ETHICS AND POLITICS   203

VII. ETHICS, METAPHYSICS AND RELIGION   233

    A. INTRODUCTORY; B. GRACE AND FREEDOM; C. MORAL DISCOVERY; D. CONCLUSION

INDEX OF NAMES   278

A STUDY IN ETHICAL THEORY

CHAPTER I

INTRODUCTION

1. It is often said of one of the greatest of living British philosophers that, when asked what the subject of philosophy was, he could do no more than point to the books on the shelves of his library and answer, 'What these books are about.' He could do no more than point to the volumes and suggest that an answer might be found by reading them. The negative implication of his reply is clear: there was, on his view, no essence of philosophy which could be distilled from the contents of the volumes and presented as the substance of the subject, no hard core discernible after differing containing shells had been stripped away.

Yet are we to infer from this that philosophical works are bracketed together as τύχη ὁμώνυμα, things which just happen to have the same name, like rackets on the tennis-lawn and in the under-world, or bulls from the Vatican and in the farmer's field? Surely not; if there is no extractible specific or generic essence of philosophy, yet still there is a kind of union between works properly called philosophic. If the notion of philosophy is one with shifting, even radically changing, boundaries, yet still we can distinguish between what is and what is not philosophical. Even if in the 17th century philosophy was often confused with physics, and in the 18th century with psychology, there is a continuity between what was then so confused and what to-day is sharply and clearly identified as the study of the logic of our language, or the plotting of the logical geography of our concepts.

If we confine ourselves to moral philosophy, the differences and the unity are even clearer. That Plato and Aristotle,

Price and Hume, Kant and Bentham, Green and Moore, Prichard and Lowes Dickinson, Scheler and Nowell-Smith have written works which are properly studied in moral philosophy departments in Scottish universities is beyond question. That they thought they were doing the same thing is, however, very far from clear; indeed we might say that we know that some of them were not, and also that they themselves knew they were not.

Thus the late Professor H. A. Prichard argued most forcibly that much of the work moral philosophers had done before 1912 was based on a profound mistake: viz., on the supposition that some difference might, or should properly, be made to our conviction that we ought to do a given action by learning that it was, or was not, to our advantage, or to that of the society to which we belonged. Such very different moralists as Plato and Butler, John Stuart Mill and Mr. H. W. B. Joseph have all, Prichard thought, argued as if our conviction that a particular course of action was our duty were, or should properly be, bound up with our conviction that its performance, either directly or by way of result, promoted the welfare of the society of which we were members, however differently that welfare might be conceived. Some of his own most important work in the field of ethics was devoted to laying bare the pervasiveness and the gravity (in his view) of this mistake; it was also and at the same time concerned to insist that in so doing he was being loyal, in a peculiarly exact way, to the moral convictions of the ordinary man, or to the deliverances of our ordinary moral consciousness.

The careful student of Prichard's article in *Mind* for 1912 on 'Does moral philosophy rest on a mistake?' or of his inaugural lecture on 'Duty and Interest', cannot resist the impression that he is deliberately, almost self-consciously, conservative, and that he is moved by this anxiety to protect the moral convictions of the ordinary man, to the bracketing together of work in moral philosophy that is of very different inspiration. Thus few could seriously suppose that Jeremy Bentham and Bishop Butler were actually saying the same thing; or that—a slightly more sensible thesis, but still one that is very far from serious plausibility—the most important thing about these moralists is found in certain sentences where a near-fortuitous coincidence of expression creates the impression of some underlying agreement in sentiment. Yet the readers of Prichard's work, and still more those who were privileged to follow the minute and subtle argument of his lectures, were left with the impression that, where moralists as different as Bentham and Moore, Butler and Green, Joseph and Laird, were concerned, the most important thing to be grasped was that all of them had sometimes let fall sentences which suggested that they had some sort of sympathy, however peripheral to their central concern, with the thesis that actions were only morally binding upon us in so far as they tended to promote human welfare on the whole. If, for instance, in the concluding paragraph of his inaugural lecture, Prichard avowed a certain admiration for Kant's ethical writings as 'having the root of the matter in them', it was because Kant was, in his judgment, free from this error.

Whether Prichard understood those whom he was criticising is, of course, a very genuine question. Few would deny that in some very obvious senses of the word 'understand' he did not. Thus emphatically he did not allow himself to be affected by any thought of the sort of questions that Bentham, for instance, was trying to answer or that beset Mill more sharply than ever when he found that, after all, 'poetry was not misrepresentation.' The whole argument was one that passed him by; the Benthamite radicalism, and the reaction against it which Mill certainly experienced, were outside his perception. Yet can we deny that in other senses Prichard did understand what he was discussing? Or, at least, must we not admit that our grasp of utilitarianism is enlarged by the study of Prichard's massive and sustained crusade against it? To speak of so rigorous and exact a thinker as a crusader may raise a smile; he was not a preacher as T. H. Green or Henry Jones were. Yet his readiness to classify as utilitarian the most diverse styles of argument in ethics sometimes reached the point of an obsession, and the use of the evocative word 'crusade' to refer to it had at least some justification.

Prichard wrote as a moral philosopher about what moral philosophers before him had done and said that much, even most, of what they had done was mistaken. He was not at his best as an historian of philosophy; to that weakness his lectures on the history of the theory of knowledge and his book on Kant bear witness, for all their great acuteness and interest; for him, where moral philosophy was concerned, the issue was not what a moralist was trying to say, or what questions he was trying to answer, but whether what he said was true in the sense of agreeing with what we *knew* to be the case. So over against our clear conviction that what we knew to be our duty we knew to be binding on us, irrespective of what might be its consequence in terms of measurable benefit to ourselves or our society, he set various positions which seemed to him to obscure this central, luminously evident conviction. So set together, these positions seemed to merge one into the other; and, for instance, Joseph's sense that our actions must somehow contribute to the actualisation of a form of common life regarded as self-justifyingly good, and Moore's insistence that, if they are to be our duty, they must promote the existence of states of affairs in themselves intrinsically excellent—both these positions alike seemed perilously akin to Bentham's demand that rights and duties be measured and judged by the single humanly acceptable standard of the greatest happiness principle.

Of course one could answer Prichard that that was not what either Joseph or Moore were saying; one could describe the precise structure and the nuances of the doctrines of these two moralists, showing how deeply they differed one from another as well as both from the philosophical radicals. Yet did, or did not, the fact that to so penetrating a mind as that of Prichard they betrayed these similarities reveal anything about the doctrines in question?

Further, Bentham and Mill themselves were men who profoundly affected the social and political life of these islands; indeed their work belongs to the history of our culture as well as to that of philosophy in the narrower sense. Their teachings were criticised not only by Green and Bradley, but also by Matthew Arnold and, by implication, by Charles Dickens. Moore also, through his influence on Keynes and on the 'Bloomsbury circle', played a rôle in British life that was not simply that of a 'philosopher's philosopher'. When Prichard, however, came to grips with their several doctrines, he worked on them as if they could be examined sufficiently and criticised decisively by methods which deliberately averted from their wider ramifications. His criticism, whether of Mill or of Moore or of Joseph, comes very near to being simply a continued accusation of the logical confusion of distinguishable concepts. Duty, for example, is not the promotion of interest; it is not necessarily connected therewith. The charge he would bring against those who argued otherwise was one of a violation of evident conceptual frontiers. If we make the effort, we can rid our minds of the sort of confusion that inevitably follows any blurring of the clearly definable frontiers of what we know things to be. They are what they are; and we know that they are.

Yet for all his realism, for all his insistence that knowing makes no difference to what we know, and that we do know, and know that we know, that duty is duty and interest interest, Prichard does, by the very rigour of his analysis, somehow reshape the material with which he is dealing. One can put this very simply and untechnically by saying that no one, after reading Prichard or listening to him, can see in quite the same way again the problems raised by the utilitarian attempt to make duty depend on interest; again, after reckoning with what he has written and said, one can never be quite at ease in the presence of the suggestion that, after all, a teleological ethic need not have the slightest truck with utilitarianism. He has got round under our defences, opened our eyes to neglected facets of the reality, deepened our sense of the vortices in the language wherewith, and whereby, we carry on so much of our business of living together, which may at any moment suck us down or twist us round. Moreover he has done this by an exaggeration of similarity between very different views, carried through with the sort of minuteness which we are inclined, and rightly perhaps inclined, to write off as purely academic.

It is impossible to distil the essence of moral philosophy, to extract the core from the different shells, but it is possible to point to conversations, even to conversations where a man casually overhearing what was said might say that one of the participants did not know, and would not learn, his fellow's language; or where that participant at least showed by his behaviour that, if he took part at all, he would refuse, as a price of his participation, to talk idiomatically, or to copy his fellow's accent. Yet even when the delicate nuances of individual attitudes and positions in respect of the end and sense of human conduct are forced to conform to the iron laws of Prichard's dichotomies, something emerges, something is said. And something by implication is shown about moral philosophy; that it may start in all sorts of places, have its origin in various impulses, but that sooner or later its practitioner is involved in various sorts of conversation, sorts of conversation which have their logics which it is also the business of the moral philosopher to map. Thus with Prichard it may start with resolving to say something about the fundamental mistake committed by those who try to ground obligation in interest, and it may end by bringing out in a way at once exaggerated and illuminating how pervasive a thing this impulse has been and is, how present in different forms, in different disguises, in very different traditions. The obstinate refusal to 'understand' is the occasion of a contribu-

tion to 'understanding'; for he also helps to 'understand' who
rejects 'understanding' where *tout comprendre semble tout par-
donner, et rien ici n'est pardonnable*.

Conversation: the word has many associations in philosophy. There are the Socratic dialogues, the dialectic of
Plato, of Hegel, of Marx, of Kierkegaard; there is Wittgenstein's dictum that a language is a way of life, Wisdom's that
philosophy is talk about talk. Now at the outset of this
enquiry into the scope of moral philosophy the suggestion
has been put forward that sooner or later the moral philosopher finds himself involved in various sorts of conversation,
at once involved in them and compelled to be self-conscious
about them, at once talking and talking about his talk. Thus
Prichard, we say, makes his contribution; and this he does in
two ways, at two levels, when he argues against the utilitarian grounding of duty in interest. This, he says, is not
ontologically true; this is not where, in the moral universe,
duty belongs. To continue the metaphor, the territory of
duty is not part of the realm of interest; or, to change it, the
pressure of our obligations upon us is not a singular, privileged pressure of our common interest. There is a fundamental independence of 'ought' from 'is', of 'obligation'
from 'inclination'. Here Prichard is describing what is
deeply wrong with the utilitarian picture of the moral
universe; he writes as someone engaged in a work of protest.
Here his contribution is one that can be taken up and made
their own by men who are trying in concrete to answer the
question how they shall live their daily lives. The overtones
and the undertones of his argument can be caught and taken
up by men who are deeply and simply puzzled by the suggestion that, after all, 'it is only, ultimately, really a matter of
interest'; they respond to Prichard's powerful plea that it is
not, that 'things are what they are, and not otherwise', that
just as numbers are not really and ultimately classes of
classes, nor tables groups of sense-data and the possibility of
more, so duties are not really ultimately long but sure roads

to the welfare of all. Thus at this level of ordinary engagement in the business of living the academic breaks in on the conversation; and when men get used to his idiom and accent, he may speak to their condition.

But Prichard also joins the conversation at another level, or perhaps rather he joins in another conversation, in which perhaps as a philosopher he is more immediately at home. Men argue about what they should do, or refrain from doing; and sometimes philosophers speak and write in ways that bear upon their arguments. But the philosopher is impelled by the nature of his pursuit to move to the level at which men do not simply talk, but talk about talk; to the level, in fact, at which self-consciousness about underlying assumptions is allowed, and indeed encouraged, to obtrude itself. The philosopher can never simply argue about a course of action, or allow himself to write as if his function were to exhort, to counsel or to warn; he has always somehow to explain why he judges one method of argument permissible, or some conclusion inescapable. Or if he fails to do so, he has to advertise that failure in such a way that it arrests attention to itself for the crucial thing it is. (This last is perhaps what Mill does when he introduces 'qualitative distinctions into the hedonistic calculus', to use the language of the text-book, and by so doing violates the canons of argument he has professed. He does not try to justify himself; but he so advertises the break in his logic that the reflective reader is compelled to see that here indeed is the central problem which Mill's pamphlet raises and that it is in the end a problem concerning methods of proof and argument. In Mill's own words it can be called the problem of the reconciliation of the intuitive and inductive methods in ethics. These methods Mill suggests at the beginning of the *Utilitarianism* as incompatible procedures; yet when he tries to describe the way men argue concerning what is valuable, he represents them as using both at the same time, and seems to find it the most natural thing in the world!)

Prichard does in his scattered writings explain why he thinks that his is the right, indeed the only, way to break in on the conversations men have with themselves and with one another about what they shall do. Sometimes his name for what he is doing is 'defending the moral convictions of the ordinary man'; sometimes he more briefly describes it as 'asserting what we know to be the case'. It is clear to the careful student of his work that he objects not simply to utilitarian morality, but to something which can perhaps be described metaphorically as the utilitarian way of mapping the ethical region; he continually seems to accuse his opponent of violating some sort of self-evident system of categorial order.

2. To some any discussion of the unity of moral philosophy will seem artificial and otiose; for to discuss such a question can easily waste time that should be spent on actual philosophical work, and be in itself a vague and sterile exercise. Yet some discussion of the matter is inevitable; for those who practise moral philosophy are engaged in a task which occupies them simultaneously at two levels. Moral philosophers, whether this be their intention or not, do clarify or obscure, or at least somehow speak to or fail to speak to, the needs of those in perplexity, of those trying to decide a moral question—say, the salvaging of their marriage, the bringing up of their children, their attitude to the claims upon them of a religious or political authority; at the same time moral philosophers must be, to some extent at least, self-conscious in respect of the principles on which they are saying what they say or are prepared to defend it as valid. As we have seen, this is true of so rigorously academic, so minute a moral philosopher as Prichard, true therefore of one who was condemned in an unforgettable, if unfair, passage in Collingwood's *Autobiography* as opening the floodgates of irrationalism by his resolute refusal to do more for his pupils than compel them to attend to a number of minute, precisely defined problems, requiring discussion that was exhaustive and

B

detailed, yet often frustrating in its barrenness of result. If what Prichard said on the subject of moral obligation and its grounds is true, if, as a matter of fact, our duties do form a group of self-evident claims in which no one is after or before another, then this is something which must be of the highest practical importance to someone inclined, for one reason or another, to bestow a peculiar authority on the claim to promote simply the welfare of his fellows at large.

To say this is not to say that all moral philosophers are to some extent preachers; the differences between Butler, who was a preacher, and Prichard, who was not, are very important. Still less is it to imply that all moral philosophers are to some extent casuists. The rôles of the moral philosopher and the casuist overlap; but they are distinct. Yet it remains true that moral philosophers are not, simply in virtue of their being academic moralists, detached from speaking in ways that affect what people are actually thinking and saying as they deliberate on what they shall do and make up their minds on the problems of conduct.

But at the same time the moral philosopher is incorrigibly preoccupied with what may be called metaphysical problems, or, in more modern jargon, with problems of meta-ethics, with the question where ethical language belongs on the language-map and indeed with the ways in which the various parts of that language are themselves related. Hitherto we have considered Prichard's views on the relation of duty and inclination; but he also held very clearly defined views on the closely related, but separable, problem of the relation of duty and goodness. Certainly the thorough-going utilitarian found the ground of duty in the promotion of welfare; but others less thorough-going, like Professor G. E. Moore, were not prepared to identify goodness and welfare, but were emphatic in insisting that duty and obligation were logically subordinate to goodness and excellence. The nature of this logical subordination was controversial and obscure; it was some-times claimed that duty and obligation could be defined with-

out remainder in terms of a tendency to promote good; but
at other times it was only asserted that the sole ground of an
action's being a duty resided in such a tendency, and that
there was a 'synthetic necessary' connection between an
action's being a duty and its having such a tendency. The
two characters were not identical, nor did the one contain
the other in the sense in which perhaps one could speak of
the character of being a bicycle as containing that of having
two wheels in tandem. Rather they were thought to be related as being coloured is to being extended, whether as the
surface of an object or as a film is extended. Colour is impossible without extension of some sort; so being a duty is
impossible without having the tendency of promoting good.
The peculiar sort of impossibility involved is that which is
referred to by the phrase 'synthetic necessity'.

Now this problem of the relation of duty and good is in
some sense a meta-ethical, even a metaphysical, problem.
That is obvious from the fact that it is hard to get any way of
stating it which does not involve a highly technical and dis-
putable notion of philosophical logic, like that of 'synthetic
necessity'. No one certainly can advance very far in philosophy without being compelled to ask whether or not there
are necessary connections which are not analytic, which are
not, that is, of the sort which obtain between being a bicycle
and having two wheels in tandem. The man who is seriously
concerned with the question whether or not to embark on an
affair with a married woman, or even to join the Communist party, may never have heard of this logical notion.
Yet the sort of question which Moore is discussing, or questions so closely akin to it as to be practically indistinguishable
from it, may and do belong to fields surely and intimately
touching life as we live it.

The fact that the point made by a moral philosopher
sometimes requires a complex professional jargon to bring it
out does not make that point of practical insignificance.
There is a delicate overlap between contributing to the

debate of the practically involved and setting out the logical order of the categories of the moral universe.

For instance, on pp. 135/142 of his work *The Meaning of Good: a Dialogue*, G. Lowes Dickinson discusses the view that good consists in ethical activity, the latter being very nearly equated with the doing of duty for duty's sake. He decides that the two cannot be so equated, that in fact ethical activity is subordinate to good, as means to end. Now, it would be hard for anyone reading Dickinson's argument not to come away with the sense that he has been encouraged to re-appraise (the idiom of the dialogue is persuasive) his estimation of moral striving, especially if he has had hitherto the inclination of the puritan to look on such striving as something good in itself, if not as *the good*. Moreover, in his ethical doctrine, at least in so far as that is contained in *Principia Ethica* and in *Ethics*, Moore is certainly arguing for the position that the character of excellence belongs primarily and intrinsically to states of affairs which do not include as one of their constituents what we would *normally* call moral striving or moral effort, and that what we would *normally* call moral striving or moral *effort* is justified only by the extent to which it promotes the actualisation of such states of affairs. If Dickinson's writing challenges the puritan, so does Moore's, even if the latter's thesis is written in a way which is much more technically philosophical. The description used at the end of the previous paragraph of the sort of thing to be found in Moore's writing may be grossly inaccurate; but to speak of him as 'setting out the logical order of the categories of the moral universe' calls attention to a feature of his work which is unmistakably there. To bring it into closer relation with what has been said in very different and much more familiar language by Dickinson, we could say that for Moore the notion of duty, which for men and women educated under the strain of a particular social and cultural tradition is very nearly identified with that of morality itself, is presented as strictly subordinate to that of intrinsic value or excellence, and that this thesis is as nearly as possible invested with the authority of a particular sort of necessary truth.

Further, in 1949 there was published an extremely interesting address by the late Lord Keynes on 'My Early Beliefs' which he had delivered in 1938. In it he revealed the importance of the influence exerted on himself and his friends by the doctrine contained in the last chapter of *Principia Ethica*. To some at least this was impressive, coming so soon after the reference by Professor P. A. Schilpp, in his introduction to the volume published in 1942 on *The Philosophy of G. E. Moore*, to Moore as a 'philosopher's philosopher'. In Keynes' paper a 'philosopher's philosopher' was presented as one who provided disciples with a doctrine, and not with a method. From Moore, Keynes and his friends did not primarily learn a method for bringing out the paradoxical character of the deliverances of speculative metaphysicians, of pinpointing what is wrong with the thesis that, e.g., time is unreal, but with something which Keynes calls a 'justification of experience', even something which could be spoken of as a revelation. There is no doubt that Moore gave Keynes and his friends a scale of priorities, a means of estimating what is of greater or less worth by reference to states of affairs discerned in their own light as intrinsically excellent.

Goodness, said Moore, is a simple, non-natural character. Indeed, in the volume on his work, that is mentioned by at least one contributor as his most important contribution to philosophy. For the philosophically educated to-day, it is the ramifications of this thesis which are significant; we are often told of the sharp and dramatic way in which it brings out the completely separate character of the languages of appraisal, of blame, of evaluation, from those of bird-watching, of rapportage, of bio-chemistry, while at the same time (I am thinking of the occurrence of the word 'simple' in the thesis) saying something almost tantalising of their similarities. Similarly, to those of an earlier philosophical generation, it was the question of the precise status that Moore was assigning to the concept of goodness which excited them; these questions were posed and worked out in terms of origin and source, of the quasi-psychological idiom of derivation and formation, of intuitive and dispositionally innate awareness. But for Keynes and his fellows the impact was more direct; for them it was a word of deliverance spoken to their need, rescuing them from the philistine crudities of Benthamism and the rest.

Here extreme precision is important; for that which had this power to deliver was both Moore's doctrine of what it was for something to be intrinsically valuable, and also his account of what things in particular possessed this quality. Keynes and his friends agreed with him in what he said on the first point and with what he said on the second. Indeed some, studying critically and minutely this very significant essay, might ask how far, for Keynes and his friends, it was possible to *separate* the content of the notion of the intrinsically valuable or excellent from those things or states of affairs which were known to possess it. Certainly to be intrinsically valuable was not to *be* the enjoyment of a personal relationship, or the contemplation of a beautiful object. In his essay on 'The Conception of Intrinsic Value' Moore has given an account of what formally it is for a thing to be intrinsically valuable. Yet there is clearly for him a very close connection between what he thought the quality of intrinsic excellence to be and the things which he thought to be intrinsically excellent or valuable. When a student of moral philosophy is first asked to discuss the question whether goodness is or is not a quality, he soon realises that it is a logical question; it may also involve very difficult considerations of an ontological character of the sort which continually impinge on fundamental logical discussions. Thus Aristotle, who discusses this question quite early in the *Nicomachean Ethics*, makes use in doing so of his own theory of categories. Indeed it has been pointed out that Aristotle's claim that

goodness is predicated in all the categories is a flat denial of
the truth of Moore's view that it is a quality. Now, whatever
Keynes and his friends received from Moore as a doctrine,
it did not at first sight look like a thesis concerning the
categorial status of a concept; yet it would be hard to
describe what they did receive without some account of
Moore's view of what it was for a thing to be good as well as
his view of what things were good.

Put the matter more simply as a question: what is the
relationship between the underlying logic and ontology of
which his theory of goodness is a part, and Moore's choice of
goods? Certainly it is for him logically possible for other states
of affairs than those mentioned above to be intrinsically excellent; there would be no formal self-contradiction in the
contemplation of beautiful objects not being intrinsically
excellent; the relationship between this character of intrinsic
excellence and what possesses it has been described as an
example of 'synthetic necessity'. There would be no other
possible way of bringing home to someone what intrinsic
excellence, in Moore's sense, is, except by compelling him to
attend to those states of affairs to which this character belongs. The sort of insight which would reveal its presence is
something very obscure; it is indeed a matter which will
be referred to later in this book. But it is tempting
sometimes to ask whether Moore does not demand the assumption of such insight as a reality because without it the
presence of such a character as he undoubtedly believes intrinsic excellence to be could not be grasped.

In this discussion, an effort has been made to bring out
something of the curious way in which the distinction of
levels mentioned in the first part of this chapter often breaks
down. To receive a piece of philosophical work as a doctrine
is clearly something quite different from getting to grips with
it as a contribution to the resolving of logical or ontological
perplexity; yet, where actual philosophical suggestions are
concerned, the two things may be quite inseparable; and this

may be because, for the man who has made the suggestion in question, what he has put forward is a much more inseparable unity than he is at first ready to admit. The use of the word 'inseparable' here gives rise to problems; it is obviously used in a way subtly different from that in which, a little earlier, colour and extension were said to be inseparably bound together. Indeed it does not seem *prima facie* at all helpful to say that, where this kind of inseparability is concerned, we have an instance of 'synthetic necessity'; for what we are trying to grasp is the peculiar sort of relationship which seems to obtain sometimes between what a man will propound in general terms as very nearly a thesis in the philosophy of logic, and what in every-day life he will, as a matter of fact, go after because he regards it as uniquely valuable. There are times when in reading Moore one is tempted to ask whether his underlying logic is not somehow made to the measure of those things which he regards as valuable; and there are other times when one is tempted to ask whether the underlying logic and ontology do not restrict his perception of the sort of thing which excellence is; and there are, of course, still other times when one wonders whether the two could have anything to do with each other; and yet these last are perhaps definitely fewer in number than the other two.

Of course it may very properly be asked what it is to receive something, in this case the thesis that goodness is a simple, non-natural quality and that certain states of affairs possess this quality, as a doctrine. Words are extremely elusive and allusive servants, and the phrase may have a variety of overtones and undertones to those who encounter it in its present use. But in this chapter it is used to indicate a particular sort of assent to a given proposition, assent of such a sort that it is allowed pervasively to affect behaviour and, in particular, choice. The question, 'Am I receiving such-and-such a proposition as a doctrine?' is one that a behaviourist could ask himself. For it *could* be answered not in terms of the intimacies of introspective self-communion, but in terms of overt response, including in the latter, of course, verbal behaviour. Pervasiveness of affect is an important factor, and also something that can perhaps at this stage only be expressed metaphorically in terms of depth of recall. For we are not speaking of something recurrent in memory, or frequently intrusive or obtrusive in conscious-ness, like King Charles's head in the mental history of the unhappy Mr. Dick. When something is received as doctrine, it is allowed to take root and to become, in terms of the familiar analogy to which the working of Kant's forms of sensibility is so often likened, a pair of spectacles through which we see things, and which are very hardly removed.

It may of course be said with reference to Moore's doc-trine (it was said with characteristic vigour and sharpness by the late D. H. Lawrence) that only a group of intellectuals would have accepted the sort of thing that Moore was pro-pounding, or developed it in the sort of way they did; it is certainly true that when something is received as doctrine, it is, to borrow a useful scholastic tag, taken in *secundum modum recipientis*. Yet however much their understanding of those needs may require correction and discipline, intellec-tuals have needs as human beings, and where Keynes and his friends were concerned, some of those needs were, to some extent at least, met by Moore, and by his thesis that goodness is a simple, non-natural quality. So a remark, to use a neutral term, which belonged certainly to the logic of ethics, belonged also to the universe of discourse in which men spoke and wrote, where it mattered supremely to them what things were good and also what sort of a thing their goodness was. A language, as I have already quoted from Wittgenstein, is a way of life, and the meaning of a sentence in part is surely a function of the language to which it belongs. So no doubt the meaning of 'Goodness is a simple, non-natural quality' is prescribed by the language-game (to use another Wittgen-steinian phrase) in which it occurs. As a remark in the logic of ethics, it has one force or meaning; as something spoken to men enslaved by the Benthamite dogma of the homogeneity of all satisfactions, it has another. But is it the same sentence that has these different meanings? Or are there two different sentences with the same verbal expression? Here one hesitates, conscious of a pull in both directions and of the attraction of competing models.

Philosophically what is crucial is to get hold of the interplay of the uses, the overlap of the level, the interpenetration one by another, of the language gained. For what Keynes received as doctrine was not a thesis in the logic of ethics; yet at the same time what he received was very close to, if it was not identical with, the thesis against which Joseph[1] said that Aristotle had argued decisively in the *Nicomachean Ethics*, and which has proved so bewilderingly fertile in subsequent discussion. One cannot separate altogether what Keynes received as doctrine from what others received as logic. Yet what Lawrence protested against was not a thesis in logic but the confirmation of a way of life.

It is sometimes said that the essence of Benthamism is contained in the thesis that 'poetry is misrepresentation'; it was certainly from some such view as that that Keynes and his friends sought deliverance, and found it in Moore's doctrine that goodness is a simple, non-natural quality. What they sought deliverance from was doctrine; yet it too was a thesis about the logic of our language, the order of our concepts. To say that 'poetry is misrepresentation' is to say that Keats or Blake do not describe as an historian or as a physicist describes; and it is of course further to imply that what is 'misrepresentation' in this way is not to be taken as seriously as what is not. It is a remark which belongs both to logic and to ordinary life; it is simultaneously talk, and talk about talk. But the manner in which it overlaps the two levels, which we would like to keep separate, tempts us to invent a special sort of discipline to which it might belong. For what else, perhaps, are we doing when we call it an epistemological

[1] *Some Problems in Ethics*, (O.U.P. 1930), p. 75.

remark, thus wishing to suggest that it is value-judgment and logical distinction at the same time?

So far, by way of illustration, we have tried to bring out some aspects of the activity, or sorts of activities, we call moral philosophy, particularly a kind of two-levelledness of reference which seems inherent in it, or in them. There is no doubt whatsoever that people are genuinely puzzled and perplexed concerning questions of value, and matters of duty and obligation. The style of these puzzlements and perplexities may vary; after all, the habit of mind of the members of the 'Bloomsbury circle' was significantly different from that, let us say, of the dwellers in a Welsh mining valley, or in a highland glen before the shock of the 'clearances'. The sort of problems that prick the conscience of one, the sort of issues that disturb and beset the curiosity of another, may be quite different. The underlying seriousness of temper that remains when a man has once, even once, known what it is to feel life on his pulses as a swing between hell's gate and heaven's gate is something that is perhaps unimaginable by those for whom the really important question is rather one of precisely defining the uniqueness of the aesthetically excellent. The point at present emphasised is that to both alike the moral philosopher succeeds in saying something. To say that he succeeds in saying something is not to say that he is a kind of vendor of intellectual remedies to suit the needs of individual sufferers from any and every sort of intellectual disquiet. What *is* true is what has been perhaps best conveyed by the idiom of cutting in on the conversations, used above. Moore in his way, Prichard in his, cut in on conversations that were about matters of deep human concern. Yet they were not preachers, nor prophets absorbed in the truth they propounded, its apostles and servants. Rather, both in their different ways were deeply self-conscious in respect of what they were saying, of its relation to other sorts of discipline, and this to the point, sometimes, of almost identifying their whole work with the formal drawing of distinctions, or, to use a more

modern phraseology, with the mastery of the logic of
different sorts of discourse. Initially it appeared as if the conversations at two levels which the moral philosopher might
interrupt could be carefully distinguished—he might contribute to the resolution of practical perplexity, he might
contribute to elucidating the logic of different sorts of discourse; at first sight it did seem as if the two sorts of contribution were separable. Yet a little further examination (of
Moore's work) suggested that in the end this was not so. The
sorting out of different sorts of discourse, the finding out what
one can and what one cannot do with them, is vitally important; and whatever may be admissible in strict logic, it is an
enterprise that may become inextricably interwoven with
the advance of moral judgment, appreciation and appraisal
themselves. Moore's thesis was a contribution to the logic of
ethical discourse, a key-move in plotting the geography of
moral concepts; yet it was also a doctrine that for some broke
the spell of Benthamism and shattered the power of the
dogmas in which John Stuart Mill had been so painfully
educated. It is fashionable to insist that if one is doing logic,
even studying the logic of ordinary language, one is not com-
mending a doctrine, or even a set of attitudes. But when one
comes to look at examples of what one would naturally call
trying to master the logic of a particular sort of discourse, in
all sorts of unexpected ways one finds the enterprise passing
over into the defence of a particular way of life.

In the following chapters of this book we shall be concerned
with various types of ethical theory; and an effort will be
made to show how, sometimes in one way, sometimes in
another, the practice of moral philosophers has in effect
followed the general lines sketched in the preceding paragraphs. In particular an effort will be made to assess the
sometimes unnoticed and unacknowledged, but always
crucial, rôles which have been assigned to epistemology by
writers on moral theory. In the above discussion there has
been only one explicit reference to epistemology as such; but

this restriction has been quite deliberate. For in the body of this book the term 'epistemology' will sometimes be used in a special, even a relatively novel, sense to indicate aspects of the arguments of moral philosophers essential to, even constitutive of, the unity of their individual work, but not by any means always presented directly as theses about the scope and limitations of human knowledge; although the choice of the term has been dictated by the fact that these aspects have sometimes been consciously and deliberately set out as their authors' theory of knowledge. It is just possible, incidentally, that this line of approach may throw light by the way on *some* of the underlying impulses which have led philosophers to develop those curious hybrids between logic, ontology and psychology which we know as 'theories of knowledge'.

CHAPTER II

UTILITARIANISM[1]

THERE is something about utilitarian approaches to the problems of ethics which gives to their discussion a continued relevance and significance. The choice of the plural, 'approaches', is deliberate; for under the rubric 'utilitarian' at least five different styles of argument must be distinguished.

A. UNSOPHISTICATED UTILITARIANISM

We are familiar with the insistence that there is a necessary coincidence between moral obligation and advantage, and that in the end there can be no obligation which does not somehow or other by its fulfilment contribute to the advantaging of mankind at large. The way, even the nature, of the coincidence is left vague; it may be contrived by a god, it may have its ground in deep-seated, almost unnoticed needs of our nature which we satisfy through the doing of those things which we regard to be our duty, and by no other path. Yet still this coincidence is demanded, and the authority of the claim made upon us by what we regard ourselves as morally bound to do is left somehow relative to its thus coinciding with our advantage.

Let us take this a stage further. We are familiar, for instance, with the demand that morality shall 'make sense', that our duties shall not form 'a chaos of unrelated commands'. There is no doubt whatsoever that sometimes, when this demand is made, those who are making it are demanding that the fulfilment of our obligations shall serve our advantage. This, of course, is not to forget that some moral philo-

[1] My debt in this chapter to Dr. David Baumgardt's most valuable *Bentham and the Ethics of To-day* is as obvious as it is sustained. I also owe much to Prof. A. J. Ayer's papers: 'The Principle of Utility', and 'The Analysis of Moral Judgments,' in *Philosophical Essays* (Macmillan, 1954).

sophers, e.g., the late Professor A. E. Taylor, whom no one could conceivably have called a utilitarian, have made just this demand in words very like those I have quoted; and the fact that they have done so shows that when men speak of morality as 'making sense', they need not be insisting on an ultimate coincidence of duty and personal advantage, in the sense of the utilitarian. Indeed it would be perfectly in order to say of Kant himself that, although he always insisted that virtue was a categorical imperative, yet by treating morality as the expression of practical reason, and by insisting on human autonomy, he was very far removed indeed from treating men's duties as something just given them to do.

Yet it is arguable as a matter of fact that when we first use the phrase 'morality must make sense', *in an unsophisticated way*, we are inclined to take it in a utilitarian sense. This opinion is deliberately presented as an opinion about a matter of fact, to be accepted or rejected as such, and the evidence to support or impugn it will therefore be empirical evidence. But it is arguable on empirical grounds that when people do begin to think seriously or critically about those courses of conduct which are presented to them as duties, their first impulse is to attempt to justify them by reference to the end of human happiness. Of course, in its beginnings, such thinking is intolerably vague; indeed the concepts by which it is carried on lend themselves with peculiar readiness to the sort of easy-going intellectual sleight-of-hand which sometimes passes for thinking about conduct. It is very easy, by a sort of casual abuse of such concepts as pain, pleasure, happiness, advantage, interest, to give to an unacknowledged tautology the force of a factual hypothesis. In elementary ethical thinking, whether we are religious or not, whether we invoke the intervention of a god who rewards and punishes or deny that such exists, we do delight to claim a necessary coincidence of duty and happiness as somehow necessary; there is something which can be called the unsophisticated utilitarianism of the ordinary man, and, however clumsy its logical structure and fallacious the arguments on which it is based, it must be reckoned with as something actual.

B. THE APPROACH TO THOROUGH-GOING UTILITARIANISM

Sometimes the thorough-going utilitarian begins from here; he makes full use of the advantage to be derived from the unsophisticated utilitarianism of the ordinary man, and goes on to give a definiteness of logical outline to this elementary woolly insistence on the necessary coincidence of duty and advantage. Some of Bentham's procedure can as a matter of fact be construed in this way.

Take the often canvassed thesis, 'All desire is for pleasure.' It is often pointed out that this is intolerably vague, that, for instance, it is not clear whether the pleasure envisaged is the greatest immediate pleasure of the agent or his long-term advantage. It has indeed, further, often been remarked that, as Aristotle's exploration of the concept of pleasure showed, the notion is one of such elusive subtlety and internal complexity that to say that all desire is for pleasure may be to assert a tautology or to claim something which is manifestly untrue. Thus, if a man says that all desire is for pleasure and is using the word pleasure in the sense of the Psalmist, who wrote of the angels of God who did his pleasure, or in the sense of the question asked by a hostess, of her guests' pleasure on a certain afternoon, he is saying something that is simply tautologous; for he is merely insisting that when a man desires something, he desires that something. But if on the other hand a man says that all desire is for pleasure in the sense in which we use the word when we speak of puritans as people who set little store by pleasure, then it expresses an empirical proposition which is quite obviously untrue; for as a matter of fact men do desire a great many things, e.g. to finish writing a book on philosophy, which are very different indeed from the sorts of activity which puritans condemn as pleasures.

All this is very familiar; but sometimes it seems just to miss 'the point'. It is certainly true that in the analysis of the concept of pleasure the development of the insights contained in Aristotle's treatment of the notion throws floods of light in all directions. But in the end it *may* miss the point of what the utilitarian is trying to do by its very delicacy and thoroughness; for the utilitarian is concerned not to deepen our insight, but to enable us to purify (or shall I say, to purge?) our notions.

The unsophisticated utilitarianism of the ordinary man is a muddle; but Bentham, for all his shortcomings, was not a muddled thinker. He knew very clearly what he was about; he believed that he was clearing up muddles, even if sometimes his enterprise has appeared to others much more like taking advantage of muddle in unsophisticated minds. To describe the intricacies in the actual working of a concept, its spread and span in the reach of our thought, is one thing; to transform that very concept into an instrument of aseptic intellectual surgery is something quite different. 'Morality must in the end be to our advantage.' Thus the plain man may muse to himself, not quite understanding the force of the 'must', only knowing that he cannot give easily unconditional authority to a mysterious something called moral obligation. It is to this mood that the thorough-going utilitarian speaks, suggesting that the concepts of advantage, pleasure, satisfaction, etc. must receive a new and rigorously determined force. They must be treated as indefinables, as notions in terms of which other notions are to be 'cashed',[1] in particular the conventional notions of ethics. If a man offers a cheque in payment for an article which he purchases, there must be money in the bank to meet the demand of the seller; otherwise we call the cheque a 'dud'. Similarly Bentham argued that if, in the world of human conduct, men tried to present to their fellows a course of conduct as something morally binding upon them, then that course must have something to do with their advantage. As a matter of fact he

---

[1] I owe this useful metaphor to Professor H. H. Price.

c

claimed on occasions that he wanted to take the word 'ought' out of the language; and although this enterprise seems in the end to have defeated him, it is a way of conveying what the thorough-going utilitarian really wishes to do; it is a way of showing what his dreams are.

There is the universe of moral obligation, of value, of traditional restraint and order; there is the universe of human advantage, pleasure, satisfaction, appeasement and reconciliation of need; there may be indeed, further, a vaguely acknowledged sense of the priority of the latter over the former. The thorough-going utilitarian is the man whose avowed programme it is to carry out the reduction of the former to the latter. But it is very important to see that in doing this he is compelled to transform the actual sense and force of such notions as pleasure, advantage and the rest.

It is worth while labouring this point by an illustration from some recent philosophical discussion concerning the relation of sense-data to physical objects. Ever since Berkeley criticised the causal theory of perception, and suggested that physical objects were, in the end, really only complicated systems of actual and possible sense-presentations,[1] a long line of philosophers, who by no means agreed with his peculiar theology, have found themselves hard put to deny the force of his claim for the identity of the sensible and the physical. Much of what we know as the philosophy of perception is no more and no less than a continued and sustained discussion of difficulties involved in accepting this identification, and the seemingly equally great difficulties in denying it. Those who have argued for it have, of course, made much of the point that as a matter of fact, where questions concerning the nature and behaviour of material objects are concerned, sense-awareness is the ultimate court of appeal. Any distinction between physical appearance and reality that has significance for human beings must be a difference realised in terms of what their senses disclose to them; the notion of

[1] I am deliberately ignoring Berkeley's truism.

physical reality must mean something in terms of what we hear, see, smell, touch and taste, or be empty of import for us. So those who, standing in the following of Berkeley, have been ready to call themselves phenomenalists have argued; and there has been something in our commonsense view to which they have made a continual appeal.

But the paradoxes of the thorough-going phenomenalist position have often been pointed out; in particular it has been insisted that, in a quite incredible way, the phenomenalist has made the actual depend upon the possible.[1] Moreover the notion of sense-datum as that of something somehow more ultimate and more evident than the familiar things in the world about us has received drastic criticism. Rather it sometimes seems as if it is the ordinary material thing which is familiar and acceptable, and the sense-datum elusive, confused and obscure.

But the discussion has not ended there; for some philosophers have boldly suggested that as a matter of fact what is really being canvassed is a thesis concerning the inter-relation of two languages, together with a claim for the logical priority of one of them. The sense-datum language has a logical priority over the language which works in terms of ordinary material things. This may seem an extravagant claim to make for a language that has perhaps never received satisfactory formulation; yet it is argued that to make any less claim is to involve ourselves in the impossible admission that we have commerce with the external world other than by sense-experience. Anyone at all familiar with recent literature will realise that the sense-datum language of the phenomenalist is something incredibly more sophisticated than the sort of thing a man might write or speak who was trying to capture a universe of sheer sensation; at least it is of a quite different sort of sophistication.

The phenomenalist is thoroughly self-conscious; he justifies himself by saying that what in the end he is defending is a pro-

[1] E.g. by such philosophers as Professor G. F. Stoat in *God and Nature* (C.U.P. 1952), and by Mr. W. F. R. Hardie in the *Proceedings of the Aristotelian Society for 1946.*

gramme of translation. Apart from holding this programme before himself as something that it is theoretically possible to execute, he will sooner or later be involved in the paradoxes of what Professor A. J. Ayer calls an 'iron curtain theory of perception'. When the notion of sense-datum enters into the outline of this programme, it is not the notion of something immediate and familiar; it is the indefinable accepted as that in terms of which we have agreed to define our notions. Almost we have transformed the familiar in the interests of a logical model; but the sanction of that model is the extent to which it enables us to escape the attraction of the inadmissible.

So Bentham could justify himself by saying quite explicitly (and indeed he does this in his voluminous writings) that unless we do try rigorously to subordinate the language of moral obligation to that of advantage, we will open the doors wide to admit every sort of superstition and prejudice. By making the language of advantage prior to that of obligation in the way in which the thorough-going utilitarian tries to do so, we transform the former language; indeed we are irrevocably committed to making it an exact instrument whereby we can measure the value of what is offered to us as an authoritative prescription in respect of what we should do. The notion of sense-datum is a technical notion; it may appear paradoxical, but it is none the less important to remember, that sense data are not to be identified with the raw stuff of sensation. Words like sight, taste, smell and the rest have all sorts of perfectly familiar uses in ordinary speech, in physiology, in optics and the rest; the sense-data of the phenomenalist are of course intimately related to them. Indeed, at the risk of an extreme paradox, it could be argued that they are 'logical constructions' out of them. The recognition of the extremely special, even contrived, status of sense-data in the phenomenalist scheme of things has, however, in the end possibly the effect of removing the sting of some of the more familiar paradoxes of his position; for it helps us to recognise what that position is. So too with the attempt by the thorough-going utilitarian to define duty in terms of advantage: it is no use attempting to take stock of this enterprise without recognising the special status in it of the notions of pleasure and advantage; within the context of the enterprise, these latter too can be regarded as 'logical constructions' out of more ordinary, and in one sense more familiar, features of our human environment.

These lines of thought may throw some light on the often mocked, even self-contradictory, notion of the 'hedonistic calculus'. Can pleasures be measured? Clearly there is a sense in which that question has only to be put in order to be seen to be a non-sense question. If one approaches the notion of pleasure as Aristotle does, seeing it as a moment in an activity, the dynamic side of an ἐνέργεια, then to speak of measuring pleasures is very like speaking of eating circles. But it is surely different if we consider the proposal of a hedonistic calculus to be but a stage in the working-out of a programme, a programme whose maxim is the elimination from ethics of any appeal to the occult or the mysterious. The proposal of such a calculus is seen to be, from one point of view, little more than a refusal to waste time over un-answerable questions of quality, a refusal to be bogged down in consideration of the claims of mysterious faculties of in-tuition as sources of ethical knowledge, when the appeal to these faculties stands condemned both by the unintelligi-bility of their supposed nature and status, and by the destruc-tive and hurtful character of the superstitions they are often invoked to support.

It will be clear that in this section of the argument there has been a most decided shifting of the ground.

The lines are now emerging of a position a great deal more sophisticated than the confused and woolly insistence of the ordinary man that 'morality must make sense', and that there cannot be an ultimate opposition between the claims of morality and human happiness. It was clearly indicated at the outset that the unsophisticated person's demand was ambivalent; it provided a starting point from which argument could develop in all sorts of different directions. Indeed it lent itself to a number of different analyses; several different answers might be given to the question what exactly it was that the unsophisticated person was asking when he demanded that 'morality should make sense', or that the 'demands of obligation should serve intelligible purposes of human happiness'. Even if he is by this demand somehow expressing a sense that morality cannot be accepted as an end in itself, it does not follow that this by itself signifies a readiness to accept a thorough-going utilitarian position.

It has been argued in the preceding paragraphs of this section that what the thorough-going utilitarian *sometimes* does is to construe the dissatisfaction expressed as a request for something which could perhaps be called a 'theory about morality'. Such a theory would attempt to do more than offer an account simply of the genesis and development of moral ideas; it would essay the more considerable task of exhibiting the logically derivative status of these notions. Such an enterprise would, it has been suggested, lead inevitably to paradox; the elimination of characteristically moral notions like 'ought' and the rest cannot be carried through. But the attraction of the enterprise remains, and it is possible to defend it by admitting its artificial, and indeed technical, character, while at the same time insisting that its impulse resides in an anxiety to eliminate appeal to the esoteric and the mysterious from the field of human conduct.

Thus, where the thorough-going utilitarian is concerned, it may be allowed that considerations of a distinctly epistemological character play a crucial part in his discussion of the problems of ethics. Indeed it might be suggested that the underlying principle of the 'hedonistic calculus' represents the way in which this underlying epistemology is expressed as a maxim of logical procedure. This calculus is a method for determining relative values; its spring is the conviction that they can be treated as exact functions of measurable differences, i.e. differences to which a precise numerical value can be assigned. The calculus is a mathematical method; where its accurate application is possible, questions of relative superiority and inferiority of worth can receive definitive answers. But the resolve to make questions of worth a matter of applied mathematics is something so strange, and so clearly artificial, that inevitably we ask questions concerning the impulses underlying it.

Moreover a moment's reflection on this artificiality clearly brings out how far we have moved, even jumped, from the unsophisticated feeling after a kind of utilitarianism by ordinary men. This jump is advertised, of course, by the admittedly technical and artificial character of the concepts involved in the statement of the thorough-going utilitarian position; but it could also be indicated by remembering that we allowed the unsophisticated utilitarian to be a theist, if his sensibility inclined him that way. For him the coincidence of duty and interest could be contrived by a god; for the thorough-going utilitarian the coincidence is something as far as possible to be made a matter of logical necessity in the name of a morality not mysterious.

C. THE STRESSES AND STRAINS OF THOROUGH-GOING UTILITARIANISM

Of course utilitarianism could be presented quite *directly* as a method for eliminating all appeal to the intuitive or the transcendent in the field of human conduct. If in the design of this chapter a different order has been followed, the aim has been to suggest the way in which an enterprise so serious and so far-reaching may impinge on the reflection of quite unsophisticated persons. We are repeatedly reminded to-day how seriously we must take ordinary language; and maybe one way in which we can do so is not to turn aside from the often woolly and confused gropings of the unsophisticated. The notion of utility is one which, in a curious way, illustrates as matter of fact the late Professor R. G. Collingwood's thesis that philosophical concepts (and the phrase need here mean no more than concepts often employed and discussed by philosophers) display a tendency to 'overlap'. If a man asks himself what is the essence of utility, the notion seems to elude him; or he finds that he is offered no more than a verbal transformation whereby utility has become 'usefulness as a means' or something of the sort. If indeed he goes further and says that the utilitarian is the man who insists that morality is a matter of means to end, he may have gone a little further; but there again a vagueness persists. It has been argued above that the ordinary man does sometimes find himself speaking of morality in this sort of way, or wishing to show morality to himself as being this sort of thing, even going further to the extent of identifying the end with happiness or wealth. He may even, of course, have also a sense of the *prima facie* otherness of the notions of moral obligation and advantage, which shows itself in a readiness to speak of their coincidence as a matter for artificial contrivance. If he is suddenly confronted with the thoroughgoing utilitarian position, he may be shocked, even while at the same time he admits that this rigorously and comprehensively developed programme has already some sort of purchase-hold on his allegiance. There is an overlap, in Collingwood's sense, between utility in the strict Benthamite formulation of the greatest happiness principle and utility in the unsophisticated gropings of the ordinary man.

Indeed a study of the history of Bentham's principle confirms this; for although the thorough-going utilitarian thesis can be presented as a sharply defined set of maxims for the definition of ethical concepts in non-ethical terms, its development has a history. There were utilitarians before Bentham; and the species did not expire, nor did it cease to undergo significant modifications, with his death. For instance, in no account of utilitarianism should a writer on ethics omit reference to Henry Sidgwick. Thus a certain indirection in approach to the central and pivotal style of utilitarian argument is justified if the reader is not to lose sight of its manifold ramifications; it is particularly justified in view of the fact that, in this book, it is with the many-levelledness of ethical theories that we are concerned, and that therefore a great deal has to be said of the ways in which they can be presented, or commend themselves. Indeed what they are as theories is perhaps inseparable from the manner in which they are thus presented, and from the ways in which they thus commend themselves.

Where thorough-going utilitarianism is concerned, however, it is important to remember that it is overtly 'censorious'; the word was one which Bentham did not disdain to use. The thorough-going utilitarian is emphatically not in favour of the sort of tolerance which suggests that, inasmuch as 'every sort of statement has its own sort of logic', we may find a road to justifying the most extravagant and the most superstitious opinions about the nature and end of human conduct. In setting out systematically the thorough-going utilitarian position, three elements in it should be clearly acknowledged.

(a) The thorough-going utilitarian believes always that it is possible to lay bare the springs of actual human behaviour. It was James Mill's boast that, given time, he could make the workings of the human mind as clear as the road from Charing Cross to St. Paul's Cathedral. 'Then Newton came, and all was light.' The desire to be the Newton of the moral sciences was a common ambition in the 18th century; and in the detailed theories concerning human psychology, and concerning the mechanics of legislation and of administration developed by the 'philosophical radicals' we can trace the inspiration of Newton's treatment of the problems of physical and astronomical science at every level. The very postulate of the homogeneity of all satisfactions is obviously suggested by the tremendous advances made in the study of the physical universe as soon as it was assumed that its fundamental laws could be set out in terms of the positional changes undergone by particles of matter endowed only with such characters as extension, impenetrability and the rest. The principle of the 'association of ideas' itself, as the very language in which it was expounded clearly shows, was offered as a kind of analogue in the field of mental phenomena to the inverse square law whereby Newton had in so brilliant a way unified the worlds of dynamics and astronomy. When the student attends to the rôle of this principle in the account which James Mill offers of the growth of the human mind, and then goes on to see the use made of it as an assumption underlying the policies of social, legal and political change advocated by the 'radicals', he is never able for long to forget the continuing power of this initial inspiration.

To some extent, of course, these things belong to past history; it is not only the model of the workings of the physical universe, which the 'radicals' took for granted, that has been outmoded; their psychology and their often contradictory doctrines concerning social justice and the mechanics of human betterment have alike also received every sort of criticism. But men still believe that it is possible to find out what men actually are like; and they still believe that the methods properly followed in such an exploration are, in some sense, analogous to those of physical science. To say this is not, of course, to commit the mistake of supposing that anthropologists and historians, for instance, use the same sort of explanatory schemata as physicists and chemists; it is only to insist that there must be some sort of analogy between the methods followed in the two fields, in respect of their individual claim to exactitude. Moreover men still believe, and insist, that the 'ought' of morality must be grounded in the 'is' of fact. What we ought to do, what can be exacted from us as obligation, must have something to do with the stuff of which we are made, and with our fundamental desires and aversions.

It may indeed appear to the reader that we are moving back again to the vaguer idiom with which this section of our study began. Certainly the oscillation between an almost uncompromising demand for the strictest and most rigorous precision in the definition of concepts and the readiness to endorse a certain vagueness, even a certain familiar and almost platitudinous quality of statement, is a mark of the utilitarian style. It would supposedly be the utilitarian's claim that even though the attempt rigorously to exhibit the 'ought' as a function of the 'is' breaks down, the attempt is always worth making; rather it has continually to be made if we are not to forget what it is that we are committed to, once we take the crucial step of allowing that the 'ought' must be derived from the 'is', and why it is that this derivation alone guarantees the freedom of our moral beliefs from all taint of superstition and irrational acceptance of tradition. If we say that as a matter of historical fact the work of the 'philosophical radicals' is *vieux jeu*, we have said something that is as a matter of fact true, except in so far as, where the history of human institutions is concerned, the past is always somehow incapsulated in the present. Few, if any, moreover would label themselves Benthamite in ethics to-day; indeed the complexity and contradictoriness of Bentham's doctrines[1] alone make the title uncongenial. But the impulse whose working has now partly been traced is a strong and pervasive one; it is in the end simply that of a disciplined and thorough-going empiricism at work in the scrutiny of human manners and morals. 'There must be some point in it'—so a man may lament the seemingly purposeless exactions and restraints of a traditional morality. It is not enough to endorse his attitude; his 'must' has to receive justification. In other words, the logical cogency of his complaint has to be shown. The thorough-going utilitarian, in the end, argues that such complaints can only be allowed logical cogency if we are prepared to derive our morality from the actual nature of the human beings whose behaviour it is to direct, and proportion

[1] Bentham's work, for all that, has an admirable toughness and vigour of quality.

its dictates to the needs, the circumstances, the opportunities, the possibilities of actual human life.

(b) If the inspiration of the 'philosophical radicals' lay partly in Newton's superb theoretical achievement, their purposes were also severely practical. Bentham and his friends offered the greatest happiness principle as a maxim to guide the legislator and the administrator in their work; in the wider territory of political philosophy, the principle was cast to perform better the rôle which, in traditional liberal theory, had been played by the notion of 'inalienable, imprescriptible natural rights'. Bentham spoke of the 'natural rights' of the French revolutionaries as 'nonsense on stilts'; his writing on the subject displays a hostility to the notion of fundamental human right, intuitively evident to the light of reason, which is sometimes theoretical and sometimes practical, and often both at the same time. The language of 'natural rights' is a confused and misleading method of referring to that greatest happiness whose promotion is the sole end and justification of law and government.

When the 'radicals' came to the actual business of deciding what was to be done, of judging, for instance, the proper rôle of governmental initiative in promoting the harmony of conflicting economic interests, they often contradicted both one another and themselves, even frequently showing the strength still exerted upon them by ideas extraneous to their own professed opinions. But even if it is hard sometimes not to be impatient with their prejudices and irritated by their actual shortsightedness, their fundamental programme is never long obscured. There is one sovereign principle by which social and political institutions are all alike to be judged; and that principle is the one of the greatest happiness of the greatest number. Nothing is too exalted by traditional standards to escape its sovereign judgment; the British Constitution itself requires not to be praised in the lyrical style of Edmund Burke, but measured, in respect of its actual working, by its tendency to increase or diminish the sum of actual human happiness. Further, when one descends from the evaluation of a comprehensive and deeply entrenched ordering of the powers of an ancient society to the more every-day decisions of policy, whether economic or penal, it is by the same principle that one must judge. Of course in the one case one is in effect asking whether a given constitution is good or bad; while in the other one may be considering the extent to which the demands of a group of strikers can be met, or whether a murderer under sentence of death for killing a policeman shall be reprieved. The problems are different; yet the principle involved in grappling with them is in both cases the same, although the circumstances and results of its invocation may be widely different. It may seem paradoxical to insist on this sameness; yet it is very fundamental to the utilitarian position to insist that there is in the end only one standard of judgment where constitutions and political acts, orders of production, distribution and exchange, and administrative decisions are alike to be assessed, and that is the tendency of one and all to promote or hinder the increase of human happiness.

Now, it is very important to remember here that as a matter of fact utilitarians have sometimes favoured conservative, and sometimes nearly revolutionary, social policies. They have sometimes been found among the defenders of the *status quo*, and sometimes in the vanguard of those who sought a thorough-going reorganisation of the underlying structure of their society. It is worth remembering in passing that the languages of Burke and of Bentham are sometimes unexpectedly coincident! But if from time to time the utilitarian finds himself making common cause with the conservative, that must not for one moment obscure the fact that he is in the end radical inasmuch as, for him, the mere relative permanence and tenacity of social habit do not provide any argument whatsoever in favour of its validity. It may be that to interfere with some particular institution at a given time will cause more harm than good; it may be that to abolish the death penalty at a time of acute national crisis would be unwise. But the unwisdom would be present simply because its abolition then would cause more damage, or threaten more ill, then its retention for a season. No appeal to its intuitive fittingness has the least relevance whatsoever; it is all a matter of where human interest lies. And where that interest is concerned, sometimes the giving of proper weight to short-term consideration of the effect of change in the immediate future will counsel caution; but often, on the other hand, the implementation of the sovereign principle will brook no delay. Of course utilitarians will have their personal prejudices like other men, and sometimes a confused devotion, for instance, to an almost metaphysical idea of freedom will give birth to unjustified hesitations in respect, for instance, of some measure of collective welfare imposed and carried through by a central authority; but the instrument whereby those prejudices may be corrected is at their disposal in the sovereign maxim of the greatest happiness. There is in utilitarian morality a kind of ruthless objectivism; in the next section this will be emphasised in connection with the utilitarian estimate of personal worth. But it is easier to understand it if we first decipher its effect in the larger letters of government and collective life; for there it is perhaps possible more fairly to discern at once the inflexibility, and yet the flexibility, of utilitarian morality in practice.

In practice the utilitarian is inflexible in the claims which he makes for his supreme principle; if that principle is spoken of as sovereign, the epithet is chosen to bring out the fact that it derives authority from no other principle whatsoever, and that any other principle to which men may appeal is essentially secondary. Thus, in practice, men often do invoke principles of distributive justice of a highly general and abstract sort; or they may speak of the claims of mercy, pity and love as if even in the large-scale organisation of human affairs these ideas must exercise a directing influence upon their conduct. The utilitarian will not want for one moment to deny that this may be, indeed even must be, so; but he will argue that in the end it is so because, for instance, the practice of a certain sort of harshness or rigidity in adherence to the demands of existing law in the treatment of those who have broken it must be self-defeating in respect of the promotion of the welfare of mankind at large. Further, it will often be necessary in matters of administration to bear very patiently with the prejudices of those with whom the administrator has to deal; in very controversial matters, touching for instance the long-established position of churches and sects in a community, or the recognised rights of trades unions and employers' associations, it may be the worst sort of folly to cut the Gordian knot in the name of truth, or of efficiency; one may simply have to pay the price of patience, and work through the institutions that are there. But there is nothing meritorious in such patience in itself; to suppose that there is could easily beget a sloppiness of mind which, even though it called itself empiricist, is poles asunder from the proper acceptance of the supremacy of fact which marks the empiricist outlook. The principle of the greatest happiness of the greatest number is the only principle which rivets legislative and administrative practice to the observed needs of human beings, and liberates such practice from the corrupting distraction of irrational, and in the end contradictory, metaphysical notions.

The principle, then, is sovereign, and its supreme status can be yielded to none other; yet that does not mean, as we have indeed already noticed, that its application must be a matter of rigid and uncritical literalism. For the utilitarian, indeed perhaps for him more than for other men, the road to hell will often be paved with good intentions; a man may indeed say that he was seeking with might and main to promote the greatest happiness of the greatest number. But such promotion, in Professor Gilbert Ryle's phrase, is a matter of 'knowing how'; the unquestioned and final authority of the principle is not a guarantee that anyone will follow it aright in the complex and frequently confused fields of public life; there are tricks of the trade to be learned here more than elsewhere, a sense of the manifoldness and even the unexpected diversity of things human to be known and continually to be reckoned with. The principle is objective as a canon by which existing institutions must be judged; but it exercises an analogous objective authority over the actions and decisions of the individual who is concerned and charged with the working and the improvement of those institutions. He will fail in loyalty to its character as supreme, if he allows his own private image or vision of what human happiness, here and now, is or could be to get in the way of a proper assessment of the actual possibilities of the situation with which he is dealing, and with the ways in which, in that situation and in none other, the cause of human happiness may best be served.

Before leaving this section, (b) there are three further points to be noticed.

(i) This discussion of the utilitarian approach to problems of government has formed a part of our study of thoroughgoing utilitarianism; it has already been remarked that there is much said in an unquestionably utilitarian idiom in, for instance, the political philosophy of Edmund Burke, in part at least justifying Halévy's description of that doctrine as a 'half-empirical, half-mystical doctrine founded on the principle of utility'; there is an unquestionably utilitarian ingredient in Burke's approach to the problems of politics, but for him considerations of utility must have due weight given them in the name, for instance, of mercy; taking stock of things as they are, cautious reckoning of the consequences of violent change in terms of actual suffering undergone by ordinary flesh-and-blood human beings is essential, if the man who would reform human society is to escape being a tyrant. The empirical, utilitarian strand is there in Burke; but it is not dominant, and no principle of utility is by him expressed as sovereign and absolute. His understanding of

human life, moreover, is much more an imaginatively
achieved vision, in which divers moments are fused together
in a kind of aesthetic unity, than a set of supposedly certain
empirical facts.

The thorough-going utilitarian is unyielding in his insistence on the supremacy, throughout the whole domain of
human knowledge, of concrete, observed fact; we may
generalise, we must generalise, inductively from what is
before us, but we begin and end with what we immediately
know as fact, whether our ultimate concern be the fundamental structure of matter or the remote arcana of human
personality.

(ii) The extent to which the notion of utility indicates
something of what Collingwood may have had in mind when
he spoke of 'overlap' in respect of philosophical concepts has
already been remarked. The social historian will no doubt
have found something artificial in the way in which, in this
whole section, the use of the notion in respect of government
has been discussed. For he may ask whether as a matter of
fact anyone has ever been a thorough-going utilitarian. Has
it not rather always been the case that when ideas have taken
hold of men's minds in human history, and seriously affected
their actions in society, they have never worked in a vacuum
but rather in soils already prepared for them? Thus the idea
of utility has been invoked in the cause of a rigorous harnes-
sing of the available and possible resources of human society
under the direction of a centrally conceived and imposed
plan; it has played, and continues to play, its rôle in the
apologetics of collectivism. The socialists' hatred for what
they call waste, the needless squandering of material and
human resources in respect for some entrenched tradition, is
something which is very properly justified by appeal to the
end of human happiness. On the other side, we have been,
and are, familiar with the way in which apologists for
laissez-faire criticise such attempts to plan and to direct the
course of economic life, the availability of resources to pro-

D

ducer and consumer, whether of capital or of goods, the flow of imports, etc., as a sure road to inefficiency and misery. In both cases the idiom is utilitarian; but does that make those who speak it utilitarians?

To push the questioning a stage further, defenders of planning and apologists for economic freedom must of course work out their defence and their apologia in detail, showing in the one case how the waste can be avoided, and in the other how, for instance, intolerable restrictions on initiative may lead to diminished production, to loss of markets and of wealth. Further, in the one case, the defender may call attention to the over-hanging threat of violence in a society wherein large sections of the community labour under the impression that they are being denied access to that community's wealth, whose very existence owes something at least to their labour; when men feel, however irrationally, that the laws under which they live are made and upheld in the interest not of the community as a whole but of powerful sections of that community, and that moreover its economic policies in particular are prescribed by men whose concern is not the common good but their sectional advantage, they may be moved to desperate remedies, and to risk anarchy and disorder to secure redress of their grievances. The man who says in such a situation that something must be done may be actuated by his sense of the demands of justice; but he may be prepared to defend the risks involved in letting justice have its way by pointing to the grave threats to ordinary security involved in acquiescence in the *status quo*. Again, the critic of planning may be concerned with what he calls the threat to freedom; it may be that what he fears most is the momentum with which a policy of planning, with its inevitable errors, break-downs, unanticipated difficulties and inefficiencies, will compel the greater and greater concentration of power over human lives in the hands of a central authority. What he may fear and morally reject may be tyranny; yet it will be inefficiency and disorder that he will stress in his attack on collectivist ideas.

In both cases it is possible to discern a kind of uneasy shifting in the idiom; sometimes government is virtually identified with the promotion of the maximum advantage in society at large; indeed the identification may come almost to the point of suggesting that what government ultimately *is* may be expressed in those terms. Just as in the theory of moral obligation the 'ought', for the thorough-going utilitarian, should be swallowed up in the 'is', so in government notions like justice and liberty must at least be eclipsed and over-shadowed by that of the greatest happiness; they cannot be allowed co-ordinate, let alone superior, standing. For after all are they not, in themselves, in some sense metaphysical notions? Against such the thorough-going utilitarian has set his face; and if those who use his idiom are still under their sway, then they have not seen what he is really demanding that they should do. We must, in ending this section, ask what is implied by the obvious difficulties felt by those who most obviously want to speak the language of utilitarianism in the domain of government, in making that language their sole idiom.

(iii) The utilitarian always asks for justification; he will not receive the authority of government as something in any sense self-justifying. There is no doubt whatsoever that here the thorough-going utilitarian finds ordinary men respon-sive, at least at first, to what he is saying; he makes a contri-bution to a conversation that has a very long history, sug-gesting that the pretentious claims of established traditions shall be measured against their promoting or hindering human happiness. It is possible now to see how, in such a conversation, the thorough-going utilitarian asks the man whose reflection he interrupts to move step by step, rather like this: first, to admit that the increase of human welfare is the sole end of government, and that social and political in-stitutions are in the end to be judged by that criterion and none other; second, gradually to come to see that the pro-motion of that welfare is what government is (after all, what

is government itself over and above the work of government?);
and then, finally, to recognise that the understanding what
that happiness is is a matter in no way, in principle, different
from the understanding of the workings of the physical
universe. Of course for the thorough-going utilitarian the
three stages are logically distinguishable one from another; but it is in the third that he makes his decisive contribution to the conversation at the second level mentioned
in the previous chapter (although of course the contribution
is foreshadowed in the second stage). It is at the third stage
that the decisive suggestion is made that, in the end, the
universe of moral discourse does not stand somehow apart; if
that discourse has any validity, or any reference to the actual,
that is only because it is a part of ordinary descriptive
language, and the universe to which it refers, fundamentally
homogeneous with the world around us. Of course praising
and blaming someone are not in the least like describing
what he has done; but praise and blame as events belong to
the world, and so do their consequences; so too do the uses
we may make of such activities as mechanisms for en-
couraging or correcting human behaviour. In the end, the
thorough-going utilitarian insists that, where conduct,
whether individual or collective, is concerned, fact shall have
authority over any sort of nebulous intuition or received
tradition; and it is from reflection on the foundations of the
physical sciences that his conception of what it is for something to be a fact has been derived.

Now, it is a familiar chapter in the history of political and
social philosophy that even men as close to the most uncompromising exponents of this creed as John Stuart Mill
rebelled against it. In his *Autobiography* Mill has left us his
own account of his revolt; and historians of the development
of his ideas have traced how the line of his writings follows
the movement of his intellectual growth, as he reveals that
in the *Autobiography*; but perhaps those whose interest in
these problems is primarily philosophical may be wise to

concentrate their attention on, for instance, his essays on Bentham, and on Coleridge, when he writes with a kind of superb detachment, 'all passion spent upon the mountain top', or even on the familiar essay *On Liberty*. Bentham had taken the principle of utility and made it the foundation of a building; or rather he had made of it an instrument whereby every sort of question relating to human existence could be resolved. Even to-day, with a little effort of historical imagination, it is possible to see how men could receive such a teaching as a liberation; in the first chapter it was argued that when men receive a doctrine, they will receive it *secundum modum recipientis*; perhaps, indeed, sometimes the manner of their reception is inseparable from what they receive, and vice-versa. To believe in the principle of utility was to see oneself set free from all sorts of besetting confusions and superstitions concerning the authority of moral ideas and institutions; the logical comparisons used in an earlier part of this chapter were introduced to convey in the most formal manner possible what it was that thus attracted men as a thing of liberating power. Of course this is not to forget that from the first there were Gradgrinds and Bounderbys among the utilitarians; or that there were men prepared in the name of utility to defend the working of children in the mines, etc. But it is to emphasise that the down-to-earth, matter-of-fact, quality of utilitarian doctrine came to men as a way through the mazes of inherited complexity in social and in legal institutions; moreover, where for instance penal law, or many aspects of the position of women in society, were concerned, the appeal to observable happiness and pain seemed to offer a touchstone by which every sort of obscurely based and irrational tradition might be branded as the superstition which it almost certainly was, and even cast out from among men. It will be clearly realised from the above that the attraction of the greatest happiness principle lay not simply in its practical simplicity as a device for getting reform and improvement, but also in its theoretical basis; its liberating power was inseparable from the underlying epistemology which conveyed it, and was itself conveyed by it.

In the end it was this epistemology which Mill could not accept. The style of the essay *On Liberty* reveals this as clearly as the much advertised inconsistencies in the *Utilitarianism*. Of course, as a political tract, Mill's essay is open to the criticisms of Fitzjames Stephen and of T. H. Green; but the liberty of which he is writing is something that occasionally suggests more that kind of ontological creativity of which Russian writers like Solovyev and Berdyaev have written than anything else. It is a matter of language and of style; for it is by his language that Mill acknowledges a kind of *mystery*[1] in human freedom; the very way in which he conveys his fear that genius may be subdued or silenced or rendered sterile by the pressure of mass standards is evidence of this. The crisis of his twentieth year, of which he writes in the *Autobiography*, remains obscure; but, at least in part, we may say that suddenly he found the utilitarian outlook intolerable. It was no longer a method of liberating men from the bondage of ancient superstition, and of bringing a humanly orientated efficiency into the working of political and legal institutions; it suddenly appeared as a view of life which confined men's minds and threatened in a terrifying way to limit the possibilities open to them. The whole utilitarian doctrine had offered itself as something intended to set men free from the domination of superstition and to make their ways more human, and therefore more kindly; but in his twentieth year the fulfilment of his hopes suddenly seemed to Mill to presage the coming of a closed rather than an open society.

Mill's temper was always agnostic; appeal to fact, to the deliverances of observation, to the confirmation of theoretical construction by induction and observation, was, for him, an instrument whereby men's minds could be freed from the tyranny of unfounded and often cruel superstition, and their institutions purged from senseless complexity and inefficiency.

[1] In M. Gabriel Marcel's sense.

But if appeal to sensible fact brought liberation, it seemed also to imply that poetry is misrepresentation, and by implying this it threatened at once to confine human perceptions in a way that was intolerable, and to threaten human life with an impoverishment that likewise could not be accepted. So across his writings Mill raises the problem of ethical intuition; and it is perhaps not sufficiently remarked how often, for him, that problem is one with that of keeping open the human horizons, of preventing men's image of what would be the most satisfactory possible state of affairs from obscuring from them the vast realms of possibility that were still untouched by their creativity. As Mr. Isaiah Berlin has clearly shown, the true liberal requires to make a very special use of the distinction between the actual and the possible to convey what is really the centre of his belief and concern. Mill made it very clear that he could not be an intuitionist in ethics; but he used the language of intuition when he had to protest against the philistine narrowness of his creed. Socrates is superior to the satisfied fool. For Mill that superiority is fundamental; but what sort of a fact is it? It is not the sort of difference that can be registered on anything remotely analogous to a thermometer; it seems at first sight impossible to set out the sort of methods by which that superiority might be discerned, certainly if the methods are modelled on those of the exact sciences. So the movement has come full circle; it is in defence of the lonely creative exploration of the man of genius, who is somehow discerned as having his own law, that the authority of fact is set aside.

So Mill remains, in his political theory, inconsistent; he is in the end a utilitarian, but one who is also deeply enough concerned with human freedom and dignity to question the completeness of his creed, even explicitly to query its epistemological foundations. Similarly his essay on Coleridge shows that, where human society is concerned, he found himself compelled to acknowledge an intractable complexity in its stuff which seemed at first, and indeed in the end, to accord ill with Bentham's maxims of rigorous, critical analysis. The longevity of a tradition concerning behaviour is evidence, Mill allows, that it may answer to something in human nature; but what sort of logical empiricism is this? To admit respect for such evidence as an intellectually valid habit of mind is to impugn the authority of fact; it is indeed to start on a road leading in the end to a denial of the sovereignty of the greatest happiness principle.

(c) There is, of course, something analogous to this movement away from thorough-going utilitarianism in Keynes' welcome of Moore. Where their theory of moral obligation was concerned, Keynes and Moore, for Prichard, would be utilitarians; for both alike accepted the subordination of moral obligation to the promotion of good ends. Moreover, in his approach to questions of social policy and the workings of human governments, Keynes shared to the full the initial utilitarian insistence that here we were concerned with means and not ends; the things of intrinsic worth lay elsewhere, in the appreciation of painting, or in the cultivation of friendship. These were not political activities, or matters of planning and contrivance; they were on another level, and Keynes had learnt from Moore their distinctive quality. And this, he insisted, was a lesson which inoculated him and his friends against Benthamism, and against 'its *reductio ad absurdum*', Marxism.[1] The mention of Marxism as the *reductio ad absurdum* of Bentham's doctrine is significant; for if there is one feature above all others characteristic of the Marxist to-day, it is his eagerness to treat every issue as political, where of course politics is seen as the promotion of the class war. Of course there is in Bentham nothing like the philosophy of history which Marx took over from Hegel; yet there is perhaps something analogous, in the feverish yet disciplined preoccupation with politics of the contemporary member of the Communist party, to the earlier Benthamite sense of the all-embracing character of the work of reform, and the

[1] I owe this explicit formulation to my colleague in Aberdeen, Dr. J. H. Burns.

promotion of the greatest happiness of the greatest number. For both alike, contemplation is something peripheral, indeed something which may prove destructive of a proper preoccupation with the purpose to be advanced.

Here again it is a matter of paradox to say that in thoroughgoing utilitarianism, looked at as a theory concerning human society and the manner of its proper ordering, there is an easy obscuring of the relation of means and ends; for initially the utilitarian's doctrine commends itself as one which measures the claims of laws and institutions upon us by the extent to which they promote our private and personal well-being. But that private and personal well-being is something which seems perilously to lose its quality when its determination is left to Newtonian methods; so in Moore's intuition Keynes found something that seemed to preserve, by the sharpness and clarity of its deliverance, the excellent whose quality we discern by means of it. To say this is to say something of the rôle of intuition in Moore's doctrine; it is also, of course, to bring out again the fact that even those who will not return to more traditional modes of thought, from the thoroughgoing utilitarian position, yet still cannot rest in it. Even if what it leaves out cannot be said, the effort to say it has always to be made; and nowhere is this more impressively advertised than in the concessions made, at the level of political theory, by those who in some at least of the fundamental styles of their theory acknowledge the worth of the utilitarian determination to judge the traditional by the observed.

'Intuition' is a name; but to use it in the setting of this discussion makes it clear that the issue raised is one of epistemology, both in the rather special sense of the first chapter and in other more hackneyed uses. Words show their sense by the way in which they are used; and sometimes one meets something like the return of a word that had been expelled from respectable society to the lips of those who still belong to the circles and the traditions of those who had insisted on

its banishment. The word 'intuition' for the utilitarian referred to a claim to know by methods quite different from
those of the experimental or exact sciences; the idea of
'natural rights', for instance, was defended on the ground that
these rights were intuitively evident, and that whereas the
actual rights, for instance, of property-owners in a given
society was a matter for empirical investigation by students of
the law, or for definition by judges, these fundamental, basic
rights were evident to the 'light of reason'. Against any such
view, as we have now abundantly seen, the utilitarians
vigorously argued; but now 'intuition' returns as the name
whereby we knot together a whole group of discontents.
Thus, for Mill, there was something wrong with a view which
did not reckon, or allow for, the superiority of Socrates over
the fool; there is the related, but different, issue raised by
Moore in his very difficult theory of the intrinsically excellent; there is, moreover, the besetting sense that, where law
and government are concerned, utility is an important consideration indeed, but one that is invoked in a shadowy
context provided by such other authoritative notions as pity
and justice. No doubt these problems have to be separated;
and if one brackets them together as 'the problem of ethical
intuition', one is perhaps doing no more than suggesting that
'intuition' is a logical construction out of these discontents.
But it remains perhaps significant that the word which most
naturally springs to our lips in this connection is a word
which at least *prima facie* indicates a 'form of knowing'.

D. UTILITARIANISM AS AN 'ERFOLGSETHIK'

If utilitarianism is of high importance in the history of
political thought, it must never be forgotten that it remains,
in the narrower field of ethics, the classical example of an
Erfolgsethik, that is, a doctrine which judges the worth of
actions as moral by reference entirely to their consequences.
Now in a sense, in earlier sections of this chapter, this has
already been admitted; for mention has already been made

of the ruthless objectivity of the utilitarian standard. The
very notion of the hedonistic calculus, with its attempt to
assign to satisfactions a definite numerical value whereby
they can be compared as greater or less, is evidence of the
hold over the imaginations of the utilitarians of the ideal of
complete objectivity; to treat the extent of a satisfaction as a
function of its purity, intensity, duration, propinquity, etc.,
may raise a smile; yet the effort to do so is a clear indication
of the impulse, running right through the utilitarian enterprise, to escape from the elusive, the nebulous, the private, to
the obvious, the clear, the public. Although the notion of an
Erfolgsethik is one of a higher degree of formality than that of
utilitarianism, there is a curious congruity between the two,
analogous perhaps to that which we have noticed in the case
of Moore, between his goods and the nature of their goodness;
thorough-going utilitarianism seems a coat well cut to fit the fig-
ure of an *Erfolgsethik*; the two seem to consort singularly well.

Of course much has already been said that bears on this
aspect of our discussion. It may be sufficient here to mention
three points.

(*a*) If we make the moral worth of actions a matter of
what those actions bring into being in themselves and by
way of result, we tend to obliterate the distinction between
action and event. For what matters, at least where the
morality of the action is concerned, is not primarily the
motives, acknowledged or unacknowledged, of the agent, but
what he has brought into being, the changes he has effected
in his environment. In morality, 'outer' governs 'inner';
there is a standard by which we can judge what we have
done, and, more important, which we can ourselves learn to
use. This standard of the greatest happiness is one that is
valid for all men; for its authority is in its conformity with the
observed facts of the human situation. By appeal to it we can
know when we have failed, or when we have succeeded
morally, in what we have done; we are not at the mercy of
some mysterious, private, inner faculty of conscience; the

standard is public and worthy of common acceptation. Again, in periods of difficulty and perplexity, when the traditional obligations of which we are conscious seem to conflict, we have a standard by which we can judge between them, or even whereby we can learn to question both alike as without proper grounding in fact.

(*b*) Morality for the *Erfolgsethiker* is a matter of consequences, not of motives; and of course the word 'consequences' is here being bent to an unacknowledged, quasi-technical use. In ordinary speech, 'consequences' is used for results, foreseen or unforeseen, of what we do; thus a man may be blamed for not foreseeing that the consequences of failing to check the petrol in the tank of his car might include a breakdown in open country, or pitied because the careful holiday he had engineered for his children led to their deaths in a railway accident. The lines in ordinary discourse between 'action' and 'consequence of action' may not always be clearly drawn; but they are there. In a way, the *Erfolgsethiker* sharply ignores them; he is not interested in the nuances of ordinary use, but rather in introducing the word 'consequences' to bring out that for him what matters in morality is the way legal and moral, political and social institutions work out in terms of human happiness or the reverse. There is a paradox, of course, here; for in the end it is human beings presumably who are happy or unhappy, satisfied or in pain. But, where morality is concerned, it is not the inward, personal questionings of the individual that matter, but the promotion of a public welfare to which he must attune himself.

It is very important to notice that there is a quality almost of the austere in the utilitarian distaste for anything which might smack of the romantic cult of the individual, or the self-regard which often goes together with a developed personal scrupulosity.

(*c*) For the *Erfolgsethiker*, morality is, before all else, 'a system of public advantage'[1]; it is a set of mechanisms and devices whereby people are enabled to live together in a way

---

[1] The phrase is Godavia's.

that secures, e.g., the greatest happiness for all. It is, of course, a system which is open to continual improvement; but the lines along which that improvement will be found are tolerably clear. Whatever we prize or set store by in human life derives its worth from the contribution which is made by it to the promotion of that system. Thus for the *Erfolgsethiker* the study and the evaluation of the virtues of justice, temperance, prudence and courage will always be subordinate to the clear indication of the end, quite external to the individual, which these habits serve. It is often said, in criticism of the utilitarian, that because of his sympathy with an egoistic psychology he practically comes to the point of identifying moral excellence in the individual with a kind of detached and impersonal devotion to the interests of all; of this point much more will be said in the chapter on Butler. But, for the time being, it is perhaps worth making the point that, for the *Erfolgsethiker*, it is what is promoted and brought into being by action that comes first; for him, virtue for virtue's sake is silly. We know what makes for the advantage of mankind; no doubt we have read, or met, men who in their lives have advanced that welfare. We do well to extol these men; indeed we are no doubt wise to attend closely to the difficulties which they had to overcome, to the habits of mind which they had to cultivate, even sometimes to admit the element of good fortune which contributed to their achievement, and which cannot be properly anticipated in our own case; but the worth of these men, and indeed their significance for us, lie in what they achieved and brought into being. Our allegiance is in no sense given to them as individuals, but rather to the cause which they promoted.

So the line runs clearly; as far as possible the distinction between act and event is obliterated. Of course there are very important differences between doings and happenings; but, for morality, acts are events of a peculiar sort, and the moralist's concern is with their proper ordering. For this an impersonal, objective standard can be found; and its sway extends from the purpose of an agent in an individual, short-lived situation to the inmost set of his heart and will. Of course responding to a particular situation is one thing, and learning to be just and compassionate, honest and sceptical, quite different. But a good man is good not simply because he manifests in his behaviour certain dispositions, but because those dispositions serve a commonly admitted public advantage. A good man then is in the end a man who brings into being states of affairs of a certain sort; his excellence is not in himself but depends on what he does. Enough surely has been said to show the analogy between this movement of thought and the already observed concern of the utilitarian to subdue the claims of morality under the sovereign dominion of fact, to exhibit moral notions as logical functions of exactly definable factual concepts.

But what of Socrates? In terms of an *Erfolgsethik*, his worth resides in what he achieves for the betterment of mankind, in what he makes possible in that respect; his infinitely patient self-questioning is significant simply because, through it, roads have been opened for the increase of human happiness which must otherwise have remained closed. Similarly, when Mill writes of liberty, he sometimes defends its extension simply because without its wide diffusion, and relatively uncircumscribed exercise, possibilities of human advancement might be lost. There is no escaping the fact that we are in the presence here of an unacknowledged conflict of principle in Mill's thinking; it may be, indeed, from this conflict that some of the more familiar contradictions in his ethics spring. To argue consistently as an *Erfolgsethiker*, Mill must refuse to allow that any human life can be in any sense its own justification; for any ethic of consequences, the justification of a life is in what it achieves in the way of perceivable result; what is true of the fabric of our duties and the manners of our society holds also of the laborious self-discipline of the saint. Both alike have their only sanction in what they achieve in terms of human welfare.

We may perhaps go a stage further; we have noticed that
the thorough-going utilitarian takes his stand on the familiar
'empiricist principle', which has received very varied formula-
tions, but which has always somehow demanded that propositions concerning matters of fact shall be established by
sense and introspection (if the latter be allowed as a proper
means of commerce with the given). Indeed there is good
ground for saying that utilitarianism is, before all else, a kind
of obedience to the demands of the 'empiricist principle' in
esteeming the universe of worth, and of moral claim. Moore,
of course, broke vehemently with any attempt to derive the
intrinsically good from pleasure and pain, satisfaction and
discontent. Mention has already been made of some of his
arguments on this point, and their character will be the subject of further discussion later. But there is one point which
should be emphasised Moore was no hedonist and yet his
understanding of moral obligation conformed to the pattern
of the *Erfolgsethik*. Indeed the sheer self-containedness of his
intrinsic goods made it possible for him almost to sharpen the
distinction of means and ends, in terms of which he set out
his justification of moral effort[1]; and Keynes and his friends,
as we have seen, found in that part of Moore's doctrine something which, so to speak, effectively put political activity and
busyness in its place—a very subordinate place! Certainly
there is a great deal in Moore that involves a decisive break
with any form of 'empiricist principle'; but although this
may sound very paradoxical, it sometimes seems that in his
ethics he would like at least to endorse the kindred principle,
'metaphysics is impossible'; at least, if it is not impossible, it is
irrelevant, a questioning that distracts the attention and
obscures the real issue.

The thorough-going utilitarian would like, as we have seen,
to remove 'ought' and its cognates from the language; his
ideal is a language of fact that is all-embracing. But even in
those moments when he presses furthest towards this goal at

[1] It was the sharpening of this distinction indeed that made him so penetrating a critic of utilitarian 'busyness'.

the risk of every sort of confusion and muddle, he never quite lets go a sense of the universe of logic as something without which he cannot say what he means to achieve. Mill's account of mathematics is one of the weakest parts of his work; yet there is something strange about this if one remembers the Newtonian inspiration of the great utilitarians, and even the rôle of the hedonistic calculus in their work. For that rôle was not, as we have argued, peripheral, but constitutive. One might almost say that a sense of the significance of applied mathematics is a kind of ghost which haunts the stage of the utilitarian argument; for when we read the utilitarians, we are conscious that while, if they are to be consistent, they should be thorough-going sensationalists, yet their world is so very unlike the confused and confusing universe of mere sensation (this has already been noticed, of course, particularly in connection with the artificial character of psychological hedonism). The ideal of clarity, of exactly drawn lines between the admissible and the inadmissible, dominates the utilitarian; and it is still there in the *Erfolgsethik* of Moore. In both there is an analogous refusal to allow that, in any sense, the spiritual life of the individual man shall be its own justification; this is true of Moore, in spite of the worth which he attaches to certain states of consciousness and to the cultivation of friendship.

Both variants of *Erfolgsethik* are rigidly absolutist; there is in neither the least sympathy manifested with any form of ethical relativity. If Moore's hostility to pragmatism is clothed in explicit argument, there is an analogous repudiation of such a view in the earlier utilitarians. Of course we judge the worth of actions and the quality of characters by results; but we do not judge them by any and every result, but only by the contribution they make to the advance of that happiness which is what men desire. The sovereignty of fact is fundamental; indeed sometimes Moore's realism seems a kind of logical poem intended to impress this sovereignty still more clearly than it could be conveyed by the language of a more traditional empiricism. To insist that metaphysics is impossible may sometimes be very nearly equivalent to acknowledging the authority of such a style as this in ethical reflection. It may be an expression of a resolve to turn away from musing and perplexity concerning what one is, and what posture becomes one under the sun, to the pursuit of attainable goals of publicly recognisable good.

E. UTILITARIANISM AND METAPHYSICS

It has continually been remarked that the thorough-going utilitarian is a rare bird; and that the notion of utility well illustrates Collingwood's thesis concerning the overlap of philosophical concepts. But where there is sympathy with the utilitarian position, there is a movement towards its thorough-going form, just as in Aristotle's table of categories whatever is is related to substance. Enough has now been said for something at least of the essential emphasis of this thorough-going utilitarian position to be clear; and it is surely revealed as something quite definite. First and foremost it is a sense of the relevance of scientific method in the study of human conduct, and in particular to the evaluation of the norms by which we guide and direct our behaviour; it is a sense of the authority of that method as a liberating, because an enlightening, power. The relentless rigour of utilitarian argument, at its best, is an expression of this conviction; and it is impressive to be continually reminded how powerfully that argument can be sustained. Thus, for instance, once the peculiar standing of the greatest happiness principle is grasped, it can be shown, in the complexity of human life, to authorise much that would at first sight seem incompatible with it; for instance, a proper humility towards the quality of one's own purposes and the purity of one's motives. Further, if one takes over some at least of the insights of Moore, or at least recognises the importance of the questions which he is putting, one may be able to modify the utilitarian thesis, without destroying its essential outline; for there is perhaps, as was sug-

E

gested above, something of a *rapprochement* discernible between the styles of both sorts of *Erfolgsethiker*.

But of course that is not the whole story; there is the problem of Socrates; there is also the vague sense that to pursue the utilitarian method to the end is to forget the setting of the pursuit. Mill saw this when he wrote of Bentham and of Coleridge; there was a complexity in things human that the Benthamite methods would by-pass, a manifoldness in human nature that was somehow ignored by the confident insistence on the authority of a single principle; and there were other and related questions. It was no accident that, for all the clumsiness of their actual argument, their frequent ponderousness and obtuseness, the idealist critics of the utilitarians questioned, in the end, their understanding of the spiritual life of men. Of course the idealists made the enormous assumption that that life was somehow self-justifying; and by that alone they moved on to quite different ground from that on which the utilitarians were wont to argue. They could, of course, claim that Mill had already in effect begun to do this in what he said, for instance, on the subject of liberty and in his insistence that the life of Socrates was, in some sense, of worth in itself. For, after all, what was that life, what is any life? We have already moved on to the ground which the defenders of a *Gesinnungsethik* have made their own; we are already asking, or coming to the point of asking, whether purity of heart may not be its own justification.

Frequently in this chapter we have referred to the thesis that metaphysics is impossible. Usually we have been emphasising the close congruity of that thesis with the utilitarian sense of the sovereignty of fact. Almost to speak paradoxically, we have sometimes suggested that the thorough-going utilitarian would subordinate goodness to fact; if such speech is a logical near-outrage, it may succeed in bringing something out of the extent to which the utilitarian at once claims to be dealing with things as they are and at the same time to be bringing human morality under their sway, thus also, of course, securing human happiness. Where there is some sort of rebellion against the utilitarian claims, this rebellion may proceed in the name of the autonomy of human goodness, of the experience of the saint as somehow its own justification. But how are these things possible? What can we say of an experience that is its own justification? Moreover can we lightly escape reckoning with the thesis that metaphysics is impossible? Later in this book other forms of this thesis will be discussed; to deny the possibility of metaphysics is not the monopoly of the verificationist and his ancestors. For the present it is with some aspects of the utilitarian presentation of the thesis that we have been concerned. The man who rejects the utilitarian claim must ask himself whether there must not be something in his thinking corresponding to it; he must even go further and ask himself whether in the life of the saint there must not be something akin to the utilitarian refusal to rest in spurious mystery and obscurity. It is the seemingly self-justifying character of the life of the saint which sets a question-mark against the utilitarian programme; it is such a life that suggests that the whole problem of human conduct requires discussion in a different style. But to say that is not by itself more than a bare denial—at least it is not much more. A first step further might be to ask whether or not what we had extracted as the abiding temper of the utilitarian outlook could be realised, as it were transposed on to a new key; what would it be like, we may ask, to question the possibility of metaphysics and characteristically metaphysical attitudes towards human conduct in a context where spiritual life, including moral effort but extending beyond it, is accepted as somehow self-justifying? It is with such matters that later chapters in this book will be concerned.

At least this discussion of utilitarianism may have served a little to illustrate how hard it is sometimes to separate the contributions moral philosophers make to conversations and arguments concerning every-day practical complexities from the whole body of what they say concerning the nature of moral discourse. For the utilitarian in the end has to say, if he is thorough-going, that morality can only make sense if we stand outside it and see it as something which validly constrains us only in so far as its dictates serve empirically acceptable purposes of human welfare; indeed in the end it is the serving of those purposes; and if the ordinary man is serious in his demands, he must pay the price of turning his back on metaphysics. He must come to discern the hostility between metaphysics and a true human pity, and then relentlessly accept that pity only as valid which accepts the sovereignty of the greatest happiness. It is by the style of argument, in the end, that the inwardness of the position is conveyed.

CHAPTER III

KANT

A. INTRODUCTORY

To move from the discussion of the utilitarians to the discussion of Kant's ethics is, at first sight at least, to make entry upon a different world. Yet there is one very important similarity in temper between the two methods of approach, which should be mentioned. The thorough-going utilitarians are uncompromising in insisting that the moral worth of actions be found in their consequences; whereas Kant is equally insistent that it is for the policy of life affirmed by the the agent in his action, and not for what he achieves by means of the latter, that we are entitled to claim value in the first instance. He is uncompromisingly the champion of a *Gesinnungsethik*, and in this respect his emphasis falls poles asunder from that of the utilitarian. Yet the two have this in common, that they both alike favour a strongly formalist[1] approach to the problems of conduct. Of course they are formalists with a difference; and, as we shall see, Kant's understanding of the form of the moral law is closely bound up with the rôle he casts for the notions of form and matter, in their polar interplay, in his whole philosophy. There is nothing remotely like this in the utilitarians. But it was already remarked in the last chapter of this book how skeletal and programmatic their fundamental position remained.

It was not for nothing that use was made, in expounding their central contentions, of an artificial logical scheme. The device did more than make possible concentration of attention on the continuing strength of their argument; it brought

[1] With the difference between these formalisms we shall be concerned later.

out features of their professed understanding of the relations of ethics to psychology too often neglected by facile *reductio ad absurdum*. It belongs to the deepest insight of the utilitarians to see the attempted metaphysical grounding of ethics as at once logically inadmissible and, where the promotion of human happiness is at issue, sterile and even destructive. It might even be claimed that the deepest obscurities of the utilitarian position lay, and were continually recognised as lying, about the relation of happiness to fact. Mill grew up in the strong conviction that acknowledgment of the sovereignty of fact would serve the cause of human happiness, and then in ways to which his writings bear manifold witness, shifts, changes and enlargements in his understanding of that happiness put repeated question-marks against that assurance; thus, as we have already seen, epistemological problems were raised for him to which in the end he offered no solution. In the end he never repudiated the fundamental utilitarian conviction that the way of virtue lay ultimately through the application to the changing circumstances of human society of a single principle, infinitely flexible, universal in scope, and of unambiguous authority. The supremacy of the greatest happiness principle is by no means unlike the supremacy claimed by Kant for his supreme moral principle; thus it is the supremacy of one way over all others of seeing the practical problems of human life, and the supremacy too of one way over all others of criticising one's response to those problems.

For Kant a man must submit the inmost springs of his conduct to the judgment of law universal; for the utilitarian a man must never hesitate to discard the most cherished promptings of traditional moral sentiment in the name of a more exactly perceived estimate of human welfare. Both Kant and the utilitarians in their very different ways stress the rôle of self-criticism in conduct: for Kant, particular impulse continually distracts men from acknowledgment in their action of the sovereign universal; for the utilitarians,

every sort of prejudice and traditional feeling can distract
men from the proper weighing of the consequences of what
they intend. For both alike, human frailty, very differently
perceived admittedly by each, calls for a relentless discipline,
and both alike in their ethical writings try to outline
the formal principles of such. For neither, in the nature
of the case, can what they offer be something applied
once for all; for both, in different ways, it must have the flexibility proper to a supreme principle intended to illuminate,
and to illuminate absolutely, the most different sorts of perplexity.[1]

There may be something paradoxical in thus emphasising
the formalist character of the utilitarian approach to ethics;
but the paradox is mitigated when the essentially formal
character of the concept of fact, perhaps the pivot of the
utilitarian system, is recalled. In the previous chapter, in
order to bring out this crucial point, deliberate use was made
of the tools provided by modern logical analysis; a use which
had abundant historical justification in the manner in which
those tools had been originally devised to make good de-
ficiencies in the fabric of an empiricist philosophy. When we
speak of the concept of fact as a formal concept, we are
insisting that 'fact' is not the name of anything in the world;
rather it is a way of indicating a certain kind of relation, or
relations, in which what happens in the world may stand to
our concern about it. Thus Professor H. H. Price has
spoken[2] of a fact as 'an event, or set of events, viewed as
making a given proposition true or false'. To speak more col-
loquially, facts are what subtle theorists must bark their shins
against; and, where conduct is concerned, acceptance of the
authority of fact shows itself in a resolve to allow the actual
routes to human happiness, determined at once by human

---

[1] Cf. here the fascinating paradox of Sidgwick's combination of hedonistic
utilitarianism with belief in a categorical imperative.

[2] In a review in *Mind* (July 1935) of Professor John Wisdom's *Problems of
Mind and Matter*. The ambiguity of the word 'formal' should be remembered
when fact is spoken of as a 'formal concept'.

nature and by human circumstance, to prescribe the moral rules by which men are to live.

B. KANT'S ETHICS AND HIS THEORY OF KNOWLEDGE

Yet, of course, the differences between Kant and the utilitarians are fundamental; and they are concentrated in the fact that Kant is, as remarked above, uncompromisingly the champion of a *Gesinnungsethik*. Moreover in the unity of the critical philosophy,[1] Kant's moral theory is cast for a very special rôle, and it is impossible to understand it without seeing what it is that Kant claims for moral experience as he presents it; if he differs from the utilitarian in insisting that moral worth belongs pre-eminently to the motive, and not to the consequence, of action, he differs also in insisting that in morality we are committed to the unconditioned. Just as the theory of knowledge contained in the first part of the *Critique of Pure Reason* provides both the ground of and an introduction to the criticism of the possiblity of metaphysics, which, as the book's title suggests, is its primary concern, so that work as a whole is both introduction to and ground of the moral philosophy which follows it. The two belong together; the subtle agnosticism to which Kant argues in his first Critique provides the context in which the peculiar quality of moral experience can be discerned. There is something of the same sort, of course, in Butler's treatment of human ignorance in his Fifteenth Sermon; but in Kant there is something at once of the painstaking minuteness and the sheer virtuosity characteristic of the philosopher of genius, who makes it possible to see a whole group of seemingly dis-

---

[1] In what follows the writer has dared to depart from the problems of Kantian scholarship, and to speak of the issues raised by some aspects of the critical philosophy; but it remains true that such boldness is only possible for him because of the magnificent labours of Kantian scholars, especially Professor H. J. Paton, who have vindicated the unity of the critical philosophy against such distracting and exhausting errors as, e.g., the 'patchwork theory of the transcendental deduction'. The debt in which any British student of Kant's writings stands to Professor Paton's work can hardly be over-estimated.

connected problems together in a new light. If Kant is an agnostic in respect of the possibility of our providing any sort of theoretical answer to our questioning concerning the nature of ultimate reality, this agnosticism achieves a quality peculiarly its own both from the doctrine of categories in terms of which it is worked out, and from the acceptance of the unconditional authority of the moral order for which it prepares the way. There is a sense in which his doctrine of categories is the gateway both to Kant's characteristic understanding of the nature of human knowledge and to his insistence that, in acknowledging the moral law within us, we are all the time enjoying commerce with the unconditioned, made all the more secure by our accepting those conditions which doom to frustration any effort we may make to describe what it is with which in such commerce we have to do. And yet although the possibility of description is absent, still we recognise in the authority which thus unconditionally constrains us the voice of our own nature as rational beings, and not the brusque, sheerly unintelligible dictate of a despot. There is in Kant's writing here, as we shall see more clearly presently, a continued recognition both of the uniqueness, indeed the mysteriousness and strangeness, of that with which in the moral order we have to do and, at the same time, of its character as rational.

1. *The categories of understanding.* In the first chapter of this book some suggestions were made about the rule assigned by writers on moral theory to something called 'epistemology'; the word was, of course, borrowed from the traditional vocabulary of modern philosophy, and put to a relatively novel use; this may easily lead to serious confusion in respect of Kant's work, inasmuch as he is often presented as the 'epistemologist *par excellence*'. Certainly, as was indicated above, his theory of knowledge provides the gateway into his whole system; if British students have been wrong to write as if the whole critical philosophy were concentrated in the first half of the *Critique of Pure Reason*, they are none the less right to

insist both on its intrinsic importance, and on its besetting influence on the whole texture of his argument. But it should be clearly understood that if we look in Kant for something which could be called epistemology in the special sense of the first chapter, this would have to be found rather at the point at which his theory of knowledge and his ethics pass, as it were, into one another. This language is unfortunately metaphorical; but it calls attention to something which any-one who has tried to teach Kant's ethics will certainly know. In a course of lectures which he gave at Oxford in the early months of 1934, shortly after he had arrived in this country as a refugee, the late Professor Ernst Cassirer spoke of the rôle of the notion of autonomy in Kant's ethics as analogous to that played by the notion of the spontaneity of the under-standing in his theory of knowledge. Such a remark, very illuminating as it certainly is, would be epistemological in the special sense given to the term at the end of the first chapter. For it serves to throw a clear light on the sort of relationship which, for Kant, certainly obtained between the forms in terms of which we necessarily represented the order of the world around us, and that moral law within us by which we acknowledged ourselves unconditionally bound and of which we were nevertheless the authors.

It used to be said of Kant that the evident disproportion observed between his theoretical and his practical, philosophy was the expression of a change of mind experienced be-tween the writing of the first two Critiques, and variously attributed to his distress at finding the religious faith of his servant impugned by his arguments, and to his fear of the Prussian state police. Certainly to those who have read about him, rather than read his work, Kant's name suggests one who combined a sceptical unwillingness to allow validity to theoretical statement concerning the ultimate origin and destiny of the world with a confident, even a dogmatic, readiness to accept the authority of an unconditional moral law. But the actual state of the case is much more subtle.

Thus in his theory of knowledge Kant is emphatic that discursive understanding is spontaneous; its ways of working, which interpenetrate one another in such a way as to form a special sort of complex unity, are its own. Even if he denies to understanding anything of the nature of what Einstein calls *Durchdringskraft*,[1] he insists that by its power the limits of the world of our experience are set. Almost, if pressed to to justify confidence in causal law, he will answer that such confidence is proper because of a non-causally ordered world we could not say how it would look. The completeness and finality claimed by Kant for his table of categories has often been criticised; but it was a completeness and finality claimed only because the philosopher insisted that the order of the world of our experience was grounded in the power of understanding to describe in this way and not in that, and to admit to the status of object of experience only that which it had first conformed to the law of its own forms.

Of course, for Kant, understanding is discursive; it cannot posit its own matter, but is dependent upon what falls to be within its grasp from without. Various metaphors have been used to illustrate this fusion of spontaneity and dependence; for instance the meshes of a net, methods and instruments of measurement, the questing beam of a searchlight (the last-mentioned by Professor Karl Popper). All alike endeavour to bring out what for Kant is fundamentally significant in human knowledge: this is, the fact that, when we know, we describe, and if the ways of our describing are necessarily in our own power, that which we describe is still something coming to us from without. Such understanding is for Kant contrasted with what he calls intuitive understanding; indeed his procedure, in some ways, strangely recalls that of those scholastics who try to lay bare the characteristic features of our human knowledge by contrasting it with the knowledge enjoyed by angels, and even by God Himself.

[1] 'Penetrative power'. See Einstein's essay in the volume on *The Philosophy of Bertrand Russell*, ed. P. A. Schilpp (U.S.A., 1944).

We may not, Kant says, suppose such an understanding to exist; but we can conceive it as a bare possibility, and by so doing we may the better take stock of the inherent limitations of our own. We can conceive an understanding which posits its own objects, and for which in consequence those objects are transparent; here it would be out of place to speak of the laborious work of description, the ordering and inter-relating of concepts, the gradual improvement of our ways of representing the workings of the natural world. If this use of the language of transparency[1] is metaphorical, at least it helps to bring out, where such an understanding is concerned, the peculiar immediacy of its knowledge, an immediacy suggesting at once its simultaneous comprehension of the whole and even the unique mode of that whole's presence to its perception. Of course, for Kant, such an activity is something which we can only deploy in negative terms, as the limit of our own familiar activity; but the enterprise of deployment is worth-while for the sharpness with which it compels us to acknowledge the peculiar polarity, in our own empirical knowledge, of spontaneous form and sensuously presented matter. Kant's readers who know the language of the prayer which speaks of God as one 'to whom all hearts be open, all desires known and from whom no secrets be hid' may well insist that what Kant is doing is no more than to illuminate the character of human knowledge by contrasting it with something that is spoken of more naturally in the language of devotion than in the kind of discourse in which Kant's theory finds its home. But it is perhaps characteristic of Kant's genius that while he is concerned with that exact and rigorous thinking which he found manifested in Newtonian physics, he sought to bring out something of the first importance concerning the standards of that rigour and exactitude, which he could only bring out by insisting on their peculiar limitation through the evocation of an omniscient, creative intelligence. Those standards did in a sense decide what

---

[1] It should be remembered in connection with another use mentioned later.

could be admitted as objects of experience for us; indeed, one would have to say that in a sense, for Kant, they *were* our understanding. But in their authority there was an element of relativity, and this Kant tried to throw into clear relief by this image (if I may so call it) of an intuitive understanding.

Thus the spontaneity of understanding is something to which Kant must deny the name of creative; for to use such a name would inevitably imply the utterly false view that, in knowledge of the world around us, we were in some sense the makers of what we perceive. For Kant, as much as for any realist, knowledge of the empirical world is a finding, not a making. The truth of the propositions we entertain about the properties of things in that world, and the relations between them, are verified or falsified by reference to what is perceived as happening. For Kant, truth is fundamentally correspondence between proposition and fact; certainly this correspondence was not, in any sense, a kind of picturing of elements in fact by elements in proposition. But whether what we supposed was true we only established by tests that took us right outside the world of supposition, and brought us into direct commerce with what our senses revealed to us as present. If Kant likened the procedures of the laboratory to learned Counsel's interrogation of a witness in court, who is confined to answering the questions put to him and only allowed to tell his story in his own words when it suits Counsel that he should do so, this did not mean that he found in these procedures the remotest hint of a deliberate retreat from the authority of the sensuously presented; if there was artifice and contrivance in the procedures of the laboratory, corresponding somehow to the basic form of human questioning and description, these were orientated to an end outside themselves, namely that of finding out what was actually the case.

If we speak of Kant as an idealist, we must be careful to remember that he was also emphatic in his insistence that we could never from general propositions deduce the nature of what is the case; he is only an idealist (apart from the special sense in which his peculiar doctrines of space and time demand that he should be called such) because of his intense concentration upon the subjective as such. He is deeply interested in human knowledge as such, the characteristic dignity and limitation of specifically human enquiry into the nature of what is. He will not take the fact of human knowledge as a springboard for speculation (the argument of the Paralogisms is definitive here); but he will ponder upon it in all its aspects, devoting to each of its most characteristic forms of expression in turn attention sometimes surprising often obscure and yet frequently illuminating. Of course it is an axiom with Kant that we are at home with ourselves, and that where the fundamental laws of our understanding are concerned, *there* we are transparent to ourselves. Unlike his successors, such as Hegel, who in so many ways moves in a different world, he was immune from the sort of perplexities and scepticisms which sooner or later follow the admission of a measure of historical relativity. Where his categories were concerned, which he had derived from the anatomy of the forms of judgment carried out by the masters of the traditional logic, he had all the logician's assurance of dealing with that which was independent alike of the quirks of individual psychology or the accidents of historical circumstance. Yet he found in human knowledge, and especially in the interplay between spontaneous understanding and passive reception of a given, something whose power and whose limitation alike fascinated him; and in a way that still captivates his readers and continually enlightens them he threw into the clearest relief the fashion and the consequences of this necessary complementarity.

It is in his theory of the necessarily discursive character of the understanding that his criticism of those traditional metaphysicians who operated quite uncritically with such concepts as substance, causality, necessity, possibility, existence, etc., is rooted; these concepts had a quite indispensable rôle

in human enquiry into the nature of the world, but the very
character of that rôle, as well as the distinctive limitation of
that understanding whose concepts they were, rendered them
totally unsuited for the task of admitting men to the order of
the unconditioned.

A thorough contemporary study of Kant's philosophy
would have to decide on the viability of such an enterprise as
his attempted metaphysical deduction of the pure concept, of
the understanding; to many it would certainly seem a high
presumption to speak of such a thing as the understanding
itself, let alone to attempt the exposition of its basic forms.
Philosophers as different in temper as the late Professor R. G.
Collingwood and the members of the so-called 'Vienna
Circle' have agreed in seeing in Kant's table of categories a
misplaced and uncritical attempt to fetter an inherently
flexible understanding in a quite artificial bondage; yet it is
hard sometimes to escape the sense that, in any serious effort
to describe the world, we are in some way or other committed by making it to the use of certain concepts; their
elusiveness and formality may continually tantalise and
rebuff the attempts we make to pin down their content in the
way in which we often succeed, in a measure, in pinning
down the content of even the most abstract of ordinary descriptive concepts. If there are categories in the sense in
which Kant supposed there to be, this very elusiveness may
be one mark of their peculiar nature; they are everywhere
and nowhere, in their nature radically formal and not
material, and in representing that nature we must have
recourse to every sort of subterfuge and extravagance of
metaphor; speaking of them even as a kind of 'dynamical
syntactic order', if thereby we can convey the way in which
they fuse in their notion, a unity of structure and an expression of the essentially active, self-regulating, questing character of the understanding.

2. *Relative and absolute*. Kant's doctrine of the primacy of
the practical reason turns on his theory of the understanding;

indeed the latter could be spoken of as a kind of propaedeutic study for the presentation and the grasping of the latter. The writer who makes the claim for characteristically moral experience which Kant makes must provide himself the context within which alone that experience can be received for what it is; it is a commonplace to say that for Kant morality is a categorical imperative, and modern writers frequently congratulate him for the insight he displays in recognising that the proper formulation of the ethical proposition was to be found in the imperative, as distinct from the indicative, mood. Certainly for Kant it was of the highest importance to perceive that the imperatives of morality were imperatives relative to no indicative whatsoever; the distinction between the categorical and the hypothetical imperative lay very near the heart of his moral theory. But it would be a complete mistake to suppose that for him the distinction was simply one of verbal form, or that the moralist's task was completely fulfilled when he had found the place of the characteristically moral imperative on the language-map. Of course he had to do this; the importance of distinguishing imperatives that were relative to purposes entertained by an individual agent, or by the society of which he was a member, from imperatives that were not so relative was a quite crucial enterprise. But the existence of the latter sort of imperative was, for Kant, something that seemed to take away from men the possibility of any sort of detached neutrality; at the level of the categorical imperative we were no longer talking about ways in which this or that element of our experience might be represented; we were ourselves confronted by the question of our validity as human beings. We were pitchforked willy-nilly from the level of the conditioned to that of the unconditioned.

The character of this sudden, yet constant, transition from the relative to the absolute we could only bring home to ourselves by the painful, yet necessary, criticism of our theoretical gropings after the unconditioned. Moral experience for Kant may be sudden and peremptory; like Mr. Arthur Koestler[1] in his Spanish prison, listening to the ceaseless butcherings of Franco's murder squads, we are made vividly and dramatically aware of the unconditional authority over us of a universe in which due regard is paid to the dignity of human nature, in which respect and not contempt has sway. We recognise the obligation to affirm in action the authority of such a universe upon us, even if we cannot deploy the detail of its life, or even by pictorial imagery cement the claim its membership makes on our allegiance. In such an experience as the one Koestler so unforgettably describes, the transition is sudden, and by its very suddenness assumes a kind of dramatic force which creates a set of images, in his case that of a gravitational field, to convey it; but Kant saw that although the transition could sometimes reveal itself to us with this peculiar poignancy, it was also one in which we were continually involved as human beings. The metaphorical background of transition is spatial, a movement from one level to another; and it would not be far-fetched to suggest that Kant sees men almost like climbers poised precariously with one foot on one ridge, one on another, compelled (if the metaphor does not seem fantastic) to make no effort to bring their feet together. In men's experience of life the awareness of the categorical imperative may break suddenly and sharply upon their dedication to, and absorption in, the service of a purpose, whether individual or collective; but in the constant, steady routines of their human life the sense of its demand upon them may also certainly continue as a kind of unconditional background to the relative, now increasing, now diminished, satisfactions they may win from the pursuit of their theoretical enquiries.

Kant certainly did not belittle either the dignity or the significance of those enquiries; his work in respect of their character constitutes a watershed in the history of the logic of the exact sciences, and men of the quality of Albert

---

[1] Compare his essay in *The God that Failed* (1950).

F

Einstein and Karl Popper agree in acknowledging a debt to him. But there was for Kant an element in moral experience that was quite *sui generis*; here we were in hourly touch with what in the end seers and metaphysicians alike had been talking about. The element of relativity in human knowledge at once revealed the peculiar character of its authority and served, by its recognition, to throw into clearer light what we have spoken of above as the uniqueness, the mysteriousness and strangeness of that with which, in the moral order, we have to do; in the same place reference was made to the subtle agnosticism of the first Critique. Perhaps we are now in a position to see more clearly what is meant by agnosticism in such a connection; it is not the name of a wistful temper that expects, with more or with less confidence, a revelation; still less is it the name of an attitude which contentedly writes off questions concerning human origin and destiny as unanswerable. It is rather a confidence of the transcendent import of moral experience, which is grounded in a rationally achieved comprehension of the powerlessness of theoretical activity to impugn its inescapable uniqueness. We are, Kant says, continually conscious of the impulse to use the concepts of our understanding to scale heights of the unconditioned, to set free such notions as substance and cause from the limitation to which their necessary relativity to sense binds them, and by their means capture at least the outlines of the absolute and unconditioned. But the fruits of such an enterprise are at best ambivalent, and at worst antinomous; and it is near the heart of Kant's doctrine that such a recognition, so far from paralysing the imagination, works to liberate the will. Moral goodness is for Kant the sun of the universe of value; such is the clear teaching of the opening sections of the *Grundlegung*. But when we recognise the imperative to pursue the way of such goodness against the background of due acknowledgment of the limitations of our most fundamental theoretical concepts to descriptive and interpretative tasks, we gain a deeper view of its transcendent dignity and import.

Here quite simply we come to ourselves, not knowing what
we are but clear beyond shadow of doubt what, by our action
here and now, we must endeavour to make ourselves.

3. *First remarks on Kant's treatment of freedom.* It is at this
point that first reference should be made to some features of
Kant's treatment of freedom. His attempted reconciliation of
a rigid determinism with freedom in the sense of the libertarian is riddled with difficulties, to some of which reference
will be made later in this chapter. For the time being it may
be remarked that Kant's work here only begins to become
intelligible when it is seen as the crucial aspect of his confidence that it is metaphysical agnosticism which before all
else safeguards the transcendent character of morality.
'Ought implies can'; every first-year student of philosophy
knows that Kant said this. But perhaps fewer realise that he
said it with a clear perception that in freedom there was
something intellectually scandalous; it was indeed for Kant a
primarily originative causality, something utterly unlike the
relationships of cause and effect we found, or thought we
found, or tried to find, in the world around us. Men and
women were somehow first causes of what they brought into
being; if the late Baron Friedrich von Hügel was partly
justified in speaking of Kant as 'the philosopher of Protes-
tantism' (and some reference will be made later in this
chapter to possible influences of the Lutheran doctrine of
justification on his thought), his treatment of freedom
showed, as the late Professor A. E. Taylor loved to point out,
that in the controversies concerning grace between Jesuits
and Dominicans it was on the side of the *synergism* of the
former that his sympathies were enlisted. Nothing could take
from men and women this authorship of what they were;
they knew themselves originative authors of what came into
being by their actions through the awareness of the moral
law as constraining them absolutely *hic et nunc*. If their view
of the universe *as a whole* conflicted with this immediate,
constantly renewed awareness of themselves as morally con-

strained, it was that view which must be challenged; and it was Kant's claim for his theory of knowledge that it revealed any view of the universe *as a whole* as something inevitably riddled with contradiction, such as must follow any attempt on the part of discursive understanding to escape the limitations of its inherent nature.

For Kant, determinism was in the end the name of a method; it was the name of a wholly indispensable method without which, he believed, any serious attempt to set out the workings of the universe around us must crumble. No doubt in recent controversies concerning the forms of physical laws his sympathies would have been with those who treated laws of a deterministic pattern as more fundamental than those of a statistical;[1] he would have been inclined to judge the latter, in some sense at least, a *pis aller*, and in this we need not hesitate to judge him wrong. But the argument concerning determinism and indeterminism in physics would have been for him an argument quite irrelevant to that of the status of human freedom; arguments in detail concerning the proper methods of the exact sciences were of the highest importance; but for the philosopher who was concerned with the significance of moral action what was important was, not to decide between determinist and indeterminist in physics, but to grasp the nature of the controversy and the irrelevance of its solution to the solution of the problem of freedom.

Kant would indeed have had no little sympathy with those who saw the controversy between determinist and indeterminist as one related primarily to the syntax of the language of physics; but he would have insisted that to see the controversy so was to see the irrelevance of its outcome to our grasp of what, as moral agents, we are. The metaphysician, for Kant, was continually tempted to convert a method of investigation into a view of what the world was ultimately like; and some of the recent deliverances of modern-style metaphysical determinists and indeterminists would have

[1] Contrast, e.g., von Mises in *Probability, Statistics and Truth*.

furnished Kant with telling illustrations of this sort of ontological illusion. No doubt his treatment of what he calls 'the notion of cause' is lamentably unsophisticated and dated; none the less he did see with extraordinary perception the extent to which, for instance, the determinist of the school and style of Laplace was wedded to a quite uncritical confusion between fundamental methodological ideas and much older ontological conceptions. The notion of cause had been used for generations by philosophers now in one way, now in another: to define men's situation in being, to indicate their ultimate origin, to convey their final destiny. But the notion as the theoretical physicist employed it, and identified it, in his employment, with the conformity of events in nature to exactly formulable laws, was of a quite different order; it was indeed Kant's conviction that it was the physicist's use of the notion that gave us a kind of key to the understanding of its inherent nature and limitations. But the physicist needed the philosopher to bring home to him the revolutionary consequences of his own transformation of the notion, and to free his scientific work from the sort of unnecessary confusion which followed entanglement in the pseudo-problems generated by an uncriticised use of concepts.

Once we have seen the character of determinism as a method, we have taken the proper measure of its claim upon us; and we can deepen our perception of the characteristic features of this claim, when we have traced the character of the notion to its remote source as a concept of an inherently discursive understanding. We may not be able to see how we can describe anything except we invoke it; its use in description, and in the explanation which supervenes upon description, may be indispensable. But description is not the whole of human life; there is also what Kant calls 'the moral law within', whose authority, moreover, we know in the demand to complete integrity which comes to us continually in respect of our theoretical activity itself. We must not cheat. Here is an authority which binds us absolutely; yet we know that we cannot describe the relation of that authority within to the world around us of which we are part. *For what we describe, we can only describe by making it part of that world.* The relation of the world of freedom to the world of nature is something which we cannot comprehend; yet we can recognise the grounds of this incomprehensibility, and take confidence therefrom inasmuch as we have seen it rooted in the limitation of our fundamental theoretical concepts to the condition. Freedom is not something we can *know*; here Kant recalls the theologians who spoke of what they called 'the negative way'. We grasp that it is; but *how* it is necessarily eludes us. Yet, as we shall see, Kant will not allow freedom to be sheerly mysterious. But it is none the less his deep conviction that, because the speculative movement to the unconditioned is so deeply wedded to the use of the notion of cause, a proper criticism of that notion, a thorough putting it in its proper place, helps to reveal the unacknowledged sympathy of any metaphysician with some kind of determinism; and consequently the vindication of the concept of freedom as something ultimate in itself must take the surprising path of identifying the criticism of the absolute claims of the determinist with something very near the criticism of metaphysics itself. If the physicists of Kant's day had confused principles of method with ontological structures, their confusion was partly explained by the failure of philosophers all down the ages to measure up to the paradoxical, and inwardly deceptive, style of the metaphysical quest. It was not only Laplace, but also the thorough-going ontological monist, who left no room for freedom in his world; and the principles in accordance with which he criticised the former were, he believed, equally fatal to the claims of the latter. For Kant there was a deep-seated contradiction between the metaphysical temper and the temper of the man who saw himself standing under a moral law which, although he was its author, he must freely himself affirm. Kant's criticism of metaphysics is the means whereby he throws into the clearest possible relief the transcendent quality of freedom, of creativity, and the means whereby he effectually refuses any temptation to downgrade the ultimacy of the notion.

4. *Kant's view of morality as absolute.* In pointing out the inadequacy of speaking of Kant's recognition of the imperative character of human morality as if it were no more than a giving ethical language its proper place on the language-map, it must be remembered, of course, that for him such language is irreducibly imperative; but this irreducibility is of a quite special sort, one which indeed can only be grasped when the relation of Kant's theory of knowledge to his ethics has been set out. Certainly, for him, we cannot derive the 'ought' of morality from the 'is' of fact; yet this radical discontinuity is something which has, for him, the quality of a most preciously won and precariously held insight. It would hardly be an exaggeration to say that for him it possesses something at least of the dignity of a revelation of what ultimately is. It is absolutely pivotal to his argument to tie the discrimination of ethical from factual language to the criticism of metaphysics. If we merely content ourselves with pointing out, for instance, that no multiplication of instances of a given state of affairs, say the cultivation of habits of sympathy and forbearance by the members of a given society, by itself somehow conveys the *morally obligatory* character of their cultivation, we do certainly point out something important about the unique status of the notion of moral obligation; we bring out the 'apartness' of the languages of sociological description and of morality. But for Kant it was still more important to bring out the differences between the pseudo-descriptive language of the metaphysician and the language of moral goodness and obligation.

For Kant, men were inherently metaphysical animals; the distinction between Reason and Understanding which he draws in the first Critique advertises a crucial feature of the human situation. It might be said that, for him, continuing metaphysical malaise was at once the surest index of men's worth, and of their poverty. The restless dissatisfaction with relatively unsystematised description of the world around them, which drove men on to simpler, more economical and more comprehensive orderings of their explanatory concepts, was, on Kant's view, only one fruitful manifestation of this besetting *nisus* towards the unconditioned; but what was a matter of pride was also a profound occasion of temptation, and here the issue was one which ranged beyond the mere threat of intellectual error in a limited sense; the suggestion that our concepts could somehow be enlarged so as to capture the unconditioned was an illusion, and it was an illusion which was most dangerous in that it obscured from us the actual commerce with the unconditioned we continually enjoy. And this obscuring worked in two ways.

(*a*) Firstly, we were tempted all the time to suppose that the absolute and unconditioned must remain the preoccupation only of an intellectually enlightened and specially trained élite; something which touched life most intimately at all times and at all places became a kind of remote and almost esoteric specialism. Further, what was the matter of perennially serious concern tended to be seen as a question or set of questions that could tax speculative ingenuity to the uttermost, but which could yet never receive an answer. Idealist and realist, spiritualist and materialist, theist and atheist, might argue ceaselessly, producing new and at first sight exciting variations on familiar themes; but although what they wrote and said in one sense bore witness to men's besetting, restless concern with the unconditioned, in other ways their thought only served to bring such concerns into a kind of disrepute, even to imply the startling and unacceptable consequence that there was something almost frivolous in an anxiety to attain a purchase-hold upon the ultimate. Kant's criticism of metaphysics enables his readers to see how such an impression is necessarily created by the very ambivalence of the metaphysical pursuit itself; it lays bare some, at least, of the sources of that ambivalence.

(b) Secondly, the suggestion that our concepts could be enlarged so as to capture the unconditioned obscured not only the reality of our commerce with that unconditioned, but the *manner* of that commerce; it was something which we knew always as an imperative laid upon us, never as a part of the world, or of another world in which we had somehow become at home. For Kant, the absolute for human beings is always realised as a *Sollen*.

If it is a commonplace to present Kant as the unflinching champion of an ethical absolutism, it is less often made clear that one of the insights which makes his work permanently valuable is the way in which he brings out, by the order of his argument, what ethical absolutism actually involves. The first part of the *Grundlegung* makes clear that it involves the supremacy of characteristically moral excellence over all other forms of excellence; but the third part, taken in conjunction with the extended argument of the first two Critiques, reveals that it also demands that we find in characteristically moral experience that about which the metaphysician had been trying to speak. It is also a commonplace to speak of Kant as pre-eminently the critic of any sort of ontological metaphysics, of any attempt, that is, to give an account of the ultimate constituents of being as such; the contrast is often drawn between his doctrine of categories and Aristotle's. But it is less often remarked that this hostility to characteristically ontological metaphysics, which pervades the first Critique, is closely related to Kant's conviction that it is at the level of *Sollen* that we have commerce with the ultimate; there is, for him, something suspect in the suggestion that what is ultimate can be found, e.g., in the delineation of the modes of an analogically participated being. What is ultimate is what engages the allegiance of our will without possibility of question or cavil.

And here again reference must be made to his treatment of freedom. It would be a bold statement, but one which the direction of his argument goes no little way to justify, to say that for Kant it is his overwhelming sense of the reality of freedom which sets him on edge in the presence of supposed ontological delineation; of course, to speak of Kant's sense of the *reality* of freedom is almost to be guilty of a solecism. For reality is, after all, in his view one of the categories of modality, correlative with possibility and necessity, and bound in its use to the limits of possible experience. If we allow such an overwhelming sense to Kant, it must always be within the context of the supremely authoritative *Sollen*. Freedom is not something we can talk about, not a dignity we can claim for ourselves as a certain professional or social standing in a particular society of which we happen to be members; it is something of a different order altogether, 'implied', in the familiar phrase, 'by ought.'

C. THE RATIONALISM OF KANT'S ETHICS

Yet at the outset of this chapter it was possible to point to certain similarities between Kant's doctrine and that of the Utilitarian; and it is important at this juncture to recall the fact. For Kant there is in freedom something ultimate, something mysterious, something for whose reality we must be prepared gladly to sacrifice the spurious delights of exhaustive description of the formal nature of what is, that by its supposed completeness would admit us in some measure upon the unconditioned. The sacrifice, of course, is not blindly made, but achieved in fulfilment of the demands of the self-criticism of reason. We come to see that metaphysics is impossible; and when we see this we see how it is that morality must rest in the air, be without foundation, outside itself; and in itself it is a matter of the individual's painful self-discipline and growth. When we have carried through the criticism of metaphysics, we are able to see what the peculiar ultimacy of morality is, what indeed becomes of a notion of the ultimate and unconditioned when a home is found for it at the level of the *Sollen*. Yet such acknowledgment of something strange, unique, even precarious, does not undermine Kant's underlying rationalism; he remains, as Dr. Karl Popper continually reminds us, a son of the Enlightenment. Our freedom is something which we enjoy, or to which we are committed, as rational beings, imposing or trying to impose upon our fluctuating and tumultuous appetites the disciplines of law universal.

For Kant, creativity is a mystery; it is something for which room must be found in our view of the world, even at the cost of the most radical criticism of the way in which we have *prima facie* received and accepted that view. And it is not simply a matter of room in the sense of some little space not occupied by something else. Here is the heart of the human matter, and woe betide us if, in the name of speculative conceit of any sort we forget the fact. Here idealist and theist could be every bit as much offenders as materialist and positivist. Yet this creativity is not something to be viewed in the manner of the romantic; Kant would have no sympathy with, e.g., Carlyle's cult of the hero, or the sort of espousal of the tragic for its own sake which we find to-day in certain currents of existentialism. Certainly the suggestion that there is any virtue in blind obedience, or acceptance of the hardness of the human lot with an almost masochistic delight, is something totally alien from Kant's own austere humanism. The ethics of the *Führerprinzip*, even if the supposed authority of the 'Leader' were given a quasi-religious dignity, were for him an obvious violation of the character of morality as we continually knew it from within ourselves; to obey the 'Leader' in a mood of violent self-disregard and exultant, supposedly heroic contempt for the ordinary routines of human happiness had, for him, no worth at all. To find in morality something mysterious, even awful, was not to be converted to a sombre, even a pessimistic, estimate of the human situation. Certainly Kant acknowledged the presence and the force of what he called '*radikal Böse*' in the human heart; and we might (he thought) well doubt whether the course of human history could show us even one example of the perfect fulfilment of the demand of the moral law. Moral failure was only too common; and sometimes indeed we found in the circumstances of human life altogether outside our control much to perplex and torment us, even that which threatened to undermine our own individual sense of the authority of that law of which we were the bearers. Yet to face these perplexing questions from within an assured grasp of what morality essentially is was something altogether different from being tricked, through a failure to understand morality aright, into finding in those questions themselves somehow the justification for identifying moral virtue with a kind of heroic toughness. In such an attitude there was nothing whatsoever of creativity as Kant understood it; only a masquerade made possible, as any and every such, by the failure to attend seriously to the implications of the criticism of metaphysics. A man may fall under the spell of metaphysical illusion as much when he somehow attaches supreme ontological import to the fact of death as the inescapable horizon of human life, as when, by some alleged intuition of the necessary relations of being, he claims to discern the necessary dependence of the world upon an infinite first cause.

Men are laws to themselves, not in the sense that by their action they confer on events an arbitrary pattern of their own devising, but in the sense of being committed by their rationality to discipline themselves in certain ways, to order at once their emotions and imaginations, and their comings and goings in relation to their fellows, in accordance with universal principles. There is nothing arbitrary about morality for Kant; if its status is that of an unconditional 'ought' there is nothing about that 'ought' remotely suggestive of the fiat of the despot. If its demand over-rides our purposes, individual and collective alike, it is still transparent to us for what it is; we are engaged by it because we are rational beings, and by that engagement are set at once in a unique and ultimate relation to our fellows. Kant shares to the uttermost the universalism of the Enlightenment, with its strong indifference to the particularities of nation and race, religion and cult. Indeed he gives to that indifference a new depth and inwardness, learning much from Rousseau, but also reviving in a new way the more ancient tradition of 'Natural Law'; and that not simply in the sense of what Bentham dismissed as 'nonsense on stilts', but rather in the sense of that which itself underlay the arguments of those writers whom Bentham criticised. For the notion of a 'law behind the law' which so aroused Bentham's intellectual wrath was in one respect only a partly debased variant of the more elusive and pervasive tradition of a 'natural law', to which Kant gave his allegiance in his own highly individual and original, yet not in the least idiosyncratic, style. Whereas, whether among the mediaevals or among the writers of the Enlightenment, the notion of a 'natural law' was often developed out of explicit relation to a *Gesinnungsethik*, in Kant[1] it is with the fundamental law of human self-discipline that we are concerned, and among his forebears it is perhaps to Plato that he is sometimes nearest.[2] It is the form of the good life as such that he seeks; and it is in the moral law that he believes to find it, something touching the individual most intimately so that nothing in him escapes its sovereignty, but at the same time relating him to his fellows in the uniquely authoritative communion of the 'realm of ends'. Yet we altogether misconstrue the nature of that realm, and the character of its constitution, if we think of either out of the context of the imperatives which convey their authority to us. If this authority is one with the authority of our rational nature, it is still over-riding in its dignity and scope. Our every heroism, endurance, act of humility and self-disregard, our every loyalty, fidelity, and supposed human wisdom, our particular attachments, our friendships, our special affections —all alike receive what validity they possess, in the end, from their conformity to its authoritative and universal order.

[1] As also in Butler: see Chapter V.

[2] Yet only sometimes; for he would have accepted the searching criticisms of Plato's political theory implicit in Rousseau's *Contrat Social*.

Nothing that we may dignify as somehow belonging to our spiritual life can escape the searching scrutiny of its judgment.

Kant is neither optimist nor pessimist, and if he will allow no weight to any attempt to derive from some general supposed ontological or material principles the moral order of human life, his sympathies are no more with those who identify virtue with the cult of the tragic, even with the embrace of despair, finding somehow in the intractability of the world around men to their aspiration the sanction of a particular moral attitude. Kant was compelled to take that intractability very seriously; but as a problem, as a barrier set to the way of moral obedience, never as the starting point of a new style of metaphysics from which an ethic could be derived which would justify, in terms of heroism or supposed human destiny, enlistment in the murdering bands of a Hitler or a Mussolini. To say that life was bounded by an inescapable horizon was true, but ethically insignificant; what mattered was that we should come to see the sense, if any, in which we needed to give to the concept of horizon in order to deepen our purchase-hold upon the character of our peculiarly human ethical experience, for instance, in respect of our membership at once of the realm of nature and the realm of ends.[1]

D. KANT'S CONTRIBUTION TO THE ENLIGHTENMENT OF WORKADAY, PRACTICAL PERPLEXITY

The time has certainly come to bring this discussion of Kant's ethics into some relation with the account given in the first chapter of this book of the contexts to which ethical discussion belongs. It may be recalled that in that chapter it was suggested that the moral philosopher might interrupt conversations at two levels: thus he might contribute to the resolution of practical perplexity, and he might contribute to the elucidation of the logic of different sorts of discourse; and although at first sight it might seem as if the two sorts of

[1] See next chapter.

contributions were separate, a little further examination suggested that in the end this was not so. With these tentative conclusions in mind, it may now be profitable to recapitulate what has been suggested about Kant's doctrine.

What is it pre-eminently that Kant offers to those in practical perplexity? We need not expect that he will speak with the same force and point to those in any and every sort of such perplexity; after all, the moralists who were mentioned in the first chapter of this book contributed pre-eminently to conversations bearing on particular aspects of the ethical field. It has already been insisted as characteristic of Kant's ethics that they combine, in a very striking way, a simplicity and absence of sophistication with a quite unusually sophisticated technicality in exposition. A first reading of the *Grundlegung* makes an instantaneous appeal to those who are convinced of the uniquely authoritative status of the moral order; they find in Kant's austere and uncompromising presentation of its claims a coherent and sustained exposition of their own inmost convictions. Similarly, however unfair their judgment may be on the actual content of Kant's teaching, we have to reckon with the contrary reaction of those who are repelled by what they judge to be the implications of his view that, where human agents are concerned, only actions done from a sense of duty have moral worth; while some readers find in his writing a presentation more pointed than any other of the very essence of morality as such, others can only remark a seeming indifference to the deeply complex and subtle springs of human action and choice. To the latter, human nature seems at once a richer and untidier thing than can possibly be captured in the net of Kant's theory. If neither the former nor the latter find what they read in his text humanly indifferent, it is surely to those beset with a more advanced style of perplexity that he most immediately speaks.

1. *Kant and the morally serious, but religiously agnostic, person.* George Eliot's conversation with F. W. H. Myers in the

garden of Trinity College, Cambridge, is often quoted as a remarkable expression of the temper of characteristically Victorian agnosticism. To speak of God as 'inconceivable', of immortality as 'unbelievable', and yet of the moral law as something at once peremptory and certain, is to speak a language not far removed from the lips of many who combined a sense of the luminous authority of duty with a deep perplexity, almost a convinced aphasia, concerning the *arcana* of human origin and destiny. We know not whence we come or whither we go, or what we may hope for; but this is clear beyond doubt, that what we do is not a matter of indifference, but stands under a judgment absolute and inescapable. We must reject any attempt to represent the nature of such a judgment in terms of a traditional religious mythology; but its unique status and authority are alike conveyed to us in a way that admits no cavil. Moreover, to those who think in such terms, the conformity with the moral order in which they express their faith is not understood simply as the fulfilment of the letter of a received code; it is something achieved only when the inmost springs of thought and imagination, of emotion and feeling, are subdued under its supreme direction.

To those who are inclined in these ways, the conviction of the uniqueness and the primacy of the ethical, Kant speaks as no other philosopher; and he does so not in the text of the *Grundlegung* in isolation, but by his whole, laborious exposition of the unique character of the moral order, and of this exposition his criticism of metaphysics is almost the heart and centre. It is indeed this intimate relationship between the criticism of metaphysics, as Kant understands it, and the vindication of the primacy of practical reason that differentiates his criticism of the possibility of metaphysics from that which receives expression in the thorough-going utilitarian insistence on the sovereignty of fact; indeed, as will appear later in this book, it is, in part at least, the way in which they each of them understand the notion of the 'impossibility of metaphysics' which distinguishes Kant and the utilitarian one from the other. Proof of the existence of God,[1] or of the immortality of the soul, lay for ever, on Kant's view, outside our reach; and that we came to recognise when we grasped the unnoticed, unacknowledged contradictions in the concept of such proofs. As soon as we had made this impossibility of proof our own, we were at least half way to the realisation of the actual nature of our commerce with the absolute. Because we saw what it could not possibly become, we were made confident and unafraid in our acceptance of its daily demands upon our will.

Of course, for Kant, the notions of God and of immortality received a kind of re-admission as 'postulates of practical reason'; but they came back only after his demonstration of the impossibility of metaphysics had been carried through in such a way as to show that the very limitations of human knowledge served to throw into the clearest possible relief the actual character of moral obligation. It was not the case that when these limitations were properly grasped and accepted our assurance concerning the authority of duty was put in jeopardy; rather it was strengthened and deepened by being shown at once quite independent of particular conviction concerning the nature of what is, and itself supremely the norm and standard of all commerce enjoyed by human beings with the absolute whatsoever.

Thus Kant speaks most pointedly to those whose sense of the absoluteness of morality has survived the onset of metaphysical agnosticism; he does so by showing that if that agnosticism is properly understood, it will be seen as providing, in effect, the setting within which the authority of the moral order is realised as absolute. Thus it could be said that, for some at least of his readers, what is most important in Kant is his transformation of the notion of agnosticism. It is no more the name of a kind of wistful straining after the unattainable, of a kind of regret that we cannot, to speak crudely, jump out of our cognitive skins. It is a something which, as was sug-

---

[1] If the very concept were not antinomous.

gested above in a different connection,[1] has a *certain* kinship
with the *via negativa* of the classical theology, a purification of
our concepts from every taint of anthropomorphism, to the
intent that we may at least see what it is that, in our attempted use of these concepts to scrutinise the unconditioned,
we are attempting. Of course Kant so understands the rôle
of thought in knowledge as to condemn in advance such
attempts to futility; but we must, in his view, have the feel of
the metaphysical impulse, make our own in the same moment
its character and dignity, and its inadmissibility. We must
take the measure of its import for human life in the same act
as we lay it down without regret. We must know both why
and how we try to reach, by the unfettered use of the concepts of understanding, a place whither by their employment
we cannot hope to come. If a man sets down Kant's first
Critique and calls himself in its sense an agnostic, the position
he adopts is something at once similar to and different from
the agnosticism of those who have not undergone the same
discipline; it is something to be understood in the end in
terms of a new self-consciousness concerning the nature of
conceptual thinking as such, and it is something which provides supremely the context within which the evident and
transcendent authority of the moral law, and the realm of
ends, can be grasped.

2. *Kant's rationalism again, in the light of the immediately foregoing.* For Kant the authority of the moral law is altogether
independent of the nature of what is; to suppose otherwise is
to commit an offence against distinctions of logical type which
he is at laborious pains to draw. Yet, as was remarked above,
if his understanding of the moral life is austere, it is not for
that reason to be identified with, for instance, the cult of the
heroic, or the interior cultivation of what is sometimes called
the 'tragic sense of life'. If freedom is the ultimate and
mysterious centre of his whole 'world-view', it is a freedom
grounded in autonomy, in men's power as rational beings to

---

[1] This theme is taken up again in the last chapter of this book.

be laws unto themselves. At the outset of this chapter the kinship between some parts of his doctrine and some aspects of utilitarianism was stressed. Indeed some may judge there to be a contradiction, or a near-contradiction, between what was said there and what was more recently remarked on the difference between Kant's and the utilitarians' rejection of metaphysics. How can there really be a kinship between an ethic which subordinates moral principles to the supposed sovereignty of fact, and one which criticises metaphysics in order to bring out more clearly the transcendent uniqueness of the moral order? To speak in more familiar language, it is surely extravagant to expect to find underlying similarity between a doctrine which pitilessly insists that obedience to the moral law *hic et nunc* is self-justified, and one that is traditionally presented as the very standard and type of a teleological theory of ethics. In Kant one finds a stern and austere scepticism concerning the authority of any particular human purpose, whether individual or collective; whereas for the utilitarian no ethical tradition, however exalted and entrenched, can ever be regarded as sacrosanct in fact of the over-riding claims of human happiness. Moreover it cannot too often be remarked that in Kant we have, *par excellence*, the champion of a *Gesinnungsethik*; whereas the utilitarian insists, without compromise, that the moral worth of actions be judged by reference to their consequences.

It may be pleaded that as a matter of fact most of this was acknowledged at the outset of this chapter; for it was made clear then, *inter alia*, that the similarity between Kant's view and that of the utilitarians could only be admitted when the latter were prepared to give to their supreme moral principle a genuinely formal character, stressing what was called there its essentially programmatic nature, and to develop their understanding of its function as an instrument of personal self-discipline. It might even be said that in the history of utilitarian morality we can detect currents of thought pulling strongly in the direction of a position not, in the end, far removed from Kant's;[1] whereas there are most certainly others whose tendency is quite the reverse. In the second chapter of this book it was suggested that the notion of utility could be represented as having a place on the sort of conceptual scale which Collingwood called a 'scale of forms'; it was insisted that there was a certain restlessness, almost a floating quality, in the concept of the utilitarian position. And such it may now be suggested can also be said of that agnosticism to which it is tied. Thus we may call a man agnostic who denies, on the basis of some general 'principle of verification', the possibility of transcendent assertion; but there is, as remarked in the present chapter, a world of difference between this sort of positivism and the more subtle doctrines of Kant. Yet it is also true that in the writings of John Stuart Mill, in particular, there is discernible an agnosticism of a very different temper, one that is as much on edge in the presence of thorough-going positivism as of any other doctrine. If, for instance, in the essay *On Liberty* Mill remains ready to justify toleration by its fruits in promoting a greater measure of human happiness, he also writes constantly of it as if the very character of human existence as such demanded that men should treat one another with a peculiar sort of respect; we are not far from Kant's conception of the realm of ends, and it is perhaps no accident that it is in these passages as much as in any others in his writings that we are reminded how, for Mill, agnosticism is the name of something much more complex than a mere denial of import to transcendent assertions on grounds of their supposed unverifiability. Of course, in the end, the notion of human happiness is cast by the utilitarians for a rôle which Kant cannot allow; if a utilitarian moralist flirts with the idea of a supreme formal principle, such a principle is always somehow bedded in the acknowledged worth of human happiness. But even here Kant is not all that far away from him, at least in sharing with him a sense that a callous, unreflective acceptance of

---

[1] Some would certainly wish to mention Sidgwick in this connection.

the necessity of pain and suffering in the name of the most exalted moral tradition is something profoundly unreasonable; and the roots of this irrationality can, for Kant as much for the utilitarian, be found in uncriticised reliance on the authority of the supposedly self-evident, even if Kant's disentanglement of the nature of that reliance is more subtle and more unexpected.

All this may seem itself unnecessarily laboured; but no account of the perplexities to which Kant speaks can claim an even partial completeness that fails to emphasise, among them, the demand, certainly experienced by some, for a reconciliation between the admission of the demands of morality as, in a unique sense, transcendent and unconditional, and what may be loosely termed a humanist viewpoint. There is no doubt that the family of ethical positions and attitudes called by the common name 'utilitarian' have managed, with greater or less consistency, to convey to those who have studied them the sense of being concerned to relate the sharp and often disturbing demands of morality to the needs and aspirations of actual human nature. Whereas those who, for very good reason, have criticised and rejected these positions, have seemed to want to replace them by a harsh and fanatical ethic of obedience for obedience's sake. If the utilitarian tends to identify prudence with the whole of virtue, his critic too easily finds in unreflective, uncriticised endurance a self-justifying value; if the disciple of John Stuart Mill seems often blind to the heights and the depths of human existence, his critic seems far too lightly to esteem the necessarily close alliance between a disciplined sense of pity and an informed perception where human happiness is to be found.

It could be claimed for Kant that he has, however tentatively and incompletely, tried to overcome these oppositions and, in a measure, to achieve the reconciliation indicated. Certainly he insists that moral virtue is not something of worth because it pays high dividends; it is an end in itself. By it our purposes are judged; they are not its justification any more than the material success or failure of the enterprises to which the authority of the moral law commits us. But the realm of ends, to which as moral agents we belong, is something not far from the aspirations of any one of us, in so far as those aspirations stand in proper subjection to the authority of a practical reason which a properly critical philosophy has reinforced. Metaphysical agnosticism reveals the authority of the moral law as unique and mysterious; yet at the same time it enforces the lesson that, in the name of that law, we can only be constrained to those courses of action which serve the more sharply to reveal and uphold the dignity of rational beings as such. There is for instance a temper of contempt for things human, for the grandeur as well as the misery of man, that is as unconditionally prohibited by the moral law within us as any arrogant attempt to contrive the future of mankind, after our own image of its welfare. That moral law, whose peculiar authority the criticism of metaphysics helps more than anything to reveal, commands before all else respect for persons, and endorses that style of endurance before all other which enables the individual to reconcile himself with his fellows without constraint or falsehood.

There is unfortunately in much of the immediately preceding an air of obscurity and elusiveness, which seems peculiarly out of place when one is trying to lay bare the practical worth of Kant's ethical teaching. But it is of the first importance to realise that what gives Kant his continued appeal is not something which he shares with Prichard, or aspects of his views which suggest the writings of contemporary moralists like Martin Buber and some of the existentialists. Certainly Kant did not believe that honesty must be shown to be the most profitable policy before we can be properly constrained to its practice; certainly he did believe that there was in a man's relation to his neighbour something altogether unique and mysteriously authoritative. But he did not so subscribe to either of these provisions as to tear

morality out of its context in human life as a whole. There
was nothing particularly virtuous in contemptuous indifference to general policies for ameliorating the lot of
mankind; and although, at the level of moral experience, we
were admitted to a commerce with the transcendent elsewhere denied us, we altogether misunderstood its nature if
we allowed it to breed in us a contempt for a disciplined
empirical study of our physical and social environment, of
the acknowledged and unacknowledged springs of our behaviour. We must never allow ourselves so to receive the
uniqueness of the moral order as by that reception to be
betrayed into an unreasoning disdain for the much which
could be done to alleviate human distress, and to advance
the growth of habits of gentleness and forbearance among
men. Indeed we altogether misconceive the character of the
unique and transcendent demands of the moral order, and
indeed the very nature of that order itself, if in its name we
advocate either contempt for exact thinking, or the cultivation of suffering for its own sake. Only a proper appreciation
of the delicate interplay between metaphysical agnosticism
and the recognition of an absolute morality will keep us
straight here. In the end Kant only endorses the arguments
of the utilitarian in so far as they too convey a sense of the
intimate mutual involvement of these two perceptions; when,
for instance, Mill in his essay *On Liberty* probes the very nature
of that human intellectual situation which makes toleration
something very near a categorical imperative, and very far
removed from an agreement to differ in weariness of the
painful and destructive consequences of ill-conducted controversy.

If this brings out at once how much and how little Kant
succeeds in saying to those in a situation akin to George
Eliot's, it will not entirely have failed of its purpose. For in
the end what Kant offers to one in such a situation is a
method of introducing a greater measure of consistency and
order into beliefs already held; he offers something very near

to what Bradley called, speaking of metaphysics, 'the finding of bad reasons for what we believe on instinct'! What must morality be like if it is to be transcendent and unique, absolute and unconditional in status and in demand, and yet not something received as a blind and unintelligible demand to affirm certain sorts of value? What must human knowledge be like if, from within its pursuit, we are to be aware of the moral order as something all the time given to us quite independent of the detail of our discovery, and yet as something to which the continued extension of the frontiers of human knowledge is most searchingly relevant, which must indeed, in its own name, uphold the ever extending pressing back of those frontiers? The ambiguity of the relation of morality to knowledge, for Kant, must now be plain; if he cannot concede the sovereignty of fact as the utilitarian, he can no more admit the sheer indifference to that which is properly demanded of us, what we know of our actual conditions and of what we may surely, in the future, learn. To take some particular ordering of human values and give it final import, to regard as authoritative for all time some particular balancing, one against the other, of particular human virtues, is to ignore the essentially unfinished character of man's knowledge of himself and of his world; it is to forget that, in Burke's words, it is of the very nature of moral principles to demand that, in loyalty to them, we sometimes in different situations lay aside the rules which ordinarily convey them to us. It was Kant's sustained purpose to lay bare in formal character, and therefore in potential relevance to the most diverse situation, the supreme moral principle of all; and, as part of that purpose, he had continually to return to its differentiation from any sort of theoretical insight into the unconditioned. If morality was absolute, its absoluteness was that of a task given us; and the moral philosopher helped the perplexity of ordinary men most when he revealed both the consequences and the context of this fact. To speak of absolutes, and yet not to acquire the accents of the would-be

spiritual despot, or the apologist for the acceptance of un-
reason or indeed of evil in the name of a supposed proper
appreciation of human existence—it was something of that
sort which Kant attempted, and his worth to the morally perplexed is pre-eminently to those among them who would
neither, in the name of supposed 'depth of insight', speak the
flamboyant idiom of romantic or existentialist self-justifica-
tion, nor yet, in the name of a supposed rational self-restraint,
confine themselves within the boundaries of what is permitted
by the thorough-going utilitarian.

3. *Further reference to freedom.* And of course, as has been
said above, the pivot of his view of the world is his understanding of freedom. We see perhaps most clearly the conversations to which he contributes and the manner of his
contribution if we never let go of that perception. Mention
has already been made, in this connection, of Mill's essay *On
Liberty*; but in view of the debt to Kant acknowledged by the
Russian thinker Berdyaev, it may not be out of place to recall
also here Dostoevsky's image of the 'Grand Inquisitor'. The
freedom of which Kant wrote was not far from that conveyed
in the Russian novelist's unforgettable picture; it is an
authorship of what is done, and origination of what comes to
be. For Kant, as much as for the mediaeval theologians like
Richard of S. Victor who saw in freedom a kind of human
participation in the very creativity of God, it is the ultimate
fact about men that they are free. Of course, as was brought
out above, there is a sense in which we do not know what we
are saying when we say that men are free; and yet we do
know what we are not saying. Here Kant's quarrel with a
certain sort of utilitarian would come full tide; for, apart from
such unique and deeply original works as Mill's *On Liberty*,
the utilitarian would tend to treat freedom as the name of a
problem to be dissolved by a proper discrimination of sorts of
human action amenable to various forms of direction and
control from other sorts of action not so amenable.[1] With such

[1] Compare next chapter.

an attitude Kant could have no sympathy; it failed to allow any proper weight to what, for instance, human action *was*. Here was something which only the most patient scrutiny could capture, something touching man so intimately that no effort was too great to take hold of something of its inwardness and character. But we could never allow that the slow, painful searching effort to measure up to the fullness of another person's claim upon us was simply a special sort of *event*; it was something in which we came upon ourselves as we could in no other way.

If we speak of morality as absolute, what we say may mean no more than an indication of this unique and transcendent fact of freedom. There is no doubt whatsoever that Kant does effectively speak to the needs of those who would see freedom so, or not let go of their sense that thus it may be. And again he enables them rejoin their perception with a sense of the proper authority of reason. This is not simply a matter of his reconciliation of determinism and free-will; it is much more the way in which he insists that the recognition of the transcendent import of the moral order, and in consequence of that causality on which it rests, does not by a kind of false magic withdraw a man from involvement in the routine of ordinary existence, and from exposure to the shocks and challenges presented by an advancing knowledge. If we say that we are free, we are not in confessing that fact somehow escaping from the necessity of correcting our understanding of our nature and environment by the resources of exact thought; still less are we suggesting we stand in no need of the aid of properly informed policies for improving our lot and that of our fellows. We are not treating some supposed metaphysical insight as if it were a substitute for the ordinary routines either of observation and knowledge or of reform and amelioration. The bare reality of freedom is not something which conveys us to a kind of metaphysical heaven where we do not have to bother with these things; it is, of course, not a 'bare fact' at all! Rather it is almost the context within

which every human concern and initiative has its place, and
indeed receives its peculiar character as a human concern
and initiative.

Kant gives men renewed understanding of that in which
the supposed absoluteness of morality may consist; he asks
them in fact to ponder what else it can consist in. He brings
out in a uniquely searching way what he judges this absoluteness to be, and what he is sure that it is not. Before all else
he denies that it is the assertion of the supreme worth of
blind will; it is rather the primacy of practical reason, the
supremacy of the rational insight which informs our practical
engagement one with another over that on which we must
rely in our theoretical pursuits. But this supremacy is not
something which is properly understood if it is judged to
involve a kind of writing off of theoretical reason; rather by
its meaning we should be able to perceive anew the latter's
dignity and worth. All through his exposition he is alive to
the unexpected character of the demands he must make of
those who will follow him in treating morality as absolute;
above all they must be prepared, now in one way, now in
another, to detach morality from any kind of dependence on
metaphysics; and inasmuch as the varieties of such dependence are manifold, so the work of detachment has to be done
now in one way, now in another. If in carrying out this work
we think we see an unsuspected *rapprochement* between Kant's
ethics and those of the utilitarians, we must not be deterred;
in as far as both find themselves driven to adopt and to commend a *programmatic* style of exposition, both alike are doing
justice to the extent to which an ethic that claims universal
authority must convey its principles in terms of a form to be
realised, a task to be done again and again, rather than in
terms of a code to be fulfilled.

4. *Some aspects of Kant's view of the relation of ethics to religion
in the light of the foregoing.* Of course the crucial character of
Kant's claim for morality is only disclosed when its relevance
is perceived to the question of the relations of ethics to

religion. At first sight it is easy to suppose that Kant's austere morality is the necessary ally of a religious view of the world; nothing could be further from the truth, and it must be said that the practical importance of Kant's contribution here to the ethical debates of ordinary men is found more in the severity of the shock he administers than in the enlightenment he immediately brings! This, of course, is implicit in what has already been said of the way in which he brings out the absolute character of morality as he conceives it; the moral law binds us, apart altogether from any religious sanction that we may invoke. Rather it binds us to the task of ruthlessly scrutinising, in the name of its own principles, the sanctions we invoke supposedly to uphold it! The root of morality is in our nature as rational beings; we are ordered to it because we are what we are. Provided we have a sure purchase-hold on the limits of our knowledge, nothing can take from us our assurance of its authority, and of our own dignity as its servants; nor can we be led astray into giving to something less than itself the weight of authority that the moral law alone can command, provided that we see that law for what it is—formal, not material. But if such insight enables us to hold fast to the dignity of the moral law as something much more than a means to the smoother functioning of human society, at the same time it altogether debars us from treating its authority as relative to the supposed disclosures of revealed religion. Our allegiance to what the latter demand of us is entirely conditional on their conformity with the dictates of law universal; a moral enormity is not redeemed by being presented as the commandment of a god; rather it is that god who is discredited. If we give acceptance to the teachings of a religion which demands of us either the approval or the practice of things contrary to the moral law, we cannot appeal to the supposed superior insight brought by faith, to justify our departure from the evident dictates of morality. If we say for instance that Samuel was justified in his treatment of Agag because of what God had commanded, then

we are simply saying that in certain circumstances the demands of morality are not absolute; and if we say this we are,
of course, denying the general proposition that morality as
such is absolute. We are saying that as a matter of fact there
is something to which morality is relative, something which
in effect absolves man from its practice, even properly commands them to withhold their obedience from it. This, of
course, may be so, although Kant himself was convinced
that, in a quite unsophisticated way, men knew that it was
not and that the authority over them of the moral law, with
him, was absolute. If, however, we allow ourselves to suppose,
as a bare possibility, such a state of affairs, we see from the
briefest supposition that it is sheerly incompatible with the
treatment of morality as absolute. Granted that what for
Kant was absolute was an infinitely flexible form of self-
scrutiny, yet the concession of absoluteness to such a form
necessarily gave to it the right to say the last word. To give
the weight that Kant does unquestionably give to the moral
law within is to bring all religious insight whatsoever under
the judgment of the moral order, to which men belong and
of which they are the bearers. Just as much as any ethic
which upholds a particular balance of emphasis between this
virtue and that must submit to the authority of that order,
so must any view which, in however disguised a way, presents
morality as a means to achieving a proper relation with the
divine; for if morality is properly seen as such, then its
sovereign authority is gone from it.

Certainly Kant will allow that the treatment of morality
as a divine command has a significance greater than that, to
borrow Matthew Arnold's language, of 'cementing the
alliance between imagination and will'. If, for him, God is
before all else the guarantor of the conformity of the realm of
nature to that of ends, and if this function of His cannot be
grasped except as a postulate of practical reason, this does not
involve the philosopher in justifying religious belief simply on
pragmatic grounds. It is as if he sought sometimes to treat

the idea of God somehow cosmologically, yet never to allow himself by the attempt to be betrayed into writing of the relation of the world to Him with the uncriticised confidence of Aquinas. The agnostic temper of his first Critique is never lost; yet the God of whom he writes is always the guarantor of men's acceptance of themselves as standing under the moral law, of which they are themselves the authors. There is never the remotest hint of compromise with the suggestion that this law constrains us categorically because it is the expression of the divine will, or even with the view that religious belief somehow conveys a special insight disclosing dimensions of the moral order withheld from those who are without it. But, for all that, religious belief confers on those who hold it a kind of assurance that the changes and chances of this fleeting life, the accidents and disasters to which inheritance and environment alike expose us, shall not have the last word. If for Kant the moral law within is something that is, for men, the very measure of what is ultimate and transcendent, and is recognised as something with whose authority over them they enjoy an unbroken commerce, yet there are aspects of the cosmological problem to which he is far from indifferent; he is on edge in the presence of any variant of the view that somehow the world, either by the bare facts of its existence or by determinate features of its actual ordering, points to its divine author;[1] yet he is too alive to the menace which continually threatens from without, the progress of men's self-discipline in accordance with the law of reason, to suppose that in the end the relation of the world to God can be left out of account.

If in this section of his writing he comes perilously near contradicting what he has previously said of the separateness of the realm of nature and the realm of ends, he would perhaps justify his uncertainty by emphasising the essentially secondary nature of what he is now about—secondary, that

[1] How far would he have accepted the view of a modern Thomist that God is the name of the problem the world sets?

is, to the vindication of the sovereign authority of the moral
law. Certainly no careful student of his writings can fail to
wish that he had attended more to the need for revising, in
the light of what he is prepared to concede of significance to
the exploration of the relation of the world to God, some
aspects at least of his treatment of the notion of time; this
because it is impossible for such a student to escape overhearing in these sections of his work at least the echoes of a
characteristically religious eschatology.[1] It is the revelation
of the world as an environment in no final sense alien to what
they know they must try to be for which men wait; the mood
of the religious man is perhaps, before all else, one of expectation. The natural language to use of such an attitude is
almost Pauline, or even, when attention turns from the idea
of God to that of immortality, the language of such prayer
for the dead as speaks of the 'completion in the departed of
the good work begun, but not fulfilled'.[2] For Kant, of course,
such a work is *their own*; it is not God's work in them; Kant
can *never* depart from his conviction that the absolute which
constrains us is that law within us by which we measure the
supposed perfection even of the 'Holy One of the Gospels'.

There is no gainsaying the fact that such an approach to
the relation of ethics to religion emphasises more sharply their
contradiction than the more familiar styles of naturalism. It
is of the nature of an absolute ethic that it must do this; it
can no more surrender its sovereignty to theology than to
metaphysics, in the sense of an anatomy of being, or of a
general view of the nature of the world. Those writers on the
philosophy of religion, and on the problems of faith and
revelation, who have stressed a note of self-confident and
almost irreverent humanism in Kant's writings have not
always been wide of the mark; there is something which must
invite the protest of the necessarily *receptive* and humble

[1] I owe very much here to Hans Urs von Balthasar's discussion of Kant in his
very valuable *Prometheus* (Kerle).
[2] *Scottish Book of Common Prayer.*

religious spirit in the suggestion that God somehow guarantees men's conviction of the supreme authority of the law within them. There is a kind of arrogance here, and also more than a hint of the clear subordination of what is personal—namely God, and men and their relation to Him— to something which is formal and universal, even in a special sense abstract—namely the law of reason. If the last mentioned is sovereign, does not that very acknowledgment displace God from the supremacy over men and over their world? Such questions are seriously posed, and later in this book we will touch on some of them again.[1] But for the time being it may simply be repeated that in this relentless insistence on the secondary character of religious belief Kant is being consistent with himself.

It is, of course, continually important to remember the extent to which Kant belonged to the age of enlightenment, and gave by his work a renewed depth and searching quality to its insistence on the independence of reason from any sort of positive dogmatic bondage. A critic may well wish to remark the extent to which his sense of what is of worth, the state of mind he esteems, even the fundamental form of life realised by the morally good man, have borrowed their contours from the assumption and controversies of his age. There are not wanting those who would insist (drawing on the later insights of Hegel and Kierkegaard) that he has given an absolute status to what is significant only as a moment in a dialectical movement. Thus it has been suggested that what he does in effect is to bestow an unconditional status upon a morality shaped initially, in respect of its fundamental assumptions, as a protest against a religious ethic, capable now of justifying the moral enormities of persecution, now of counselling acquiescence in the rule of any and every sort of despot somehow excused as the only existing bulwark against anarchy. Certainly it would be a mistake, in any attempt seriously to understand Kant, to

---

[1] In Chapter VII: *Ethics, Metaphysics and Religion.*

forget how pervasive and attractive for him was the idea of freedom; and this attraction certainly in part derives from the vivid presence to his consciousness of the problems of the age in which he lived. Yet his peculiar vision of man as free, and as free because he is the author of that law under whose inescapable authority he stands, has proved capable of illuminating generations and individuals remote alike in time and place from the circumstances in which Kant wrote.

Thus if a man wishes to insist on the reality of the 'religious basis of morality' after reading Kant, he will most certainly be clearer how easily such a 'basis' can undermine rather than uphold what is said to rest upon it. Of course there are, as has been said, many places where the defender of the characteristically religious ethic may claim that Kant has failed to do justice to what he is seeking to affirm. The emphasis that the believer lays on a special sort of réceptivity will be discussed again later in this book; but here perhaps another point should be stressed, namely the rôle for which Kant casts the notion of law in his ethics. Certainly he knew the tradition of natural law, and in one sense stood clearly within it; it might even be said that in his doctrine of an immanent law universal, of which men as rational were the bearers, he took hold of the imaginative mediaeval vision of the fabric of a common human life, woven into one by the thread of a divinely-grounded law, and somehow 'interiorised' it.[1] This law was no longer glimpsed, as certainly it was in the writings of Kant's near contemporary, Edmund Burke, as something cosmic in its reach and status; it was rather a rational form to whose authority men themselves subdued the particularities of appetite and prejudice. So he speaks continually of the reverence evoked by the moral law *within*. But for all its intimacy to the individual, it remains law; and if Kant is in his way as much preoccupied as Luther with the besetting problem where a man can achieve confidence that he stands right with the ultimate ground of

[1] Cf. p. 124 above; see also Chapter V.

existence, the answer he would give to that problem is sharply opposed to that of the reformer. If the publican in the parable went down to his house justified rather than the Pharisee, that δικαίωσις lay neither in his bare acquittal by God, nor even in the latter's free acceptance of him as contrite; for Kant, the publican's 'justification' was inseparably one with the integrity he had achieved by his rigorous self-scrutiny and unflinching honesty with himself; and it was through the law (the law of his rational being), to whose judgment he submitted himself, that he achieved it. It cannot be denied that even those whose approach to the problem of ethics is in no sense tightly tied to acknowledged religious presupposition find something disturbing in Kant's uncompromising rigour at this point. To these matters we shall return later.

Yet there is no doubt that by his formalism Kant does, more than any other moralist, succeed in showing what is claimed when absoluteness is claimed for morality. At the outset of the *Grundlegung* he argues for the superiority of moral over other forms of excellence, and his account of what that excellence must be is throughout tailor-made to safeguard its supremacy. It is something realised in the policy of life affirmed by an agent; and to that extent it is independent of material success or failure. Kant will have nothing to do with any view which finds the essence of morality in a 'system of public advantage'; yet for all that, there is nothing in it to encourage the ethic of the *Führerprinzip*, whether the 'leader' is conceived in religious or in political terms, or, more loosely, is identified with some inherited pattern of discipline and behaviour.[1] Kant contributes thus by bringing out clearly, more clearly perhaps than any other moralist, the kind of thing which a man is claiming when he claims absoluteness for morality; he does this admittedly by identifying morality with a special sort of

---

[1] Prof. Karl Popper is right to stress his attachment to the Enlightenment. Cf. *The Listener*, March 1954.

disinterestedness, but one that has all the time to be conceived formally, continually a *faciendum*, never a *factum*. The ultimacy of the mood of *Sollen* is very closely bound up with Kant's subtle yet uncompromising formalism; and both alike serve to bring out what he means by morality as absolute.

5. *Conclusion of this section.* So, at the same time as he uncompromisingly vindicates morality as absolute, he establishes the sense in which that absoluteness is, and is not, mysterious. It has a character of uniqueness, and the freedom which it presupposes is something altogether *sui generis*; yet we are not pitchforked by acknowledgment of the unconditional authority of the moral law into a world in which the clear light of reason yields to the fiercely championed obscurities of supposed *Erleben*, or of 'intuition' in the sense in which that word is used, as it certainly *sometimes* is, as a virtual synonym for *Erleben*. If we grant that our absolute is grasped as a form of self-discipline, bearing imperatively upon us, we are not likely to be tempted to convert it into some kind of object of unique and incommunicable insight. We altogether misconceive what is absolute and unconditioned if we abstract it from its context in the categorical *imperative*; if the 'realm of ends' demands our uncompromised fidelity, it is not as the concept of some transcendent utopia which we have somehow seen and must work to realise on earth, but as an aspect of that relation of disinterestedness we must affirm *vis-à-vis* our neighbours, in the changing variety of particular situations.

E. KANT ON THE RELATIONS OF ETHICAL TO NON-ETHICAL DISCOURSE

In what has been said, the contribution Kant makes to the other conversation, viz. the conversation concerning the precise relation of ethical to other forms of discourse, is already implicit. In a very special way his contributions to the two conversations are woven closely together; thus we cannot detach his vindication of the absoluteness of the moral order, and the peculiar character of that absoluteness, whereby he speaks in a deeply relevant way to those who find themselves in a position akin to that of George Eliot, from his answer to questions concerning the relation of ethical to other sorts of language. It is not enough, as has been said above, to say that for Kant the former is irreducibly imperative in mood; for it is also the language in which, on his view, we express and bring home to ourselves our fundamental commerce with the absolute. It is this, of course, which is thrown into clear relief by Kant's theory of knowledge, where the phrase is used, not in the sense of the first chapter of this book, but to indicate the contents of the first Critique. For Kant, through reflection on the relations of ethical to non-ethical language we achieve an answer to our underlying perplexities concerning the language we use to refer to that which is relative, and the language which touches what is absolute. Clarify the relations and interplay of the former sorts of language, and one has achieved insight into the relations and interplay of the latter sorts. Yet the two problems of relationship are not to be identified, and, as we have seen in the order of his exposition, Kant's exploration of the nature of characteristically metaphysical language precedes his direct attack on the problem of the nature of ethical language; it has often been insisted in this chapter that his negative assessment of the possibility of effectual metaphysical enquiry provides the setting into which his doctrine of morality as unconditional falls. The notion of the unconditioned is supposed already in his readers' minds when their attention is strictly focussed on the achieving a proper self-consciousness concerning the limits of their knowledge, and the power of its characteristic concepts: Kant does not identify *tout court* the problems of the relationship between ethical and non-ethical language on the one side, and between assertion concerning the unconditioned and assertion concerning the relative on the other; there is a problem of the possibility of metaphysics which has, even for

Kant, a certain independence of the problem of the status of ethical language. The notion of the absolute, in the sense of an ideal, final, and unconditionally valid completion of the fabric of our knowledge, enters our thinking apart from the sense of an ethical imperative; we are somehow the prisoners of a restless urge to reach a vision of things as they are, beyond the possibility of criticism and revision, and we know something of the power of these bonds upon us;[1] if we show failure of understanding the characteristic powers of our basic descriptive concepts in even entertaining such dreams, these illusions are still part of the human situation, and Kant is always impatient with the kind of empiricism which treats their force too lightly. If they are of the nature of phantasies from whose distracting influence we must be freed, yet their presence in our minds is part of our characteristic human dignity.

Thus it is one of the most fundamental differences between Kant and the contemporary logical empiricist (of the temper, let us say, of the late Professor Moritz Schlick, whose work on the nature of human knowledge betrays a strong Kantian influence)[2] that the former cannot condemn as a mere 'corruption of consciousness', whether rooted in failure to grasp the logic of our language or in some other sort of breakdown, men's concern with what is absolute and unconditioned. In a way it could even be said that for Kant the notion of the asbolute and unconditioned are there, 'floating' as it were in the human mind, concepts without a home, without use clearly understood or mastered; and it remains for the critical philosopher as something very near the heart of his task to take hold of them and rivet them to the ethical, inasmuch as there, and there alone, they find significant employment without shadow of ambivalence or threat of antinomy. And in doing this, a work that is one of clarifica-

---

[1] How far is this equivalent to the tug of being of which certain neo-Thomists speak?

[2] Cf. his *Allgemeine Erkenntnislehre*, Vienna, 1918.

tion and almost of rescue, if one can speak of rescuing a
concept from abuse, Kant believes that he is somehow loyal
to what men have always known, when they had achieved
at once proper self-consciousness and consistency in respect
of what they thought of their human situation. It is easy for
us with our deepened and ever deepening sense of historical
relativity, and of the tremendous transformations succceeding
generations have known in respect of what they have come to
see to be the conditions and nature of human knowledge, to
smile at Kant here, to insist how confined and uncriticised
his horizons, and so on. And yet, on the other side, it is a
mark of the depth of his philosophical culture that by his
brilliant, if sometimes elusive, use of the notion of form he did
try to safeguard himself against these inevitable shortnesses of
view. Even the utilitarians, whose canvas was in certain ways
much more restricted than Kant's and the range of their
sympathies much more limited initially than his, safeguarded themselves against the charge of narrowness and
unwarranted confinement of perception by finding the means
to give to their fundamental moral principle a skeletal and
programmatic character;[1] as we have constantly insisted,
Kant did the same, even if, as we have done previously in this
chapter, we must concede deep differences between the way in
which he conceived the formal and that in which the notion
must be understood by those who treat, e.g., satisfaction as a
'logical construction'. It may be arguable that, for all his
datedness, Kant does provide, in outline at least, certain
principles, used now in one way, now in another, by men
attempting the disentanglement of ethical from non-ethical
language; and if it must be insisted that these are not the
only principles by whose means such a disentanglement can
be set in hand, it can be pleaded that the very method of this
book emphasises the variety of approaches to the central
problems of ethics, even while also acknowledging a deep

---

[1] Again, the difference between the formalism of the utilitarian scheme as
outlined in Chapter II and that of Kant must not be forgotten.

community between the different issues with which different moral philosophers have concerned themselves. It may profitably be repeated here that Kant's contribution to the two sorts of conversation distinguished in the first chapter do not fall apart, and those are perhaps readiest to see his contribution to the latter sort of conversation who are not without real understanding of the issues debated in those of the former sort to which he particularly speaks, those, that is, who (in Collingwood's sense of 'understand') would claim to 'understand' what George Eliot said to Myers.

F. CONCLUSIONS

This chapter is already over-long, and may be judged both unfairly selective and unduly discursive, incomplete and yet clumsily repetitive. But it is informed by a conviction that the position which Kant takes up in respect of certain ethical controversies is of quite fundamental importance. Thus in the end Kant will not endorse the view that the moral philosopher's work is done when he has revealed the irreducibly imperative character of ethical discourse; this, although he stresses it uncompromisingly. But he does not reject this limitation of the philosopher's task in order to claim for him the right to undertake speculative adventures in the indication of possible new directions for human life, and of new sorts of value to be promoted. It is rather that Kant comes to ethics from a very serious engagement with the *problem* of metaphysics: can we ever know the nature of the unconditioned? What is the rôle of the notion of the unconditioned in human thought and action? In a way, Kant's quarrel with the utilitarian would be that the latter too lightly esteemed the questions of the possibility of metaphysics, and indeed of the nature of fact, and therefore inevitably answered them wrong. To get the measure of a question, one had to take it seriously. Thus both Kant and Bentham deny the possibility of metaphysics; but what they deny is different. The latter, in denying the possibility of metaphysics, is rejecting an obscure, even meaningless, intellectual game, a sentimental indulgence in the effort to clothe dreams with substance. Thus, for him, the only alternative to the attempt to derive moral standards from the observed facts of human behaviour and desire must be to rest them on the supposed disclosures of some mysterious faculty of intuition; the metaphysically minded person is the person who plays around with the notion of such esoteric sources of knowledge, and in their name seeks to justify disregard for the deliverances of observation. It is hard for the philosopher who thinks like Bentham to take metaphysics seriously; whereas for Kant, as much as for Aquinas, it is significant and worth the closest attention that men try to establish metaphysical truth. We must take the proper measure of this besetting, restless preoccupation with the absolute and unconditioned; almost it is Kant's view that we cannot exorcise it, only discipline it and give it a direction that is both valid and constructive.

Do we acknowledge a reference to the absolute and unconditioned in our thought and action? For Kant this is almost a question of fact and he might accuse the thoroughgoing empiricist of refusing to admit a matter of fact when he retreats from admitting it to be the case that we do. For Kant it is no justification at all to say that we dare not admit such a reference, lest we find ourselves by the admission compelled to speak of non-sensuous faculties of intuition, and the rest; what we have to do rather is to continue what Kant throughout his whole argument has shown himself prepared to do, namely to revise our estimate of the elements within that human experience which we are concerned to discriminate and whose validity we are concerned to assess. If we do that, we shall soon see a reference to the absolute and unconditioned, obscure, yet tenacious and pervasive, in human thought and action; and we will allow a problem in taking its measure. Moreover we will readily admit that although this reference is tenacious, it is also at the same time strangely precarious, and we will further admit that there is a sense in which it is also a dangerous thing.

It is certainly true that for Kant metaphysical preoccupation is a dangerous and distracting habit of mind; it may distract men from the kind of exploration of the world about them that lies within their power, awaken in their hearts a preference for the obscure and ill-disciplined ramblings of the seer to the exact and controlled work of the scientist, and lead them in the name of an illusion effectively to close the doors on the advance of human knowledge. There is something in such preoccupation demanding a continually renewed work of criticism.

There is an analogous peril in the notion of an absolute morality, should that cease to be an absolute morality in the sense defined in this chapter and become, unnoticed to itself, the handmaid, and not the judge, of a world-view, or of a set of passionately held religious beliefs. We should never forget how sharp Kant's consciousness was of the evils against which the men of the Enlightenment protested, and how strongly he repudiated both obscurantism and the appeal to fear and superstition, on the one side, and, on the other, tyranny and persecution. If his realm of ends conveys a *vision* of the ultimate good, it is the vision of a way of life marked by the effectual banishment of such things from the ways of men, commanding their allegiance sufficiently by the bare fact of the absence of such evils. If we are to conceive morality as absolute (and it is Kant's conviction that we must do so), we must invest that absoluteness with a flexibility great enough to enable us to find in it that judge before which such evil habits of mind and will can be arraigned for what they are; and that not once for all, but in any and every guise and shape they may assume in the long course of human history. The moral task is never done.

Thus the formalism of Kant's ethics is tied to the way in which he saw the absoluteness of morality as something in fact engaged continually in competition, acknowledged and unacknowledged, with other claimants to human direction and illumination which would dispute its authority. And, of course, these claimants are necessarily much more sophisticated than, e.g., pleasure and pain, under whose twin mastery Bentham had seen human life as set. They will include indeed most visions of an all-embracing human good justifying the sacrifice of the present in the name of the supposed welfare of generations yet unborn; they will include equally attempted derivations of a proper way of human life to be commended to men as somehow congruous with the nature of what is; they will include all attempted justification of the over-riding of the clear dictates of morality in the name of some supposed higher law of human behaviour, endowed with some supposed religious sanction.

Here inevitably these concluding reflections will remind the reader of criticism often brought against Kant by elementary students of his ethics, who say, for instance, that for him morality is 'essentially negative', something whereby we are constrained to refrain from certain courses of conduct rather than encouraged to promote some way of life recognised as good in itself, or to realise certain values seen as positively excellent. To this point, expressed now in a crude and unsophisticated style, a reference has already been made when comment was passed on the rôle of law in Kant's ethics. But few teachers of Kant's doctrine will have failed to meet the comment that, where, for instance, the obligation to treat human beings as ends and not as means is concerned, it is much easier to see what this prohibits than what it commands. Thus it is clear that it rules out anything akin to deliberate recourse to a prostitute for the relief of sexual tension, the unacknowledged, yet deliberate, exploitation of a position of functional superiority to repay an old score against another, etc.; what is prohibited is clear; and if it is in part at least the formal character of the moral law that leaves the positive counterpart of what is thus prohibited vague, yet still the mere recognition of that fact does not satisfy the

critic altogether. For, after all, for Kant morality provides
the setting within which men have commerce with the
absolute and unconditioned; for him it is the very heart of
human life; there is something vaguely unsatisfying in the
suggestion that what brings men to themselves as they are is
something negative, a fabric of restraint and discipline they
must impose upon themselves. In the light of the preceding
argument, it may further be asked whether the concession of
absoluteness to morality in Kant's sense does not necessarily
always have the consequence of making the crucial human
experience something, in the admittedly loose language of
this paragraph, 'negative.' And it may indeed seem to some
at least that this consequence puts a question-mark against
our properly treating morality as absolute.

But what does 'negative' mean in this connection? There
are certainly unnoticed emotional overtones in the word. We
must not be tricked by them into attributing to Kant what he
certainly did not believe. Thus it would be very unfair to
his method and exposition in the *Grundlegung* to forget that
for him the notion of goodness takes precedence over that of
duty; if moral goodness is the fundamental form of goodness,
that very language bears witness to the precedence of the
notions of goodness and value over those of duty and obligation. There is a sense in which Kant could have allowed
place to the language of Augustine, with its obvious Platonic
background, that there was indeed a good which formed our
heart's true home, even while he identified this home with
obedience to the moral law, austere and unrelenting, in all
the various circumstances of life. If this obedience is often
something extracted from us willy-nilly, in seeming indifference to our purposes, individual and collective, and to our
private vision of men's proper end, it is, for all that, no violation of our rational nature, but the fulfilment of the demand
of its law upon us. What we find constraining us has authority upon us as the law under which, as rational beings, we
necessarily stand.

It may be worth referring here again to some points made in the first section of this study of Kant's ethics, and continually referred to in its course: namely the almost paradoxical, but quite necessary, congruity between intense moral seriousness and metaphysical agnosticism. We suppose that we know what it is to be morally serious, whether the attitude be one we endorse or reject; it is part of Kant's aim to bring out how little, in a sense, we know of what such seriousness involves. He might even concede that part of its price is a readiness to find our commerce with the absolute more in something, superficially at least, negative than in something positive and inviting our allegiance by its obviously attractive power.

It is very easy, and even fashionable to condemn Kant's ethics as individualist, even to find in them an underlying kinship with the Stoic indifference to external environment, whether natural or social, and detached concentration on supposed inward purity of motive. Nothing could be an easier, nor a more fundamental, mistake; for Stoicism, as much as the cult of the heroic, or the religious man's exaltation of certain states of consciousness as realising some kind of communion with God, is a system of values, with a determinate material content. The Stoic has a vision before his eyes of what he must become, of the way of life befitting the moral aristocrat; and this is something much narrower than what Kant esteems morally virtuous action to be. Indeed there is an offence against the proper discrimination of logical types in even appearing to treat the two as if they were of the same order. Certainly Kant treats personal integrity as something infinitely precious; but its cultivation can no more than happiness itself be converted into the all-including, all-justifying end of human life.

Certainly Kant shares with some of those whom we would normally call individualists a strong sense that no circumstance is by itself enough to discharge a man from the necessity of obeying the law within him. There is a great gulf

fixed between his ethical teaching and such destructive
superstitions as 'my country, right or wrong'; men are, by
their rational nature, committed to a common and universal
allegiance from which no particular loyalty can ever remove
them; as men, they are laws to themselves, and, for Kant,
they contradict this autonomy as much when they bestow a
kind of quasi-validity upon the commands of a despot by
accepting them as when they abandon themselves to follow
the promptings of their desires; in both cases alike, autonomy
has yielded place to heteronomy. Yet there would be a signal
failure to understand Kant if these illustrations of his teaching
were generalised to make him the apologist for a particular
sort of liberal individualist society as if such were the con-
cretion of his realm of ends. If he rejects the heteronomy of
the 'party line', equally emphatically he will have none of
that mistrust of State action in the interest of the common
welfare which bases itself on a false mystique of the 'personal'.
We are all of us familiar with the sort of pathetically dated
'lady bountiful' who proclaims her regret that the growth of
publicly conceived and executed policies of social welfare
has robbed of all true 'human' concern the relations between
those who administer and those who receive such benefits.
Of course what she means is little more than that what she
has delighted to call *her* 'charities' no longer provide her with
the necessary outlet for her consuming egotism. Even those
who were not prepared to defend the slums as desirable
schools for the achievement of heroic sanctity find it sometimes a little hard not to mourn the passing of the soup-
kitchen in the name of what they call 'truly personal
relations'. But for Kant the supremacy of the moral order in
no way whatsoever vindicates the special dignity of the
'personal' in this sense; indeed in such a situation it is the
clear demand of the moral law that the 'personal' yield
before the relatively impersonal, the particular before the
relatively universal; for thus the 'lady bountiful' will be protected against the self-deception and masquerade involved

in her rôle, and the recipients of her 'charity', who now receive of public right what is their due, preserved against a real affront to their dignity.

Thus the formalism of Kant's supreme principle gives it a kind of universal relevance, and protects us against identifying its fulfilment with the promotion of any system of value that we delineate. It is true that Kant's inspiration lies within the Enlightenment; but the principle with which he identifies the very essence of morality possesses a dynamic, compulsive force that at one moment recalls Plato's 'Idea of the Good', and at another (to quote words used to me over twenty years ago in discussion by the late Professor W. G. de Burgh) 'translates into another idiom the reminder of Christ that, when we have done all, we are unprofitable servants'. Certainly Kant's absolute is, in one sense, a fabric of self-restraint, an order of self-discipline to which a man conforms himself; and we are inevitably on edge in the presence of a view which at once insists that morality is an end in itself, indeed alone of all things is self-justifying, and yet identifies it with such a remorseless system of constraint, even while insisting that it is the expression of our rational nature. Is any room left for those things of which, for instance, Pascal wrote under the name of the 'order of charity'? Is every claim of such an order as that to a unique and peculiar dignity suspect, because of the unacknowledged cruelties and false-hoods men have unwittingly justified in its name?

If the formalism of Kant's ethics is tied to the way in which he saw the absoluteness of morality, it is tied equally, of course, to the way in which he saw temptation and the moral struggle. It is true that Kant always saw that struggle in its most diverse embodiments, as one in the end between particular and universal. Even as Rousseau, from whom Kant had learned so much, shunned the particular allegiance and attachment in society which might distract men from the morally and politically crucial obligations of citizenship, and found always in such distractions the highway of the tyrant's rise to power, so in the world of individual morality Kant set the particular over against the universal. The individual's private greed and secret lust, his unacknowledged self-regard and refusal to face the reality of his own motives—these were contrasted with the austere and searching demand of law universal. Particular interest was in continual conflict with the demand of a true disinterestedness, to whose service alone validity belonged. A reader fed on the more concrete approach to these problems characteristic of Butler, with whose teaching we shall be concerned later, may find himself antagonised by the way in which Kant seems to want to constrain the infinite variety of human weakness under the rubric of a quasi-logical formula. But here again, at the very end of our survey of some of his ideas, we meet what is peculiarly characteristic of Kant's whole approach to the problems of ethics, what indeed marks his 'theory of knowledge', in the sense given to that phrase in the first chapter of this book.

No one could accuse Kant of taking the issue of temptation lightly; it is an experience which, it might be said, for him comes near disclosing the heart of the human situation. Those theologians who, like the late P. T. Forsyth, found in Kant's 'moralism' the corrective which they required to the seeming indifference to ethical distinctions, which they judged characteristic of Hegel's philosophy of history, were in no way wide of the mark. For Kant, Gethsemane could never be charade, or pageant; such an agony had in some way to belong to the stuff of reality, and if to find room for it ontological metaphysics had to give way to an agnosticism which at least made it theoretically impossible effectually to 'explain away' freedom, there was nothing here to regret. If the only way to safeguard the ultimate reality of freedom was to make more profound and searching the empiricist's criticism of the claims made for metaphysical language to describe the ultimate structure of being, the criticism must be welcomed as a necessary first step to throwing into proper relief that ultimate. If, as a corollary of this, the moral order must be seen as something continually constraining men to allow their most cherished ideals to be broken in pieces rather than as a way of life that fulfilled harmoniously their deepest aspirations, that corollary too had to be accepted. We could have, or rather we thought we could have, the tidy completeness of a supposed all-embracing vision, or quasi-vision, of the order of being; but such, if we could come near its achievement, might take from us our precious, yet precarious and continually menaced, sense of our dignity as freely creative in our actions. Thus we should welcome that criticism of metaphysics which put a searching question-mark against the validity of our supposed syntheses, our subtle deployments of the modes of being; for by such criticism we are held fast to the ultimate mystery of our freedom.

And yet, to mention again the quotation from Professor Ernst Cassirer, the autonomy through which that freedom is possible is analogous to the spontaneity of our conceptual understanding; we find analogies to the exercise of freedom in conceptual thought. For Kant, in the one no less than in the other, there is nothing to suggest the random, the irrational, the lawless, the contingent; if freedom is creativity unique, individual, mysterious, it is also made possible by the fact that men stand under the authority of a universal and rational nature of whose law they are the bearers and to whose law they must submit. Thus Kant's 'theory of knowledge', in the special sense of this book, leaves the reader with a curious yet besetting impression of the marriage of seeming incompatibles, best simply described as 'freedom' on the one side, and 'the rational universal' on the other. It may be hazarded that if what has been said in the immediately foregoing about the characteristically formalist quality of Kant's moral theory has any validity, it is through the manner of his understanding of form that the union of the seeming incompatibles is achieved. To this matter we shall return later in the book.

CHAPTER IV

THE NOTION OF MORAL FREEDOM

AT this point it may be worth while to interrupt the comparative discussion of different sorts of ethical theory, to which this book is largely devoted, to discuss a controversy that is one of the perennial themes of moral philosophy; it is one, of course, to which already in the last chapter a good deal of attention has been directed. There is a sense in which what follows is not much more than an appendix to what has already been said; but the idiom in which it is written will, in some respects, be significantly different, and, coming where it does, the chapter may have the further advantage of adding something to what has already been said on the controversy between *Erfolgsethik* and *Gesinnungsethik*, a controversy that remains one of the most subtly pervasive and crucial in philosophical ethics.[1] It is, moreover, a controversy which the development and use of modern techniques of philosophical analysis enable us to see in a new way, in one moreover which brings the issue between them into peculiarly intimate relation to what is often, even usually, discussed as 'the problem of freedom'.

In the previous chapter it was insisted that, for Kant, men in, for instance, their effort to describe conceptually the world revealed to them by their senses were somehow transparent to themselves. Of course such language is metaphorical; but it bears witness to a persistent claim made by philosophers at least as early as Augustine that there is a special sort of immediacy in self-knowledge. Kant's attitude to his predecessors' views on this point was qualified in many ways; he agreed with Hume that we never 'catch ourselves without a perception', and certainly in the Paralogisms he

---

[1] This controversy is one of the central themes of this book.

argued most strongly against the suggestion that we somehow were justified in drawing conclusions touching our status in being, from the bare fact of our intellectual activity. Yet at the same time he claimed that we knew what it was to think, to attempt to decipher the order of the world around us to which our senses gave us access. Such at least would seem to be the underlying assumption of the 'Metaphysical Deduction of the Categories'; the argument of that Deduction takes for granted that the exposition of the nature of thought, in the sense of discursive understanding, will 'ring a bell' in the mind of the reader; and this because the reader will recognise, in the activity Kant is setting out, something with which he is perfectly familiar in himself. It remains true, of course, that, for Kant, the most important thing he was concerned to bring out about this activity was its inherent limitations.

Again in his ethics, it was emphasised how important for him was the experience of temptation; and also how he analysed this experience in terms of the conflict between the particular inclination of the agent and the authority of the practical universal. And in his argument we recognise the same assumption as in the Metaphysical Deduction, viz. that the reader will respond to the analysis, and to the emphasis laid upon the analysandum, because the experience is one with which he is himself familiar.

It is in fact such assumptions as these which differentiate Kant's method from that pursued by the modern practitioner of logical analysis; certainly there is much both in Kant's criticism of metaphysics and, indeed, in his treatment of the nature of ethical discourse which is congruous with modern logical procedure; but Kant will not concede that logical disentanglement is something carried out apart from the subject's immediate presence to, and involvement with, what is being disentangled. For Kant, thinking is more than the operation of a calculus in according with rules, and in moral action the agent is continually aware of the *dynamism* of that form of law universal to which he must submit himself. In so far as modern analytic procedures take for granted, even without acknowledgment, a sympathy with behaviourist assumptions, Kant will not endorse them. There is something which we can only call 'spiritual life' that the philosopher is concerned to explore; it is certainly no lawless, undisciplined rhapsody of the imagination, but something shaped by the laws of understanding, and the authoritative principles of reason. Moreover the exploration will take the shape very often of distinguishing the logical powers of one expression from another, of plotting the liaisons of concepts and the rest; but its issue will convey renewed perception of the posture proper to man 'under the sun'; it will have an inescapable 'existential' flavour.[1]

It would be unfair to Kant to accuse him of trying to derive the common public world of ordinary perception and concern from the private world of individual, personal experience. Whatever may be true, for instance, of Descartes, it is *not* true of Kant that for him the private, logically or temporally, precedes the public; but it is, for all that, fundamental to his argument that there is in individual experience something that cannot be conjured away, or reduced to terms of anything except itself. It is not something to which we have access as if it subsisted apart from the familiar world around us, as if it were a kind of ghostly world of strangely privileged immediacies into which we could withdraw. Thus there is no such thing as the 'life of thought' apart from the effort to describe exactly the order of the world around us; nor is there, as was insisted in the last chapter, such a *thing* as freedom on whose home we can, as it were, suddenly and unexpectedly light.

In the following sections of this chapter an effort will be made to develop further the contrast drawn between Kant's method and the dissimilar, yet similar, methods of contemporary philosophers; and an attempt will also be made to

[1] In the simple sense of dealing with life as men live it.

bring out the bearing of this opposition on the pervasive and continuing controversy between *Erfolgsethik* and *Gesinnungsethik*.

A. FREE-WILL AND DETERMINISM:
AN ILLUSTRATIVE DISCUSSION

1. *The Libertarian position.* Mr. Isaiah Berlin's recent impressive Comte Lecture[1] may not be regarded by the purist as philosophy; but it is interesting evidence of the tenacity with which, in certain moods, we all of us cling to libertarian modes of expression. At least in our polemics against these who tell us that we are conscripts in the army of historical development, we are prepared to use an idiom that is almost *simpliste* in its resistance to dissolution by those who tell us that 'the problem of freedom' has been dissolved. An idiom of protestation is something with which we find that we cannot dispense, and when we are told that something called historical necessity must make murderers of us all, we re-join the old-fashioned intuitionists in rigorous metaphysical insistence on the responsibility of the individual.

If philosophy is critique of language, it must surely take account of these sudden revivals of old-fashioned idiom. I repeat that maybe Mr. Berlin is not writing philosophy, but rather providing matter for philosophical analysis. After all, if philosophy is talk about talk, even the talk of the philosophically educated can provide grist for the mill, especially if they seem, in their vehemence, to adopt with a passionate dogmatism old-fashioned metaphysical styles. Indeed if one were writing an old-fashioned history of ethics one would have to class Mr. Berlin as a *libertarian*; for such he surely is. But nowadays taking sides is clearly seen to be no part of philosophy in the strict sense of the word; we are interested in the controversies of older days from a ringside seat. We essay something which might even be called philosophy of

[1] *Historical Inevitability* (O.U.P., 1955).

philosophy; and here our ways may divide. For if we say that
the task of the philosopher is the dissolution of problems, we
will surely welcome whatever serves to reveal the roots of a
puzzle in failure of attention to the logic of language as a
whole. But if, on the other hand, we incline to the view that
sometimes an obstinate perplexity about a particular problem points to something perhaps more significant than an
easily dissolvable confusion, we may prefer to identify the
philosopher's task with the most precise possible description
of what the problem is.

Mr. Berlin has shown by the way of his prophesying the
persistence of libertarian styles; and the attempted dissolu-
tions of the problem of freedom are relegated to footnotes in
which the dissolvers are accused of *ignoratio elenchi*. To any
inclined to dismiss the thorough-going libertarian position as
nonsense, the vehemence of his language may compel a
reconsideration of, for instance, what 'position' means in this
connection.

'I could have done otherwise'; and here I am simply
repeating, in a different style, an argument set out in the
introductory section of this chapter, which runs rather like
this. We are, it is said, 'nearer' to ourselves than we are to
stones and waterfalls, cows and cats, in the sense that we know
from within what is is like to be a human being, while we don't
know what it is like to be a material thing or an animal.
Sometimes the expression of this point is generalised, and
we are told that in our thinking, our willing, our choosing,
we are 'transparent' to ourselves. Thus, if it is suggested that
human thinking can be represented by the model of a Kelvin
tidal predictor, we can immediately give the lie to the suggestion that this is an exhaustive and complete account of the
matter by recalling what we know from within of the styles
of our actual thinking; in such activities (to use the phrase
again) we are 'transparent' to ourselves.

So, if we are told that our actions are determined, we can
appeal to an assurance, called by Sidgwick the 'simple

affirmation of consciousness in the moment of deliberate action', that this is not so. We know this affirmation to be true; we cannot escape from it. Why should we not simply take it at its face value as something which, by its very nature, we can only enjoy where our own choices and actions are concerned? Why should we not concede the unique deliverance of what must be a unique fact, uniquely made known?

About such argument there is much to be said. First of all it should be noted that it is an argument in the sense of apologetic for an established use. We do write as Mr. Berlin has written, and speak as he has spoken; we do challenge those who submit us to the sovereignty of something or someone called historical development in the way in which he has done. (And here some light may be thrown on what was expressed above in general terms about the relation of public and private: Berlin's language is one of protest, of revolt, of repudiation. It is by the use of such an idiom that the individual asserts himself as an individual. Almost we could say, 'I rebel; therefore I am.' Rebellion may be the expression of the reality of the private in a public context; but, as Hegel said before Professor Ryle, the private demands the public as its setting.) Can our challenge be justified? Can we show that somehow it is an intellectually respectable thing to make it? So we develop our apologetic; only, of course, it is not consciously apologetic, but rather direct appeal to what we are told we know immediately.

The style of this argument is realist in the old-fashioned sense in which Prichard was a realist, when he said, for instance, talking about Kant, that knowing was not a construction, but a finding.[1] The fact of human freedom, in the sense of the libertarian, is something thrust upon us. It overwhelms us, and we cannot get away from it. This even though it is also, of course, a fact, a categorical fact, about *ourselves*.

Here a man comes to himself; it is *almost* a kind of Cartesian

[1] Kant, of course, thought so too; but Prichard did not see this.

revelation, this entering on the knowledge of what one is. Even as Descartes' *Cogito* conveyed the existence of a substantial self as a necessary implicate of his thinking, so the recognition that one could have done otherwise conveys the reality of the responsible self.

Clearly a tremendous weight is being laid on this deliverance of consciousness. It is almost the authoritative revelation of the self to itself. Sense of responsibility for what we *have* done is implied to be the most ultimate thing that we can enjoy in respect of ourselves; nothing takes us deeper than this. If the language is metaphysical, that is because the fact that it conveyed is judged pregnant as nothing else with the revealing of the core of our characteristically human nature.

It is almost as if the strength of our apologetic concern, our anxiety to justify a means of expression, were clothing itself in terms of a particular description of the *arcana* of the self. That we do argue in a particular way is something which we learn with 'our eyes and our ears' (in Professor Wisdom's phrase). It is a matter of empirical fact whether or not we do repudiate deterministic styles of expression.[1] It is also a matter of empirical fact whether this repudiation takes the shape I have indicated, whether it lays such emphasis on what we know from within. But I would suggest that there is an instructive problem here for our consideration.

Protest is a visible, audible phenomenon; the idiom of protest is in some sense the assertion of the sovereignty of the individual human person. But the assertion goes by the seemingly roundabout route of commanding attention for a particular deliverance of 'introspection'. We *know*, we say, that we are responsible, and that certainty nothing takes from us. It is something that is *private* in the sense that every individual's access to it is his own, something that must be won and held by himself alone. It is as if, to the outward

---

[1] It is in fact as much a matter of empirical fact as whether we swear, or speak with an Edinburgh accent.

insistence that the collective will of a society does not absolve an individual from his personal responsibility, there corresponded a kind of hidden dialogue within which was the evident foundation of freedom. This was the inward acknowledgment by the individual of his personal responsibility for what he did, his personal realisation of the distinction between action and event.

To this dialogue, to this conversation of the individual with himself, we are each of us, we say, present by the very fact of our humanity. Maybe this is a forced model; but it is surely true that traditional defences of the libertarian position have emphasised this supremacy of inward over outward.[1] What we know from within about ourselves cannot be shaken. We were, in speaking of what belonged to our inner life, on home ground; there we knew the ropes. Our protest stands fast because of what we know of ourselves *ab intra*.

2. *Introspection and the language of freedom.* But what if one rejects, in the modern style, the distinction between outward and inward? Does inward survive only as a 'logical construction' out of outward? Does the vehement appeal to the deliverance of 'introspective' consciousness seem in the end to be no more than a way of referring to what we are actually doing when we are protesting, when we are taking our individuality upon ourselves? I suppose that traditionally consciousness of freedom was, as in Sidgwick, the name of something which we were supposed to enjoy as a kind of immediate possession; it was the name of something which was seen as a kind of introspective awareness admitting us to the very reality of what we were. But nowadays we cannot possibly see it like that; if it seems most natural to us to describe it in terms of some sort of inner awareness of ourselves, we realise that this awareness is inseparable from overt behaviour. Perhaps we do indeed convey the character of this overt behaviour to ourselves by the way in which we try to

---

[1] Whether the libertarian be concerned with historical determinism, as Berlin, or with determinism *per se*, as Prof. C. A. Campbell.

represent its inward counterpart. Maybe the description of our 'spiritual life' in terms of an inward experience private to ourselves helps us to see something of that life's reality, that it is a part (to speak crudely) of what we are, which does assert itself whenever we try to suppress the fact of its reality and see our overt behaviour somehow wrong. For we surely do see that behaviour wrong when we forget, for instance, that in ethics language is, in a profound sense, creative, and what that creativity implies.

'I could have done otherwise.' Such a phrase might express not simply a retrospective glance at what might have been, but *an act of repentance* which it makes concrete.[1] When the prodigal said that he would 'arise and go to his father', he was no doubt, from one point of view, recording the fruit of inward communing with himself. But at the same time he was making that communing something more than a mere daydream, and he made it so by linguistic action. He said something to himself, and, by saying, he did something. Was he conscious of freedom? One may say that that is an unanswerable question, that we cannot know whether in that moment he enjoyed something which might be called certainty that he could have done otherwise and that now he was free to transcend himself, to make effective effort against the weight of his pre-formed character. Yet he spoke, and spoke the sort of language which in the end focusses what the libertarian is really claiming to be part of the human inheritance.

Such language when it is spoken means that things cannot be as they have been before. A man does something to himself, and at the same time to his fellows; in the language which Kant made peculiarly his own, he affirms himself and them alike to be members of the realm of ends. The liber-

---

[1] This section was written *before* I had read Max Scheler's profound discussion of this matter in *Vom Ewigen in Menschen* (Francke Verlag, Bern), *Reue und Wiedergeburt*. Even those who cannot accept his phenomenological method must admit the great penetration of this discussion, and its cruciality for the matters here argued.

tarian is the man who will not let such forms of speech, with their peculiar and authoritative temper, be for one moment treated as other than they actually are.

'I will arise.' It is the prodigal who says this to himself. Only an individual can use the first person pronoun in that way of himself; but that is something which he must do. He will, if he is honest, steadfastly resist the suggestion that somehow this peculiarity of action made concrete by speech can be conjured away.[1] For if he yields to this suggestion, the fabric of ordinary discourse will be torn, and the pattern of proper human relationships, so largely built by words, violated. 'Spiritual life', as so much else, is carried on in words; repentance, the sense of a 'might have been' within one's power, is as much a verbal business as the description of the moon. Only it has its own logic.

It is a *peculiar* fact about the way in which we describe our 'spiritual lives'—and here, of course, I include particularly our moral conflicts—that we do persistently present them to ourselves as an inward reality finding outward expression; this is, of course, because they are so specially our own and because the way in which we make them bear fruit, whether for ourselves or for others, is our own work and must be so. Berlin, who is writing primarily about a particular approach to problems of politics, writes of the possible elimination of this kind of discourse very much in the style of Mill in his essay *On Liberty*; he fears the consequences of its elimination, the consequent corruption of the fabric of human society; that is indeed to claim the necessity of its preservation on modified utilitarian grounds. He leaves the language of ultimacy, etc. aside; he is perhaps too much a sceptic to use it easily, yet it may be the only sort of language in which what he is wanting to say can be worked out. Most likely we have to use that language if we are to make our own something of what underlies the urgency of the claim which the libertarian is making. What the libertarian is in the

[1] Cf. here Scheler's discussion.

end insisting is that we cannot eliminate what we know of ourselves in the way in which we approach our actions when we ourselves do them. We know then that they are our own; indeed our very understanding of what the words 'our own' mean is enlarged when we thus use them of our actions. This is a knowledge which is not a mere passive awareness of something outside ourselves, but something inseparable from the doing of the act, inasmuch as it is truly ours. And it is by the language which we use in respect of it that we make it ours.[1]

Of course in what I have said so far there has been a repeated suggestion of the defensive. Indeed that is inseparable from most libertarian writing, whether it is sophisticated or not. It is a feature of such writing that it pleads, or seems to plead, for the recognition of something that may be overlooked. Of course the importance of what we are to attend to is vehemently stressed; our authorship of what we do is something very near the heart of what we as human beings are. Yet in reading the writings of those who call themselves libertarians we are continually reminded of people clamouring for some sort of room for what otherwise might be crowded out. Thus we must find place for the one who understands as well as for that which is understood, for what we know in the moment of action as well as for what we come to realise when we look back on what we have done.

Why is this? Partly, I suspect, because the very character of what we are talking about when we talk about human freedom is something which we can only know in some sense from within, *even if our very understanding of what it is to know something from within is itself enlarged and corrected by the insistence that human freedom is the very standard of such,* and because

---

[1] To *know* that an action is mine is a very strange sort of knowing, quite different from knowing that an apple or a book is mine; to use the word 'know' in such a context is a venture, fraught with intellectual peril. One can so easily be bewitched into supposing that one is referring to special sorts of awareness; whereas what one is doing is advertising one's insistence to treat oneself in a particular way.

we know enough to realise that our knowledge of ourselves and our motives is always fraught with the deepest uncertainty. There is a sense in which we do not know what we are. A man may believe in an unsophisticated sense that he is acting freely, that in what he does he is himself the author. He may be completely oblivious of the extent to which, in the moment of supposed freedom, he is acting under strong compulsion of which he is quite ignorant. No one who has passed even some of the way through the discipline of psycho-analysis can ever find it easy to accept again his supposed 'transparency' to himself. Very often when we think that we know exactly what it is we are about, we are the prisoners of some persistent infantilism which is carrying us whither we would not.

We do not see things as they are; and the process of learning even a little how they are is one in which at times at least we have to become objects to ourselves. Then we do begin to understand what is common in recurrent patterns in our lives, patterns often outwardly quite dissimilar, yet revealing to reflection an inward core of similarity, even of identity. Of course there is a sense in which it is impossible in advance to predict how an individual will behave; for it is unlikely, even impossible, for anyone to foresee the sort of situations to which he will be subject; but that unacknowledged inward stresses, etc. will make their power felt and, to some extent at least, shape the life of the individual remains true. No doubt it is easy to write of this in a language which, because it is tinged with melodrama, is deeply misleading. Of course there is a difference in type between the chains that bind a man on a chain gang and the unconscious motives which determine the individual's conduct. To plead for deliverance from what in the end we are is to talk nonsense.[1]

But there is no getting away from the fact that we are what

[1] It is a matter of coming to terms in the way, for instance, a man of genius like Shakespeare may have done. Cf. Dr. Ernest Jones' *Hamlet and Oedipus* (Gollancz). But would such have been possible apart from the language of freedom with its mythology?

we are, that our conduct does seem to fall under laws of a near deterministic form. There is a human understanding which takes the shape of bringing under law the diverse fashions of individual behaviour, and of revealing their common substance. If there is freedom in any significant sense, it must be found as something known in and through that and similar activities of self-knowledge.

There is deep insight in Kant's insistence on an antinomy between freedom and causality. Yet it is not quite enough to say that what he fastened on was the contradiction between a man as spectator and a man as agent. It is perfectly true that when we look back retrospectively over our past lives we are shocked by the continuities we can discover; and yet that when we, the same individuals, come to act, we find ourselves quite unhesitatingly accepting the illusion that we are the authors, the first beginners, of what we do. There is a kind of indifference, sometimes even consciously experienced, to the past which may be a little part of what Kant had in mind in his mysterious doctrine of moral action as timeless; an indifference to the past which seems to let us see ourselves as here and now beginners of what we are trying to do.[1] (This may be related to what some writers mentioned earlier in this book had in mind when they speak of creativity.) But in his developed treatment of freedom Kant was after something more far-reaching than the mere advertisement of this fact.

It is a common question of the critics to ask what is the sort of understanding which takes up Kant's meaning in the Critique. If we assent even in a measure to his position, what is the nature of that assent? How is it related to understanding, how to reason, in his sense of those terms? Nowhere is that challenge more sharp than here. What are we really doing when we are acknowledging that we are 'phenomenally determined, but noümenally free'? We may say that what

---

[1] And even, as Scheler points out in his treatment of repentance, masters of what we remember of ourselves. Contrast the sense in which through repentance the past is changed, in Scheler's view, with the manipulation of the record of the past by the architects of power in Orwell's *1984* (Secker and Warburg, 1949).

we are doing is partly indeed to differentiate the standpoints of agent and spectator; we understand in so far as we accept, in daily life, the differentiation. But what is such acceptance? Is it itself both 'phenomenal' and 'noümenal'? It seems to me that Kant must have allowed it to be both; for no more than anything else can receiving light from part of the Kantian philosophy escape the duality in which Kant sets all things human!

When I said that it was not quite enough to attribute to Kant a mere distinction between the standpoints of spectator and of agent, what I had in mind was, in part at least, the complex character of the being of an agent, as including, no doubt in itself, the assenting to this very duality. For it is the central argument of this section of the present chapter that what we are talking about when we are arguing concerning the freedom of the will is the status of what I have called the 'spiritual life' of the individual. On Kant's view, that life is focussed in the awareness of the categorical imperative, and in our obedience to it; but it has perhaps far less precisely defined frontiers than he allowed. It is, as I have said, a business that is quite largely carried on in words whereby the individual creates various relations with his fellows, and in creating them creates himself. It must, if I may be permitted a very old-fashioned remark, include some part of what we call philosophy itself, in so far as through philosophical work the agent achieves a new self-consciousness in respect of what it is to *act*.

There is a part of the language once loved by philosophers contrasting the inner and the outer, and exalting the former as immediate and inexpugnably grasped for what it is, which needs to be seen as a tool whereby we convey ourselves, even 'work out', our individuality. It is even worth while to make the experiment of treating such language, specially favoured by libertarians, as a move in a game, the game of insisting that the standpoint of an *Erfolgsethik* is not exhaustive. A language is a 'form of life'; and if we develop a particular style and way of speech that has a certain extravagance of implication, and threatens to create a perilous and misleading mythology, we may justify what we have done by renewed closeness of attention to the context from which it derives its significance, enabling us to use, and not be mastered by, the instrument we have developed.

3. *Moral and political freedom.* Traditionally, as we have seen, place has been found for freedom by setting it within the inner life of the individual, the sacrosanct privacies to which he can appeal without fear of contradiction from his neighbour. That has been the conventional move in the establishment of the notion, and Kant himself in his opposition of what he calls worlds is perhaps in the following of that tradition. Yet he made a great step in stating the problem of freedom as an antinomy, and making it his aim to show the context which made that antinomy inevitable. If this is not trite or, worse, idealist, I might say that freedom shows itself in the insistent recognition of antinomy here. And this is something which can only be done in words, in the language whereby men make themselves.

We have already looked at one crucial instance of his language, namely the language of repentance, where inward and outward achieve a peculiar unity. But the thing is much more pervasive; it touches the whole argument of men with themselves in, for instance, deeply tragic situations, when a man must sacrifice what he knows to be good. For instance, if we do allow that in our present situation atomic warfare is justified, we cannot do so perhaps without acknowledging a real guilt. Maybe this will be judged unhealthy; yet, if Berlin is right, it can be justified almost on utilitarian grounds as contributing to the welfare of society at large. Such hesitations and scruples may be the expression of illusion, seen from one point of view; yet in their continued articulation there is found the actual process whereby alone a society is maintained in health. Those who painfully carry on the business of debate about this problem of means must have at least in some sense the feeling that what they do is more than sound and fury signifying nothing. The business is carried on in words; the protest of the conscientious objector is nothing apart from the speech in which it is made. But that speech is itself breach with all forms of determinism, and if it is indeed truly an expression of freedom, that and the very difficulty of it will be advertised in its inward form.

To take an example from politics may seem strange; but I do it deliberately inasmuch as I want to bring out the nature of the 'inwardness' of the debate men carry on with themselves. Why should we argue? What purpose is served by the argument which we carry on with ourselves? Is it sound and fury signifying nothing? Is it something like a bubble on the surface of the world of fact? Or is it sometimes more? And here, in speaking of 'argument', we are in effect back in the presence of the issues raised in the introductory section of this chapter.

I am not talking about the outcome of this debate; I am talking about the debate itself. Is it just a kind of vague playing around with issues, or is it something more? Is argument something which is simply swallowed up in its outcome, or is it significant in itself? Those who call themselves libertarians are in the end concerned with saying that argument itself is significant; they are not the guardians of some kind of esoteric rite whose mysteries they will somehow guard against the prying eyes of intruders. If the argument is private, its privacy is not the privacy of what is sacrosanct, what must be preserved inviolate against the intrusive eyes of the irreverent; if they use an idiom which suggests that this is what they are doing, then libertarians fail to bring out the real burden of what they are trying to say.

The reader may notice that I say 'inwardness'; why do I say that? Is not even saying that begging the question? Am I not, in fact, contrasting the esoteric and private against the public and ordinary? But then I remind you of the fact that I have deliberately chosen an example from politics, deliberately made you attend to the perplexities of the individual confronted with his political obligations. If I speak of an 'inwardness', that is something to be understood in terms of the individual's perplexity, and not in terms of some kind of mysterious inner colloquy which the individual somehow has to have with himself. To speak of such a colloquy is to use an idiom, an idiom which we must understand; it is, in fact, an idiom that we use when we want to insist that such perplexities are of the stuff of life, that their endurance belongs to men. 'Ethical language' is not confined to praise and blame, exhortation and prohibition. We find this language in use not simply when we are trying to dissuade or to encourage, but all the time that we are trying to come to terms with what we are.

So far in this chapter I have been mainly concerned with the effort to extract what it is that the libertarian is saying, and to show how far it can be stated without the *literal acceptance* of the sort of appeal to introspection by which it is usually conveyed. I have wanted to show that that appeal to introspection, that reference to the concealed mysteries of the inner life, is simply a way of speech. We are not talking about concealed secrets, the rituals of some unacknowledged rite;[1] we are referring to the way in which we actually use language. I say 'use' deliberately; for if we are to understand what people are talking about who make the curious, almost silly claim that we are free, we have to see they are really saying that a certain sort of language must be taken for what it is, a certain 'form of life' accepted at its face value.

In this chapter I have tried to suggest that the heart of the libertarian's contention can be stated as a thesis about words, as the claim, made on behalf of a resolution to use a particular sort of language, that it is not made in vain.

When I say that I am responsible for what I have done, am I saying anything? Of course the ordinary use of words

---

[1] Prof. Ryle's criticism of the inward-outward dichotomy is familiar by now, but always challenging.

K

demands that I should be regarded as responsible for that in respect of which I claim or admit responsibility; but is that all that has to be said about what I am doing when I make the claim? Am I simply allowing that certain rules of my society apply in my case, *or* am I doing something to myself? If the latter, then I think that the ultimate point of the libertarian's case is conceded. For what the libertarian is insisting is simply that we should see in a special way what it is we are, or may be, doing when we use the language of ascription of responsibility to ourselves; in other words, the libertarian is trying to show that the language of repentance is not a kind of bubble on the surface of things. There is a difference between the sort of speech in which a man acknowledges responsibility for what he has done, and mere description of events. When we acknowledge responsibility in this kind of way, we are doing something to ourselves. The use of words ceases to be a kind of mirroring of what has been done; it becomes part of the action.

In the end, what is important is not showing that the moral psychology of the libertarian is nonsense; of course it is! What matters is to bring out what it is that he is contending for. Earlier in this chapter I have tried to say that the object of his concern is the 'spiritual life' of the individual; and now I come back to that theme. The way in which the contention is pushed through is that of appeal to the inevitably private and esoteric.

But the appeal must not be taken at its face value, but as part of the way in which a man tries to secure a place, the proper place, in language as a whole for the language whereby he fashions himself as an individual.

4. *Saying and doing.* Those who have emphasised the importance of 'performatory' language in ethics have often failed to see the whole burden of that for which they are contending. To say that the use of language in ethics is performatory is to say that all the time we are talking in the characteristic language of ethics about human conduct we

are *doing* something. We are, for instance, trying to stop people from committing murder or fraud. But we may encounter performance in other places than the formal prescriptions and prohibitions of positive law. The *Gesin-nungsethiker* has to do things with words too: he has to find the means of conveying himself to himself. If it seems in a way forced and fantastic to suggest established rules in such a context, that may be because one is only prepared to admit *either* a private life to which there is *immediate* privileged access *or* one which is a 'logical construction' out of public behaviour. Whereas individuality (as the *Gesinnungsethiker* understands it) may be something, in a sense, to be *achieved* as much as, for the *Erfolgsethiker*, the happiness he seeks by edict and prescription to promote.

In a way, what I have been trying to insist is that the libertarian is the man who is self-conscious at this point; that he is the man who understands that the very defence of his position is an expression of the claim it lays upon him. Why should one bother to construct the kind of wayward, psychological mythology in terms of which libertarians represent their conduct? I mean, why should one bother to introduce notions of 'effort of will' and the rest, which are soon seen to be the merest destructive nonsense? One does this because it is the only way in which one forces on oneself what it is one is trying to say; and, in this case, *saying is a doing*.

What I want to bring out is, I repeat, the possibility that the very argument of the libertarians (the appeal to the immediately known, etc.) is a move in a game; it is not an attempt to say that this is what is the case; it is rather a doing of something, a making of something. Therefore I say that the argument is in the deepest sense a performance.

It is the defence of a particular sort of language, if you like the defence of address, calling one over against oneself a 'Thou', and not an 'It'. To be an ethical determinist is not to deny a particular set of propositions; it is to live in a particular way. For the business of living is carried on in words,

and it is with the defence of a particular sort of language
that in the end the libertarian is concerned. It remains true
that the determinist sees with an overwhelming clarity the
fact that there is a continuity between conduct and character;
but he ignores the queerness of language, that language is
indeed a way of life, a kind of creating of oneself. It is the
last phrase that focusses the central part of what I am getting
at.

Those who have emphasised the importance of 'performatory' language in ethics have often inclined, as was implied
above, to a utilitarian position. That is, they have brought
out the peculiarities of moral language, of words like 'ought',
'good' and the rest; they have helped us to see that this
language is what it is and not something else. Moral language
is not a kind of disguised presentation of advantage; it is not
the case that saying that 'ought' is a concealed form of 'is'.
When we say we ought to do something, by the very use of
words we encourage ourselves to do it. In this section I have
tried to show acknowledgment of this point. But what I do
quarrel with is the suggestion that if we emphasise the language of ethics, we are thereby committed to a thorough-going
utilitarian verdict on its direction, or on the kinds of expression that belong to it. The libertarian seems to be the man
who insists that we can recognise the *uniqueness* and the range
of ethical language, and hold to that uniqueness and to that
range; the whole gallimaufry of our idioms for bringing home
the ethical to ourselves is not something which needs be made
secondary to some general conception of public advantage.
Of course praise and blame and the rest do serve as activities
for the promotion of the common good; praise and blame are
acts whereby that good is promoted. But is that all that they
are? From the mere insistence that the moral philosopher
studies language, and the language of conduct, is their uniqueness, it does not follow that that language is a kind of instrument whereby men pursue their advantage. Of course we
are right to insist on the uniqueness of ethical language; to

praise someone, to bring out by the words we speak one line of conduct from another, is something unique. There is nothing in the world like praise and blame, nothing in the world like the ascription of responsibility and the reverse. *But it is a matter of crucial importance to be clear as to the context in which the ascription is made.*

What is this context? What are these contexts? That, I think, is the real problem about which we are obscurely arguing in our discussion of freedom. No one denies, no sane person can deny, that when we are responsible, we are by that very ascription shown as standing in a particular relation to what we have done. But what is the acknowledgment of responsibility? Is it something which somehow belongs to the verdict which a society passes on our conduct, or may it be something also which in the end we do to ourselves? Those who admit that ethical language is 'performatory' have inclined usually to a utilitarian conception of the moral end. They have admitted, in a sense, certainly, the uniqueness of ethical language; they have not wanted to define the 'ought' in terms of the advantageous. They have acknowledged uniqueness; *but always in a context of the promotion of public advantage.* Blaming oneself is worth while if it promotes the end of human happiness; but blaming oneself is never admitted as something which might be, I will not say, an end in itself, but at least as a moment in the creation of the self.

What is it to be a human being? The libertarian is the man who insists that we do not prevent our answer to that question by a sort of unreal circumscription of the idiom in which we pose it. Of course he has dressed up his argument in a queer fantastic language; but in the end he is trying to ensure we do not forget the queerness of being human.

Of course if one says, as the utilitarian is sometimes inclined to, that being human is not something which is an end in itself, then we see matters of praise and blame always in the setting of the contribution that praise and blame make to the promotion of human welfare. But if one refuses that context as a final authority, one allows that maybe such language has a function in the very creation of the self. Of course freedom is not something that is revealed to a kind of introspective counterpart of what we like to call perception; of course we never know that we are free in the way in which, for instance, we know that we have earache or a cold. Knowing that we are free, admitting our responsibility is *doing* something; what matters supremely is the context in which it is done and the recognition of that context. For if we know that context, we know what we are doing when we call ourselves free. We are doing something to ourselves; if we cease to do that something we change the very understanding of our lives. The denial is also an action.

The libertarian is the philosopher who has seen this; he has understood the peculiarity of the ascription of responsibility in the setting of a doctrine which takes the spiritual pilgrimage of the individual as something significant in itself. He is calling attention to the uniqueness of a certain sort of language, but in a different way from that in which those who simply acknowledge that ethical language is what it is are doing the same. The libertarian wants to say that a particular sort of language must be protected against any sort of subordination and against various sorts of restriction; for it is in the use of language of freedom that the individual comes to himself.

The problem of ethics is in the end perhaps only the problem of a particular sort of language. Of course no one denies that it is a unique sort of language, but what sort of uniqueness belongs to it? Those who believe, in some sense, in a categorical imperative claim ultimacy as well as uniqueness for the language; they also see its stretch as covering human life in all its various expressions. They are insisting that we take this life as something which must be accepted for what it is; the very uncertainty and confusions of those who live it are seen to be in some way sometimes almost an end in themselves. We cannot speak of the use of ethical language as means; in these connections it is the defining of end. The philosophical problem is a problem both that of safeguarding of uniqueness, and of the understanding of the sort of uniqueness which is being claimed.

The libertarian in his controversy with the determinist is not someone who is protecting a particular way of speech as an idiom or accent which he as an individual favours; he is rather compelling people to attend to features of the place which ethical language occupies in language as a whole. To insist on this is not necessarily to commit oneself to some sort of Kantian doctrine in that of which goodness consists; it is rather to ask what status in being we are to assign to the concern with such goodness. It is to ask how we view what I call the 'spiritual life' of man in relation to being as a whole. As the late Professor John Laird often insisted, an ultimate controversy in ethics lies between the ethic of motive and the ethic of consequences. If we look at the problem of freedom and its curious intractability from the standpoint of language as a whole, it is this, I submit, which is most inexorably thrust on our attention.

B. SOME COMMENTS ON THE FOREGOING DISCUSSION

To some readers the discussion in the first section of this chapter may have seemed a distracting interruption, alike in argument and in style, even if the former, in certain ways, overlapped with and repeated what had already been said. All this was quite intentional; for the section was intended partly to enable the issues canvassed in the preceding chapter to be seen in a rather different light, and to be presented both in a different style and context.

1. Thus a reader may ask himself how far the approach to the problem of freedom in the foregoing section can be judged akin to that of Kant. Obviously Kant's distinction between his 'two worlds' has seriously affected the exposition;

the whole argument is conducted under the guiding light of the assumption of their irreducibility one to another, even if there is less acknowledgment in this than even in the preceding chapter of the importance, for this part of Kant's doctrine, of his treatment of time as a subjective form of our experiencing. But if Kant's influence is discernible, the emphasis so painfully laid in the preceding chapter on his rationalism is almost entirely absent. Indeed some of the things said about the language of freedom might seem more easily to apply to Fichte than to Kant; what has been stressed in the exploration of the language of freedom has been that aspect of creativity mentioned in the previous chapter almost to the exclusion of any other. And this concentration of attention might be said to have received particular emphasis in the discussion of those forms of language, such as confession or penitence, wherein the individual as it were conveyed to himself his freedom; the critical reader might have the sense of something suspended in mid-air, poised over a void in relation to nothing except itself, as if all that traditional theologians had found scandalous in the idea of a 'creation from nothing' was somehow supposed present in the simplest human action. To represent speech as creative, to conceive men as almost owing their humanity to what they make themselves by way of some of the things which they say, seems perilously akin to a singularly gross sort of mythology.

Nevertheless it may be claimed that the discussion has at least served to throw one very important one into clear relief. In the introductory section of the chapter, reference was made to the controversy between *Erfolgsethik* and *Gesinnungsethik*; it was also implied that those who practised rigorous methods of logical analysis in the exploration of ethical concepts were for the most part, consciously or unconsciously, sympathetic with behaviourism. Now the behaviourist is necessarily an *Erfolgsethiker*; that is, he measures the worth of a policy of action by a reference to its tendency to increase the amount of happiness in the world at large; his hostility to anything which can be called introspection sets him on edge in presence of the *Gesinnungsethiker's* preoccupation with motives, states of minds of agents, etc. As the student of Bentham's writings will realise, that very able and tough-minded moralist, in defending with deep insight and critical skill the standpoint of an *Erfolgsethik*, takes up almost unnoticed a position in respect of the method of psychology closely akin to that of the behaviourists.[1] So when the problems of moral freedom are canvassed, and resolved, as they often are, in terms of the way in which our language of praise and blame fulfils its peculiar and assigned function, the locus of that function is usually far too quickly identified with what it must be within the horizons of an *Erfolgsethik*; but to say that this is the only job such language can possibly 'perform', this the only sort of context to which it can possibly belong, is to beg the question under the unnoticed, yet pervasive, authority of behaviourist assumptions. On what ground do we deny that there can be no other context for such language, deny, for instance, that there can be such a thing as a sense of sin, or such a struggle as a man may sometimes think he has with himself to purify his intention, to make as perfect as he can the charity within his heart?

In the first chapter of this book, and indeed in the following chapters as well, mention was made of the conversations which a philosopher might interrupt, even if maybe his accent had to be changed in some degree to make him comprehensible, even as a man used to speaking the 'doric' of Buchan might have to modify his accents in Bridgeton or the Gorbals! The background certainly of some of the ideas set out in the first section of the present chapter lay in Kant; but in the manner in which they were set out and developed they were intended for a place in a contemporary dialogue. Indeed they were offered as the sort of interruption which might help to transform the conversation. For, of course, that conversation is usually conducted on the assumption that the problem of exhibiting the compatibility between the

[1] Cf. David Baumgardt's *Bentham and the Ethics of To-day.*

language of determinism and the language of freedom is one which can be comfortably conducted in terms of an unacknowledged acceptance of the underlying principles of an *Erfolgsethik*; whereas, of course, what Kant in effect does, in the context of such a conversation, is to challenge just that assumption. His challenge is in a way precisely the same impatience as, it was suggested in the previous chapter, he would show at the suggestion that what in the end he was saying about morality boiled down to insisting that it was irreducibly imperative in mood. To say this, we saw then, was certainly to say something about the character of human ethical language on which Kant repeatedly insists; but it was not the whole of his doctrine, but a part of it which could only be properly appreciated when the imperative element in morality was recognised as unconditional. For it was of the essence of Kant's view that in their moral experience —a matter, of course, of language as much as any other form of experience—men were projected continually out on to the sea of the unconditioned. So in the interruption he makes to the conversation, of which we are now speaking; he would allow that men needed both the language of freedom and that of determinism. Before all men he is impatient with the suggestion that we should try to confine the writ of causal order within the world about us somehow to make room for something we call freedom. Kant is a determinist, and his aim is always to show the compatibility of determinism with freedom; but he will not allow that we can do this lightly or easily by showing that, for instance, certain forms of words, the languages of praise and blame, of accusation, condemnation and acquittal, have their several necessary rôles in promoting the smooth functioning of our society; or at least if he admits, as he would in a sense be prepared to do, such rôles to such language, and a general task set to men to achieve by any means known to them, or discoverable by them, a more humane society, he would also insist that that was not the whole story, nor even the most important part of it. But how, at once comes the question, do we know that it is not the whole story? And here, inevitably, we are thrown back again on the alleged transparency of our consciousness, whether theoretical or moral; certainly the relation between this sort of transparency and the introspection so severely criticised by the behaviourist remains unclear. It may, however, be claimed that some of the discussion in the first part of this chapter does throw some light on the way in which a man working with the notion of the alleged transparency of consciousness might move with it, as a chessman with his queen; and the understanding, the tracing, of these moves may have thrown some light on what it is that those who contend for transparency are contending for, and on what we have said of their contention in the introductory section of this chapter.

2. The conversation which we represented Kant as interrupting was, of course, one on the second level of those distinguished in the first chapter; it was questions concerning the very foundations of ethical belief which we conceived him as raising in his challenge to the assumptions on which the discussion of the place and rôle of the language of freedom and responsibility was being conducted. But in his provocative lecture which furnished us with a starting point in the first section of this chapter, Mr. Berlin was addressing openly an audience concerned with less abstract issues. In him prophetic speaking to a situation was the dominant note; his references, which his lecture certainly contained to Kant's contribution to the other, more technical conversation, were for the most part relegated to footnotes. The relatively uncritical, swashbuckling temper of his argument made it quite clear whom he was hoping to reach; he was concerned to attack remorselessly the merchants of any form of historical determinism; and Hegel, Marx, and Toynbee alike come under his whip; he preaches in order to 'vindicate the dignity of the individual'; his lecture is an essay in such vindication, and, as in other of his recent writings, there is present a

readiness to embrace gladly the scandalous metaphysical language of 'open possibilities' and the rest. There is a richness and a diversity in human life, and men stand in the presence of high possibilities of achievement, of exploration of the unknown, of adventures into uncharted realms of intellectual and aesthetic experience; they are continually threatened by those who will rob them of their inheritance of scepticism and independence of mind, of acceptance of the authority of fact and yet of readiness to admit the possibility that things might have been otherwise. Of course such language is not precisely Kantian; the stress is laid more on the possibility before men of intellectual and aesthetic experiment, and less on the more austere constraints of duty. But Berlin is still defending the intrinsic significance of the 'spiritual life' of the individual against those who would treat that individual as nothing more than an element in an impersonal process. By what he writes he shows how close the *apologia* for liberalism in the political and cultural sense can come, in its idiom, to the impassioned defence of human freedom by such a libertarian as Professor C. A. Campbell; in the use of the language of 'open possibilities' by both alike, admittedly in very different contexts and styles, there is conveyed an analogous perception of the precious uniqueness of individual human existence.

In Berlin's lecture the relation between the questions of moral and political freedom becomes explicit; and in the first part of this chapter we have allowed the relationship to show itself in the very examples used. Thus the choice to illustrate, of the conscientious objector's argument with himself, was in no sense haphazard; even though the pressures which would deprive such interior debate of significance might come more from the deliberate use of power by men in a position to employ its resources than from the supposed authority of some general view of the order of the universe, (where, of course, the power used is understood as including the insidious suggestion of a cautious, even unacknowledged, propaganda as well as the more direct instruments of coercion, whether physical or psychological). Are such debates sound and fury signifying nothing?

In 1940 the present writer vividly recalls a course of lectures by the late Dr. Karl Mannheim, delivered in Oxford, in which the distinguished sociologist insisted that, as a matter of historical fact, we were moving out of an age in which the dominant styles of thought had been individualist, emphasising the introspectively revealed and the privately enjoyed, to one in which the dominant temper was behaviourist and prepared to insist on the sovereign significance of the public and the collective. Thus he instanced the reaction, clearly discernible, against the sort of philosophy made fashionable by the work of Descartes and his successors, and bracketed it with the shifts already showing themselves in psychological method and its application in the field of public life; all this reaction was part and parcel, in his view of the situation as a sociologist, of something almost akin to an ontological mistrust of the notion of the solitary individual, with his questionings and seemingly unassailable privacies of thought, feeling and choice.

Certainly we can trace the influence of the behaviourism of which Mannheim spoke, in the unacknowledged assumption conveying an *Erfolgsethik*, as the only context in which men can seriously discuss ethical issues or find a home for the language of praise and blame and the rest. Behaviourism is, of course, the name of a varied set of assumptions and methods, even of phenomena; and it would be quite unscrupulous to suggest that the modern philosopher's recommendation that inner experience shall be treated somehow as a 'logical construction' out of outer belongs to the same universe of discourse as the insistence on a thoroughly conformist behaviour, by the autocratic masters of power in a modern totalitarian State. (After all, the sources of the flight from Descartes can be found in, for instance, Aristotle's doctrine of ἐθισμός.) But there is a certain family resemblance between these very different manifestations of the priority of the outward over the inward, whether viewed as a principle of analysis or a maxim of behaviour. The autocrat will demand that a man sacrifice his own sense of the significance of his hesitation, perplexities, scruples, scepticisms on the altar of an organised public good to whose service he can be bent; and certainly there is something akin to this, however deeply humane most of its professors may be, in the suggestion that the solitary life of the individual, the aloneness in which his sudden vision of the natural world may take form or his sense of the over-riding obligations of pity press upon him to a point of unanswerable perplexity, is somehow a mere bubble on the surface of things, a ghostly by-play of individual emotion and fear that is altogether strange to, and apart from, the actual course of events.

'Behaviourism'[1] is, then, the name of a central aspect of the problem which we know as that of moral freedom; and in the same moment as we see this, we see also the importance of the point made in the first section of this second part of the chapter, and before. We see that the issue of moral freedom is closely bound up with that of the adequacy of the standpoint of an *Erfolgsethik*. We have next to discuss further how far the mysterious language of states of consciousness regarded as somehow transparent and immediately grasped for what they are, of special sorts of 'introspection' which disclose to a man in ways which cannot be impugned the reality of his freedom, are bound up with the claims of a *Gesinnungsethik*; it may already be clear to some at least how near such discussion must come to an exploration in the field of the 'theory of knowledge' in the special sense given in the first chapter of this book. When we see the controversy between *Erfolgsethik* and *Gesinnungsethik* in the context of the problem of freedom, we are ready, or almost ready, to grasp new rôles which may be played by the things called 'theories of knowledge', and this in contexts which include reference not simply to the theoretical and moral activities of men, but also to the

---

[1] This may be a new use of the word 'behaviourism'.

manner in which they exercise their rights, and fulfil their
duties, as members of political society. The question 'What is
an individual?' is one which floats, and seems to find its
home now in one context and now in another; and it is at
least possible that it is an epistemological question in the
sense of our first chapter, that is, a question which will find
at least one possible and pointed way of statement in terms
of the manner and methods of our knowledge.

3. The term 'theory of knowledge', and the cognate
'epistemology', were introduced at the end of the first
chapter of this book, where it was said that they would be
'used in a special, even a relatively novel, sense' to indicate
aspects of the arguments of moral philosophers essential to,
even constitutive of, the unity of their individual work, but
not by any means always presented directly as theses about
the scope and limitations of human knowledge; although the
choice of the terms has been dictated by the fact that these
aspects have sometimes been consciously and deliberately
set out as their authors' theory of knowledge'. And already
we have seen that in this special sense, the term 'theory of
knowledge' has been used not as the name of one identifiable
thing, or even of enterprises with specifically or generically
similar features, but rather to bring together, and to set
thereby in a new light, a whole family of enterprises. Thus
one would not hesitate to describe as 'theory of knowledge' in
this special sense, e.g., Mill's sudden insistence that room
must be found for the perception of nature vouchsafed to him
through Wordsworth's poetry as something much more than
an adornment or decoration of life, like the icing or the
pattern of the icing on a cake, and his near-readiness to
readmit disreputable words like 'intuition', long expelled
from respectable philosophical society, to advertise or to
cover this acknowledgment. It was remarked in the second
chapter of this book that one of the features of Mill's very
best work in the philosophy of ethics, such as his essays on
Bentham and Coleridge, which helps to give it its abiding

distinction and value, is the clarity with which he succeeds in
bringing out just this problem. Again in Moore's case, it was
suggested (by implication as well as by over-statement) that
the term 'theory of knowledge' in our sense lent itself quite
naturally for use to indicate his view of the nature of our
apprehension of certain states of affairs, e.g. the contemplation of beautiful objects, as intrinsically excellent in relation
to his understanding of the nature of the various entities in
the world around us, not to mention entities of another order
such as cardinal numbers, and our awarenesses of them and
the relations between them. If we attribute to Moore something legitimately described as a 'theory of knowledge' in
this sense, we are helping to indicate the close interlocking
there seems to be for him between the intrinsic excellence of
certain states of affairs and the way in which we recognise its
presence in them; it is almost as if the refusal to permit
intrinsic excellence to be treated as on all fours with the
sensibly manifested characters of events in the world of
space and time elicited the supposition of a special sort of
awareness to reveal that uniqueness, and further, as if the
nature of that awareness were itself refined by the peculiar
quality, namely intrinsic excellence, whose presence was
supposedly disclosed to it. It was even suggested in the
first chapter that awareness of intrinsic excellence was presented as something tailor-made to be the revelation of
this peculiar quality inherent in some self-enclosed unit of
experience, some near-atomic state of consciousness in
external relation to its surroundings, seen through that
awareness as endowed, in its independence, with a special
luminous quality of excellence (something suggesting even to
those familiar with the Hebrew and Christian scriptures the
Shekinah). If Moore's treatment of intrinsic goodness as a
simple, indefinable, non-natural quality manifests itself in a
series of argumentative moves, in which any attempt to
substitute for 'good', in any expression in which it occurs,
some word indicating a natural quality such as red or green,

pleasant or unpleasant, attractive or resistant, is rejected, these obstinacies are, as it were, underpinned by a more elusive, hardly stated view of the things in the world, and their relation to our experience, the former very various, and the latter acknowledged as including among its modes, almost on equal terms, this, that and the next.

In the chapter on Kant it was emphasised that when the student speaks of the relation of Kant's theory of knowledge to his ethics, the former was an enterprise of a different order from the one referred to in the first chapter; in his theory of knowledge Kant was criticising the attempt by means of theoretical concepts, of which the most fundamental, such as substance, cause, actuality, possibility, necessity and the rest, were thought *a priori*, to deploy the structure of ultimate reality, and in it he necessarily included a positive evaluation of the status and function of such fundamental concepts, and the principles from which they were abstractions, in description of the world around us and formulation of the laws of its working. Where 'theory of knowledge' in our special sense was concerned, it was even suggested that the phrase could best be used to describe Kant's whole establishment of the primacy of practical reason in the context of a radical metaphysical agnosticism.

But in the immediately preceding pages[1] of the present chapter a reference has been made to the work of those, like Descartes, Locke, Berkeley, and Hume, whom in his *Concept of Mind* Ryle would seem to be indicating when he speaks of the 'great epistemologists'; of course, in one sense, Kant is of their number, indeed in some ways the greatest of them all. But, in this as in other respects, he manifests one of the features of philosophical genius by transforming the character of the discussion he had inherited; it was easy enough to neglect this transformation, as long as it could be suggested that what was of supreme importance in his work was his answer to the

[1] In the reference to the judgment on the intellectual scene passed by Prof. Mannheim.

L

so-called 'problem of knowledge'. But as soon as it was noticed that such sections of the first Critique as the 'transcendental deduction of the categories' and the first and second 'analogies of experience' were significant not only in criticism of the undue and quite unreflective self-confidence of the devotees of the old associationist psychology, but also in preparing the way for the radical criticism of metaphysical argument which was to follow, the bearing of Kant's work was seen in a new way; (this peculiar misunderstanding of Kant's work as a contribution to the 'problem of knowledge' was a great deal more common in Great Britain in the days when the British idealists to some extent monopolised the exposition of the Critique than it was on the continent, where men like the late Professor Moritz Schlick, who came to differ very sharply from Kant, none the less showed in their writings the continual influence of his argument, and where strict Thomists like R. P. R. Garrigou-Lagrange shrewdly concentrated their attack on his attitude to ontological metaphysics.) But there is no doubt that the phrase 'the problem of knowledge' is an appropriate indication of the sort of thing a great many philosophers of the modern period spent their time on; Professor Ryle, whose sympathy with the behaviourist programme of treating the inner as a 'logical construction' out of the outer is clear in his book, treats this preoccupation as a mixture of real, though confused, insight and uncriticised muddle. There is, thus, deep insight certainly present in Berkeley's analysis of the conceptual system of Newtonian physics; where the understanding of the law of gravitational attraction and the abstract concepts, entering into it were concerned, and the relation of both alike to the things we see and hear, smell and touch in the world around us, he had the root of the matter in him. Similarly Hume made a discovery of first-order logical importance when he discriminated sharply between the relations obtaining between conclusion and premise in a deductive argument from those obtaining between conclusion and premise in even the best attested induction. In the former case to deny the conclusion, and yet to assert the premise, would involve formal self-contradiction; in the latter, however strong the evidence for the conclusion, its denial is formally perfectly compatible with the continued assertion of the premise. If Hume seems to approach this discovery in the philosophy of logic by a quasi-psychological scrutiny of the contents of his consciousness, seeking, for instance, for the impression corresponding to the idea of cause, such hesitant beginnings do not detract from the permanent worth of his conclusion. They no more contaminate his contribution to the philosophy of logic than does Berkeley's theology ultimately obscure the clarity of his insight into the nature of physical laws. There is a core which remains after the confused and confusing containing-husk of metaphysical assumption, psychological and quasi-psychological language, uncriticised reliance on the supposed privileged access vouchsafed by something called 'introspection', have all alike been stripped away. It remains, at least in the opinion of some contemporary philosophers that most of the language most peculiarly characteristic of the statement of the 'problem of knowledge' belongs to the husk and not to the core. But to this judgment we must attend, if we are really to measure up to the extent to which we accept to-day uncritically the assumptions of an *Erfolgsethik*, and to grasp the close interpenetration between the claims made by the libertarian and the standpoint of *Gesinnungsethik*.

There is so much in the old-fashioned language of the 'problem of knowledge' to provoke a smile that one feels ridiculous even in suggesting that it might be taken with a certain seriousness; but it might serve some sort of defence against being laughed out of court to distinguish this seriousness from the seriousness with which some among us can certainly remember arguing about 'knowledge', as if we were men imprisoned and shut up within the circle of our own strictly private, immediate awareness, somehow trying to break out in order to enjoy contact with the world of every-day life with which plain men and scientific investigators of the order of nature were alike concerned. We can certainly some of us remember such moods, in which even if we did not entertain the supposition of the existence of a *malin génie*, we none the less behaved very like men always threatened by the tricks of such a cosmic practical joker. Can we ever certainly know the existence of a physical world revealed to us by the private, fleeting interrupted flow of our sensation? How can we conceive the relation to the world of things in space and time of sense-data alone given to us; how can we justify our reference of presentations to objects? We are all familiar in some way with such questionings; and even if a training in the method of 'logical constructions' has gone some way towards giving us a recipe for immediately converting them into questions of logic, we can at least some of us recapture the mood in which they were almost the expression of a predicament, a cry for help, a lament still poignant, even when we began to suspect that it was logically senseless.

Of course we are now alive to the peculiar vice that spoilt the whole enterprise, the assumption of the primacy of the private over the public, the deliberate, if unconscious, attempt to construct the growth of human knowledge into a move-ment, as it were, from within outwards, with the immediate and private secure and immune from question, while on the circumference a haze of uncertainty seemed to envelop the ordinarily certain and unchallenged world of every day. The paradigm is now judged worse than caricature; it is seen to be meaningless, and the very language in which the supposed absolute certainties of private experience are conveyed is recognised as parasitic upon less refined, more earthy levels of language, from which we have gained, *inter alia*, our very notion of what it is to obey a language-rule.

So we cannot simulate the sort of seriousness about the 'problem of knowledge' which once we may have enjoyed; but still we can look back with at least a tolerant, interested regard on this curious language-game to which philosophers have given so much of their time, to this crucial manifestation of a certain way, or ways, of representing men's relationship to their world. Wittgenstein's remark that a language is a form of life has already been quoted; it would seem certainly to be one of the implications of his later work that we are more than simply permitted, we are even compelled, to study the workings of language in the closest connection with the behaviour they express and further. It might be said that the 'problem of knowledge' could be looked at as a language-game which philosophers have played, coming admittedly, as they played it, to the frontiers of nonsense, forgetting that public and private are necessarily correlative, supposing sometimes that the latter could be swallowed up in the former. The besetting temptation to solipsism of those who have worked with the 'problem of knowledge' is in no sense accidental; the solipsist, after all, is the man who thinks he has swallowed up the public in the private. But once one is conscious of the shadow of the nonsensical across one's path, one can begin to evaluate the language adventures those who have spoken and written in this way have risked. If the conception of a reconstruction of human knowledge upon a sure and certain foundation is an illusion, yet like other illusions it may tell us much of the men who attempted it; it can even be regarded sometimes as a specially revealing chapter in their autobiography.[1]

We are alive to-day not only to the hazards but to the sheer logical absurdity of the enterprise; and, further, the bias towards exalting the outward at the expense of the inward presses strongly upon us. We must, of course, distinguish what is a matter of logic from what is an influence of environment; the peril is there when the two levels are allowed to merge, and we are almost tricked into supposing that we can

---

[1] I owe a great deal in this section to Professor Norman Malcolm's article on Wittgenstein's 'Philosophical Investigations' in the *Philosophical Review* for 1954; I am not sure that I have fully understood him and, admiring his article as I I do, must apologise for any misrepresentation or misuse of what he has said.

extract from an emphasis upon behaviour, which is primarily logical, an argument in favour of a behaviourism that would conjure away the realities of the inner life altogether. As a matter of historical fact, the concentration upon the 'problem of knowledge' of which we have been speaking had its remote background in the rich profusion of works of mediaeval spirituality which took self-knowledge as their theme; Gilson spoke of Descartes' conception of God as being indeed a reminiscence, but less the recalling of some innate endowment of his mind than the recollection of something heard in church as a little boy. So with the 'problem of knowledge' we had a kind of intense preoccupation on the subject's relation with its environment, from which it was seen as somehow estranged; but the weight of emphasis in discussion fell always on the subject and its powers; the yield of the investigation was always some sort of novel or renewed perception of the way the subject dealt with external reality. Whether the language was that of inference, of the seeing of all things in God, or of the habits of imagination, 'changeless, irresistible and universal', it was still of the subject that men spoke.

What can we say now of this preoccupation with the subject, this ready acceptance of the subjective as a kind of 'home ground' whereon men could argue with confidence? Kant certainly did not see the growth of human knowledge as a movement from the private to the public; for him the world of which we spoke was by that fact alone the public world; the categories were vindicated as indispensable conditions of communication, the notion of causality itself being proved as the *sine qua non* of the dating of events in a public time-order. Moreover, as has been constantly insisted, the problem of metaphysics, of the validity of men's attempt to orientate themselves in respect of the unconditioned, was fundamental for him; it was with the status of that enterprise that he was concerned. But he shared the assumption of those who worked on the 'problem of knowledge' that he judged men's consciousness somehow transparent to itself. The public was not in any sense capable of exhibition as a function of the private; yet if he were asked how men knew the difference between, for instance, wondering whether or not there was vegetation on the moon, and acknowledging a duty to refrain from deliberately exploiting a functional inferior, he would not hesitate to say that they knew it *from within*.

Emphatically this does not mean that the acceptance of Kant's standpoint demands that we should take up an uncritical attitude towards the sort of thing we know as the 'problem of knowledge'; but we shall fail altogether in measuring up to the demands on us of such a treatment of freedom as the first part of this chapter discusses if we do not see the continuity of some of its assumptions with what informed the complex enterprise we know as work on the 'problem of knowledge'. There is no doubt that Kant would have seen in some of the writing which deals with that 'problem' some signs of that abstract intellectualism, that almost aesthetic dilettantism, which he so mistrusted, and which we found present in the speculative temper that sometimes went with metaphysics. For him the primacy of the practical reason cast its authority even over the methods judged proper in theoretical philosophy; it worked as a kind of correction, even enabling men to sift the wheat from the chaff of their speculations in a way remotely analogous to that offered by the principle permitting only those problems to stand which can be treated as somehow problems of logic. The austere note of the categorical imperative cut across the *Schwärmerei* of the man who had almost fallen in love with his own abstract intellectual perplexities and uncertainties; Kant would not altogether have approved the language in which Mr. Berlin sets out his sense of the dignity of freedom of 'open possibilities'. This because, for Kant, such freedom was less the theme of a poetic rhapsody than the condition under which alone men received, from within themselves, the authoritative voice of the moral law.

Yet the reference to the history of the 'problem of know-

ledge' has not been sheer irrelevance; there is a sense in which
it is within this tradition that Kant stands, and the very
exaggeration and extremity of some of its more thorough-
going manifestations may help to advertise what is the
peculiar 'form of life' to which it belongs: that 'form of life'
whose characteristic expression is intense subjective preoccupation revealed in the effort to subdue, as far as possible,
the language of public and overt reference to that concerned
with the private and the interior life. For Kant the latter
certainly has a special and irreducible status; but within it he
discriminates, as alone confronting men with the unconditioned, the language in which they issue to themselves the
categorical imperative.

4. 'What shall it profit a man if he gain the whole world,
and lose his soul?' For the *Gesinnungsethiker* that is one of the
supreme questions in human life; and if he flirts with a supposed transparency of consciousness to itself, it is in order
that men may properly be said to recognise when their soul
is at stake. Its salvation (to use a traditionally religious word) is
something assured by no external conformity; nor, of course,
is it a matter simply of vaguely entertained good intention. A
man may 'lose his soul' by supposing circumstance too much
for him, absolving himself from the duty of protest against
politically organised cruelty, injustice or indifference, in the
name of supposed patriotic obligation. What cannot be
secured by mere external conformity of behaviour to acknowledged rule may none the less be forfeited through omission
of particular concrete obligation.

In a way, of course, one learns more of the nature of the
soul through a phrase which thus challenges us to envisage
its possible loss than from some abstract general statement
affirming it to be, for instance, a substance. A soul is something a man may lose, and to avoid its loss he must be prepared to sacrifice the whole world; and this, of course, may
involve the laying aside of the very possibility of serving
others as he would wish to and they expect. After all it is not

the Attila or the Genghis Khan who has gained the whole world, but usually the man who has conferred great good upon mankind, whose 'private vices' have indeed been 'public virtues'. This phrase sets before us, even as its language sheds light upon the nature of the soul, the sense in which the proper possession of oneself is seen as something set as a task, an inescapable *Sollen*; it is at the level of the most searching of all imperatives that we come to ourselves, and the language of the 'problem of knowledge', which seemed in ways sometimes abstract to the point of frivolity, even if often not without its special poignancy, is seen as passing over into the language whereby a man scrutinises his purity of heart, asks himself if indeed for him the measure of success in his enterprises is more the purity of his intention than the applause of his fellows, or the outward success his labours bring him. If the *Gesinnungsethiker* makes the morality of action depend upon the motive from which it is done, it must always be remembered that, in so saying, he takes hold of the notion of motive and gives it his own special sense, that is, a sense relative to the expression in which it falls. He is saying that the moral universe is that universe in which a man's soul may be at stake; that it is such language as that, and not the language of purpose achieved or happiness increased by itself, that admits a man to the universe of morality. And here one may join the approach with that favour to the problem of freedom by Professor C. A. Campbell, whose writings on the subject are held in high respect by all British students of the problem.

For Campbell it was pre-eminently the experience of temptation, in respect of which a man knew that he could do, or could have done, otherwise, which undermined his confidence in the metaphysical conception of the world as a whole of internally related elements, each part contributing necessarily to the actualisation of the whole in such a way that nothing could be different from what it is, or differently related to other things, without everything in the world, and the whole world itself, being radically altered; thus such for Campbell was the force of the experience of a man subject to bitter temptation, that he was prepared to sacrifice his logical and metaphysical monism in order to bring out, as almost the supremely revealing fact in the world, that even a scoundrel could transcend his pre-formed character and, in the moment of deliberate action, by effort of will respond to the demands of goodness. Of course 'possibility' and 'effort of will', as Campbell uses them here, have to be understood in special senses internal to the situation being faced by the agent; but it is Campbell's argument that we are on home ground here, and can safeguard these uses by rigorous separation of their force from all irrelevant imagery that may intrude upon us through our confusing their use here from that which may be theirs in other and less fundamental and crucial contexts. But although Campbell's language and the language used earlier in this section are in their way remote from the style of the 'problem of knowledge', they share with the language of the 'problem of knowledge' the sense that there is something in men which we can only call spiritual or inner life, that there is the dimension revealed to introspection, even that there is a genuine problem, or set of problems, of rightly mastering the relations of private to public, inward to outward, that cannot be slurred over by treating the former as 'logical construction' out of the latter any more than by swallowing up the latter in the former. Descartes' *malin génie* is something in some ways very remote from moral evil; the sense of possible trickery with which Descartes makes such play has always for the modern reader the air of being somehow artificially induced. Moral evil is not like that; yet is it not also something of whose reality we learn when we enter into ourselves? *What is it for a man to enter into himself?* Is not that almost the fundamental question? If we cannot see such entering as a starting point, how are we to conceive its place, how are we to understand the language in which we speak of it? And how are we to discriminate the language about it that is valid from that which crosses the frontier into nonsense?

5. We are surely now in a position to understand the bearing of the phrase 'theory of knowledge' in the sense of the first chapter on our present enquiry. For the position reached is surely rather like this:

(a) In the history of philosophy there is a chapter which shows men preoccupied with something called the 'problem of knowledge'. This preoccupation is compacted of various elements, including certainly exercise about crucial problems in the logical analysis of the concepts and methods of the exact sciences which continue to concern philosophers to this day, but also including the working-out of deep perplexities concerning, for instance, the reality of the external world, and the nature of our certainties concerning its being. Where the latter has been not far from the centre of interest, we have had such things as the demand for a 'proof of the external world' (of which Moore in 1940 wrote so pungently).[1] In the present chapter emphasis has been laid on the intense subjectivism characteristic of such preoccupation, the concentration on the interior, private experience of the subject as if, through some new depth of intellectual discipline, assurance could be won concerning the reality of what was somehow uncertain, and the threats of the 'practical joker' dispelled. This is seen, for instance, in Berkeley, where, in the more metaphysical section of his writing, contradictions in our every-day beliefs about the nature of the world of bodies, and our knowledge of it, are dispelled when the latter is grasped as in the end some sort of communion with the infinite, creative Spirit.

Of course concentration on the 'problem of knowledge' has its history, going back to Augustine's conviction that the primarily evident realities were God and his own soul. Indeed there is no little justification for the judgment of Gilson, Taylor and others that the only truly novel thing in Descartes

---

[1] In his British Academy lecture: *Proof of an External World.*

was his 'geometrical method'! But in the contemporary philosophical situation one looks back on this sort of pre-occupation, with a certain detachment, from the standpoint of language as a whole. The conception of a reconstruction of our knowledge on the foundation of supposedly indubitably certain data of immediate, private experience is recognised as a logical illusion.

(*b*) All this is somehow remote from the problem of moral freedom, at least superficially; it could be said that if one has understood the relation of Kant's theory of knowledge to his ethics, one has grasped this point. But still, when the contemporary student comes to look on the problem of freedom, if he is dissatisfied with the fashionable contemporary methods of dissolution, he begins to notice a certain congruity between the libertarian's traditional approach to the problem and that which gave its spring to work on the 'problem of knowledge'. Both alike in different ways make play with such notions as the alleged transparency of consciousness to itself, the privileged access men enjoy to their own inner life, and so on; *it is as if some of the traditional jargon of traditional epistemology found a kind of last use in the vindication of freedom.* If philosophers were no longer able to follow the conventional routes pursued by those who worked on the 'problem of knowledge', still those who argued as Campbell did (even if they did not share his general sympathy with the standpoint of a sort of metaphysical idealism) were prepared, in speaking of, for instance, the experience of temptation, to use the language of privileged access, in order to bring out that this was something essentially private to the individual himself. Of course such use of the notions of privileged access, privacy and the rest does not commit the user to the untenable thesis of supposing that there is something esoteric and unique in the way in which such words are learnt; if the domain of the private and intimately personal is to receive special emphasis, and if a special status is to be claimed for it, that emphasis can only be laid, that claim only pressed, from within a clear recognition that public and private are correlative, and that it is a sheer mistake to speak of the latter as if it were a level on to which one could withdraw, seeking to pull after one all that belonged more obviously to the level of the public and ordinary.

Such a work is 'theory of knowledge' in the sense of the first chapter; and the many . . . similarities to, as well as the differences from, what we have remarked in the cases of Moore and Mill will be obvious. Here there is no postulation or assertion of special sorts of knowledge, to be indicated by the obscure, familiar language of 'intuition'; rather there is the partial rehabilitation of an old style of philosophising, an old sort of language, as it were in order to convey and make secure the reality of such experiences as repentance, the acceptance of responsibility for what has done and been, and the often painful probing of one's motives. In the first part of this chapter it was emphasised how much these parts of the business of living were carried on in words, how narrow here the frontier between word and deed. But such language cannot be left alone; men have learnt it, acquiring knowledge of the rules which make its employment appropriate. And then, in using it, they come to recognise that it carries with it a kind of commitment less obviously present with other modes of speech; and of this they must try to give account, elaborating in the effort something that we can only call a 'metaphysic of knowledge', a doctrine of the transparency of the conscious subject to himself that has obvious links with the assumption underlying work on the so-called 'problem of knowledge', but pointing, perhaps more obviously than such work itself, to the context of preoccupation with self-knowledge, out of which some of its most characteristic notions and procedures were drawn.

(c) The libertarian is committed to a *Gesinnungsethik*, and the freedom in which he is interested is that through which a man may be said to cleanse, or to try to cleanse, his heart and reins. Of course he must acknowledge that there is a very obvious sense in which men's motives are often far from transparent to themselves: the supposed devoted service of the welfare of others, expressed in ceaseless and unrestricted expenditure of time and energy, may mask the working, at the subconscious level, of deep unacknowledged and unresolved conflict. A man's very goodness, in the sense of what he may believe to be his own inward striving after charity in the true sense of that word, may merely bear witness to his ease and power in self-deception; there is a perfectly ordinary sense of the word 'transparent' in which men cannot say that their motives are transparent to themselves; and indeed it is precisely this kind of obscurity that gives strength to the position of the *Erfolgsethiker*, who, while not committing himself to a thorough-going behaviourism, none the less judges motives too obscure and elusive to be admissible as the home of right and wrong, good and evil.

Rather what the *Gesinnungsethiker* calls transparent may be something analogous to what was spoken of in the last chapter as *form*. Thus he might say, as the late H. W. B. Joseph once said, that good men always know how much 'they have sinned and come short of the glory of God'; such knowledge is, of course, a matter of the language they use, and of the attitude such language conveys. But such men, Joseph rightly said, will further insist that even if they are without knowledge of that in which the achievement of such a glory must consist, they yet know in outline the sort of conditions that must be fulfilled. Kant would have made the same point in terms of stress on the categorically imperative character of human morality, of that form of living to which they are commanded by what he calls their rational nature, which lays absolute and unconditional demands upon them here and now, which cannot be identified with any of the relative and limited pictures we may form of its completion. The categorical imperative touches the very springs and sources of human action at all times and in all places; indeed one might say that for Kant the very notions of springs and sources of action themselves have sense as those things which, by that imperative, we are bidden to search out unscrutinised. It could be said that for him not only does 'ought imply can', the reality of moral obligation convey to us that of freedom; but when we speak of an inner life, using the words to indicate something more than the field of descriptive psychology (the latter for him being the study of the data of 'inner sense' and the establishment of their laws), we are speaking of something of which we come to form conception under the pressure of the categorical imperative.

(d) Of course this drives us back on the problem raised in the last chapter, on the nature of the unconditioned. Can such a notion be made tolerable, even if the place of its presence is identified with the authoritative demand made upon us by a form of life that we must affirm in the ways of our day-to-day living? It may be conceded that the languages of repentance, of self-knowledge, of the purification of intention, have their place on the language map; a determinate place assigned to them, in part, by their relation to other sorts of language. 'Everything is what it is and not another thing.' But to use in respect of certain forms of imperative such words as 'unconditioned' and the rest is to take a most serious step: it is to claim for that language uniquely privileged status, even suggesting that by its use we have commerce with a unique reality, even if that reality is then identified with the universal form immanent in our own individual humanity, even if at the same time transcending what we can any one of us hope to make of our lives. Of course, as we have seen, a measure of formalism in ethics is a protection against the relativity that makes of some particular system of values, whether individual or social, the measuring rod of all excellence; but it is hard to escape the sense that those who write of unconditioned imperatives, and whose very conception of the individual takes shape under the guidance of its supposed reality, are in danger not only of the logical blunder of investing an essentially relative family of notions with absolute force, but also of the rather different fault of exalting the supposed private self-communing of the individual with himself to a very special place in their scale of values. The logical criticism of such concepts as privacy, privileged access, transparency and the rest may leave us with a sense that these notions can be legitimately used; we have to learn what can and cannot be done with them, and to be very careful when we try to take hold of what was attempted by means of their exaggerated, undisciplined and uncritical employment. We then, of course, are brought sharp up against the notion of the unconditioned, that notion which Kant employs when, in the language of his own ethics, he faces the question 'What shall it profit a man . . .', etc., and tries to bring out its special character as a question.

Yet some, for instance those who have felt the strength of the criticisms brought against this sort of thinking by Hegel and Marx, will point, with less logical sophistication no doubt, to the dangers underlying the ready acceptance of Kant's way of thinking here, and that of others who are, in some ways at least, akin to him. They will accuse his notion of the unconditioned imperative of relativity in another sense: of a relativity that touches the whole conception of *individual personal integrity* which seems to be its burden. Preoccupation with the 'spiritual life' of the individual, with the purification of motive and the rest, are distractions from the concrete earthy task of bettering the lot of mankind; there are ways whereby men turn in on themselves to the neglect of their neighbours' needs and the plight of the society to which they belong. If this is the idiom of Marx rather than of Hegel, at least Marx learnt his peculiar methods of social and philosophical criticism from Hegel; and the language used served to bring out the real continuity between this sort of criticism of the *Gesinnungsethiker* and that of the utilitarian. We are back almost unnoticed on the level in which men converse about the way in which they should live, the values to which to give priority, and the rest; we have left the level in which in a logically sophisticated way we explore the workings of our ethical language. It is important that we should see the way in which the notion of relativity occurs at both levels, and ask ourselves how the two sorts of relativity, the logical and the ethical or social, in the special sense of the latter with which we have been concerned, are related. We can reject the notion of an unconditional morality of motives because such seems to violate the fabric of our language, the way in which language is learnt and forms of life realised and promoted from its use; or we can reject the notion, as the utilitarians certainly did, almost on pragmatic ground as one that turns a man in on himself to the neglect of obvious tasks of social betterment, as one even that can only commend itself to a socially privileged élite. With the relations between these rejections we must concern ourselves again later.

So the notion of the unconditioned, so pivotal to Kant's ethics, emerges as something at once logically scandalous and, in the manner of Kant's use of it, at the same time pregnant with a practical threat; it can serve to withdraw a man's attention from the pressing, workaday needs of his fellows to the cultivation of an interior moral purity, which looks sometimes very akin to a secular transcription of the mystic's disinterested love of God for His own sake. This, although no one could fairly accuse Kant of preaching an ethic of self-realisation, inasmuch as no one more than he insists on the peremptory intrusion upon the pattern of human purposes, whether individual or collective, of the claims of the realm of ends whose sovereign authority over us we must affirm in all the changes and chances of our life. The fault supposed is rather one that must beset any *Gesinnung-sethik*.

6. In conclusion of these comments it may be worth remarking again the important difference between the denial of the possibility of metaphysics by those who are concerned to assert the uniqueness of human freedom, and its denial by those who favour the position called in the second chapter of

M

this book by the name thorough-going utilitarianism. For the latter, metaphysics is the name of all that menaces acceptance of the authority of fact; we judge metaphysical and dismiss as such whatever involves appeal to the deliverance of some esoteric faculty of intuition, whatever introduces reference to notions that cannot be 'cashed' in terms of what we perceive; to deny the legitimacy of metaphysics is to champion the authority of observation and induction, and of that exact thinking which makes itself their handmaid. It could easily be argued (and the actual pages of Bentham's writings bear this out) that such reflection, such laborious justification of strange linguistic usage as this chapter contains, fall under the same condemnation. The thorough-going utilitarian would write off what we have here written as metaphysics and waste of time; even though an effort was made to show that what was being defended was being presented in the context of language as a whole.

But the quarrel with metaphysics that one finds in Kant, and that is echoed in a curious way by Campbell, is of a different order; it is the unique dignity and status of human creativity that can only be revealed when the attempt at completeness of theoretical comprehension is laid aside. There is an echo of Kant's attitudes in Campbell's judgment on absolute idealism; and we find a comparable agnosticism in Berlin's criticism of various versions of the metaphysical thesis of historical inevitability. Of course historical determinism and natural determinism are not co-ordinate species of the same genus; but there is an analogy in the way in which men quarrel with them. Berlin is concerned with the threat to the very conception of original genius he sees in certain fashionable philosophies of history; he owes much obviously to Mill's essay *On Liberty*, a work in which its author shows a strange and unexpected kinship with that of which John Keats wrote as the exercise of 'negative capability'. But Berlin is also concerned to combat the spirit of passivity encouraged by the suggestion that there is some sort of inevitable direction in historical change with which a man must identify himself. Of course he brings out the overlap between that which Kant resisted and criticised and that which the thorough-going utilitarians so vehemently rejected; there is an overlap, as one might expect, remembering what has already been said in this book about the elements of kinship between Kant and the utilitarians. But there is also a difference, and it may be that Berlin, whose style is more akin to that of the British empirical tradition than to that of Kant (for all his great debt to the latter), sees the issue partly in terms of the threat conveyed by certain systems of ideas to readiness heroically to endure.

In the last chapter Kant's hostility as a rationalist to the romantic cult of the hero was stressed; but this does not obliterate the fact that for the moralist, especially the one who in the end rejects the utilitarian doctrine as a final account, endurance and fortitude, for all their ambivalence, raise very special issues. These virtues most certainly raise the problem of the soul, perhaps the real subject of this chapter. The behaviour of a man like Charles de Gaulle in 1940, of which we now have his own unforgettably impressive description, puts a question-mark certainly against the facile constructions of the historical determinist; of course when we speak of his tremendous effort, we are not using the word 'effort' in the sense in which Campbell speaks of 'effort of will'; the use is less mysterious. But still when one sets what de Gaulle then did and endured against the background of the pressures pushing him in another direction, one's sense of what it is that the libertarians are trying to say is clarified.

Paradoxical though it may seem, one gains a contributory insight from reflecting on the man who, after counting the whole cost and admitting the contradictions in his position, decides that he must conscientiously object to modern methods of warfare. Here too we can discern the outline of a courage that reveals to us something of the unique reality of freedom. But it should be stressed that one only gains that revelation where there is a real counting of the cost: a counting which may well include close reckoning with the question-mark set by the earthy, concrete argument of the utilitarians against any moral posturing that somehow makes itself an end in itself. Certainly Kant is as hostile to such posturing as any utilitarian; but it is, as a matter of fact, a feature of his approach to ethics, and the approaches of those who have learnt from him, that they are continually lured by a false mystique of the individual: one that can neither be called Stoic or romantic, but which breeds its own special styles of distraction from measuring up to the actual situation of men.

In these last paragraphs various issues, one after the other, have been raised to which we shall return in the sections of this book dealing, for instance, with the relations of ethics and politics. Further, the reader may have expected, in view of the use made in this chapter of near-religious forms of expression, that it would include some discussion of the relation of ethics and religion; certainly even if the grace of God is in some sense, for the religious man, sovereign over men, the language in which they speak of it pre-supposes that of freedom, and we may therefore be justified in bringing out the character of the latter first, before turning to the discussion, e.g., of the language of Paul in 2nd Corinthians. Again some may realise that the notion of dialectic is showing itself above the horizon of our discussion; that is certainly true, and in the next chapters overt use and discussion will be made of it. Again, it would be a mistake to suppose that the discussion of freedom itself is at an end; for some may say that the originating impulse behind the use of the language of freedom and its elaboration is as obscure at the end of this chapter as at the beginning.

But to summarise what we have done in the chapter we can hardly do better than say that we have tried to study the language in which, and by means of which, we bring home to ourselves that we have a soul. What is it to have a soul? How do we know that we have a soul? The last question is, in a sense, unanswerable; for the only answer we can give is in terms of a certain sort of behaviour, behaviour which is informed by the peculiar assumptions of freedom and of a *Gesinnungsethik*. This is a matter of language, itself a matter of inheritance as well as of invention. But language is 'form of life', and the justification of the language of freedom is justification of that form of life which it defines. More narrowly we can say that the languages of transparency, privileged access and the rest are justified if by their means human horizons are enlarged, human possibilities safeguarded, as by no alternative means. But what is it to be human, and how can we be sure that one way of speech, one style of self-designation rather than another, or complementing another advanced and extends our perception of what it is to be human? On what do we base our preference for that way of life to which, e.g., the distinction between inner and outer opens the road? We may admit, we must admit the manifoldness and complexity of the language of freedom. There is little doubt that we need before all else a detailed *description* of the ramifications and windings of that language: description before all else so that we know what it is we are talking about, and so that we lay bare some of the connections between the language of freedom, and the language of self-awareness. We may be reaching for something akin to a Kantian 'transcendental justification' of its continued use.

CHAPTER V

BUTLER

In dealing with Butler's ethics, there is one mistake above all to be avoided. His work is in volume very short, the fifteen Sermons and the brief, pregnant Dissertation; yet it is extraordinarily complex, obstinately resisting any effort to pigeon-hole it. The late Dr. B. H. Streeter used to say of the early Christian fathers that one could attach to their name almost any conceivable doctrine, provided one's edition had a good index and one did not look up all the references. Something of the same kind is true of Butler; one can call him a naturalist or utilitarian, one can label his conscience intuitive or discursive, one can find his religious beliefs central to his ethics or one can make them peripheral, one can find in him passages that bring him near to Kant, and others that justify, to some extent, Matthew Arnold's emphasis on his uncritical acceptance of the 18th-century *Zeitgeist*.

A. BUTLER'S EMPIRICISM: INTRODUCTORY

Is there a key which will unlock the door of the unity of Butler's ethical doctrine? Or must one take refuge in the source-criticism which would assign one piece of his doctrine to one period, and one to another? Such analysis must not be despised in dealing with a preacher who is writing not a treatise but a series of sermons, and who is anxious to persuade to virtue rather than to lay bare, in the manner of Kant, the form of moral excellence as such. Butler is a very English moralist, in the sense in which French students of European letters love to contrast the earthy empiricism of the countrymen of John Locke with the rigorous, formal *clarté cartésienne*; and his Englishness is accentuated by the fact that he wrote for his audiences in the Rolls Chapel. Perhaps his readers may sometimes regret that he was unwilling to recast his Sermons in the form of a treatise, more on the lines of the *Analogy*; and in what follows an attempt will be made to give to Butler's argument a unity which may seem to be imposed upon it rather than found in it. But this is done in order that we may learn some of those things which he is suggesting that are philosophically important.

At the outset of the Preface he contrasts his procedure with that of Wollaston, who seeks, as he says, to derive the fundamental principle of morality from the 'abstract relations of things'. For Wollaston morality was fundamentally telling the truth; the good man was truthful in all his ways, the bad man somehow a liar, a masquerader. The deceitful man, the counterfeiter, the frauds-man, furnished the paradigm of the immoral; and whatever form of viciousness one might have to reckon with, in the end it could be exhibited as a form of cheating. One could even say that for Wollaston we saw the character of action most clearly in 'performatory' speech of the order of promising, undertaking, bequeathing; there was a sense in which, for him, to act was to speak by deed. We saw what immorality was most clearly when we consider a man who promised without intent to perform, contradicting himself by thus exploiting the character of promissory commitment. The liar contradicts himself; by his lie he cuts at the threads which bind men in a common rational fellowship, but he does so by invoking, in the self-same act, the fabric which he is destroying.

By such argument we may seem to come near exhibiting immoral action as a violation of the principle of non-contradiction, and therefore definitively establishing the sense in which it is irrational. Virtue is consistency, immorality self-contradiction. To ask whether it is reasonable to be good ceases to be significant, once virtue is shown as rational self-consistency in conduct. And in this process of identification of virtue with self-consistency the reduction of all forms of immorality to lying or masquerading plays a crucial rôle. One could even say that for Wollaston the masquerade was the *schema* of the formal notion of self-contradiction whereby we interpreted it to ourselves in terms of the world of action. Take what are commonly regarded as immoral actions—murder, persecution, fraud, theft, adultery—and find in them the common character of counterfeit and imposture. Here is their essential immorality; here is that which, in them, at once corresponds to and realises the notion of self-contradiction.

The questions which Butler puts to Wollaston are fundamental: do we, if we argue like this, succeed in capturing the essential character of virtue and vice in their particular instances? Or have we in fact made of morality and of immorality things so rarefied that they seem to have become kinds of construction which we compel the actual complexity of our human nature to accept in order that the laws of that nature shall be exhibited as one with the laws of logic? Self-contradiction, lying, immorality—do we honestly think that the second does provide us with a universal *schema* corresponding to the first in such a way that we can see that first in every manifestation of human wickedness? Or is the whole procedure intolerably *a prioristic* and artificial? To this last question Butler certainly gives an affirmative answer. This he gives while certainly taking lying very seriously indeed; one of his most pointed sermons is devoted to emphasising that partiality to oneself, the half-deliberate, half-unconscious exemption of oneself from the discipline of a commonly accepted moral order, is something very near the heart of wickedness. David's conduct over Uriah is masquerade; he is pretending to himself (whatever the content of that pretence in his overt behaviour) that he is, for instance, giving Uriah a chance to distinguish himself in the service of his King, providing him with opportunity for heroism and self-sacrifice. But the source of the long story of his self-deceit is lust; his conduct is an example of that 'subtle casuistry of the passions' of which Jeremy Taylor spoke. Nathan challenges him with a story that pin-points the root of his elaborate pretence in unbridled desire, in the exploitation of royal prerogative to gratify the desire certainly, but in the desire itself fundamentally.

For Butler human nature is, of course, a unity, and immorality is somehow the violation of that unity and order. But immorality is as complex as, in the end, human nature is; and we do not understand the nature either of moral good or of evil if we insist that their essence is to be grasped in an abstract formula. David could have avoided sin more surely by discipline of imagination and emotion than by a mere acknowledgment of the paramount worth of self-consistency. The form of the good life is something as complex as the stuff we are made of, and the key to what human goodness is lies in attention to the particularities of our actual nature and the proper relations to be established between them.

This, then, is certainly empiricism, in the sense of the appeal to fact, to what we know of ourselves, and, more generally, in the sense of a readiness always to sacrifice the nicety of theoretical construction to the actuality of human behaviour, of observed or overheard judgment and use. We shall see later in this chapter that it is fundamental to the understanding of Butler to recognise that this empiricism of his is something fused very closely with his equally pervasive sense (which no student of his writings can escape) of morality as something very serious, as a law by which we are inescapably bound, immediately and luminously evident to us. It is his view that we prevaricate equally, whether we make acknowledgment of our duty, await some unachieved metaphysical insight, or insist on subordinating its commands to some conceived programme of human welfare which we invest with universal validity. In both these respects he has been thought akin to Kant, and to the traditional intuitionist insistence on the immediacy of our apprehension of moral principles. But there are certain very important differences of style, and it is no accident that in the Dissertation, when he argues against Shaftesbury's view that benevolence is the whole of virtue, he appeals to what men have been prepared to justify in the name of the supposed identification of benevolence with virtue. The catalogue of what they have so justified is quite particular; the general principle is certainly invoked as authority, but it is presented by Butler as invoked to justify what engages individual men and women in particular situations of temptation. There is certainly something monstrous, in his view, in this capacity men display for justifying in terms of general principle, their particular personal follies and wilful ignorances, lusts and cruelties. If benevolence, for Butler, is not the whole of virtue, it is partly because to treat it so is to invite men to turn aside from the manifoldness and complexity of their relations with their fellows, and to impose upon that diversity the over-simplifying image of a single generalised relation.

Butler's empiricism is shown in his insistence that we look at the particular elements of our nature, one by one, turning aside from none of them. But it is just when he is doing this that he is most insistently defending the transcendent claims of morality; as if he is sure that only when we see morality as a coming to terms with our actual nature will we esteem it for what it is, something at once quite simple and inflexibly authoritative, and yet as rich and diverse in content as human life itself. The quality of this empiricism is shown when one remembers that it is manifested alike relatively in his quarrel with Wollaston's derivation of virtue from the abstract relation of things and with Shaftesbury's identification of benevolence with the whole of virtue, and positively in the minute particularism of his argument, e.g., concerning the complementary rôles of pity and anger, of mercy and justice in human existence. For him the utilitarian is as much a rationalist as the Wollastonian in his endeavour to say what morality essentially is; and both in their answers are turning away from human nature as such. To the full implications and manifestations of this argument we shall return later.

B. BUTLER AND PRACTICAL PERPLEXITY

To what sorts of perplexity in day-to-day life does Butler speak? He was after all a preacher addressing an educated audience in 18th-century London, and presumably had their difficulties and concerns in mind when he spoke; indeed one of the things which make his Sermons difficult for the modern reader to assimilate is just the fact that they are, in a way, a period piece. Matthew Arnold in his essay well brings out their concessions to the *Zeitgeist,* and many students of philosophy will recall how hard they have found it to discover in Butler, at first reading, anything more than platitude on the one side, and a curiously artificial teleology on the other. The comparison of human nature to a watch seems to many at once contrived, dated and altogether unenlightening; the suggestion that there is an analogy between our nature and a certain sort of political constitution may have a more venerable history and be at times more helpful (at least if the reader is familiar with the self-regulating character of flexible constitutions); but it is after all only an analogy, only a way of looking at the course and principles of our behaviour. And to many it is one that simply seems to provide Butler with an elaborate device for presenting the familiar doctrine that honesty is the best policy!

Broad and Taylor agree in praising him as a moral psychologist, and his arguments against psychological egoism are both various and powerful. To anyone inclined to flirt with the cruder or the more sophisticated styles of this opinion, Butler's discourses can administer a salutary shock. His sense of the extreme complexity of our nature, brilliantly and suggestively conveyed, often with more than a touch of irony, is something easily revealed as logically independent of the framework in which he presents it. But what else is there?

For Prichard, of course, Butler is bracketed with those other moralists who have thought it their business to prove honesty the best policy, and who have laboured under the further misapprehension that they were helping mankind by attempting the proof. He is in the end utilitarian, even if sometimes in spite of himself. Certainly we must agree that he is constantly inclined to commend virtue, and this commendation often does take the shape of attempted demonstration that its practice is to our interests in the end, that in fact cool self-love, rational benevolence, and the authoritative principle of reflexion coincide in what they prescribe. Anything which could be called conflict, whether of duty or inclination, or of duties among themselves, slides into the background. In a cool hour we see how easily lust and greed, pride and self-deception make fools of us all, and under the guidance of reflection we refrain from what we intend, serving at once our peace of mind and the ease of our life with our neighbour. It sometimes does seem as if Butler, whose sermons deal often with particular matters, whether anger and pity, self-deceit and the government of the tongue, in the end comes to rest in a vague conviction that if only we learned to manage aright that nature which has been put in our own power, all will be for the best in the best of all possible worlds. Is anything permanently significant said?

The answer is in the affirmative; and it may be that it is little more than a restatement of the traditional claim made for Butler's excellence as a moral psychologist. It is part of his achievement that he *does* continually recall his hearers and readers to the complexity of their actual nature. His method is piecemeal and untidy—he omits, he repeats himself, he contradicts himself; but this he does do. He reminds us, now in one relative, now in another, how much there is within us of which we must take stock. He is sensitive to the distinctions we draw, whether in identifying the springs of our own conduct or in judging them or those of our neighbours. Almost it is as if he says in answer to the man who asks how

he should account himself, 'As you are'; and if this is a platitude, it also comes as a warning which illuminates.

Butler is the enemy of the single formula, whether it be the
identification of virtue with benevolence, or with the proper
balancing of benevolence and prudence, or with justice, or
with pity, or with piety; it is none of these things; it is living in
accordance with our actual nature. If, for instance, one reads,
one after the other, the sermons on resentment and on forgiveness, one sees this, at least if one makes the imaginative
effort of thinking oneself into the frame of mind of the man
who identifies virtue in the end with compassion or with
justice, or who tries to hoist himself or herself on to a level
where the conflict between justice and mercy does not occur.

It is perhaps an inevitable consequence of such a contribution that it eludes quick definitive characterisation; to
receive it, one has to be on the way to leaving something out,
on the way to making that sort of identification which Butler
criticises, even at a deep half-conscious level. For what a man
thinks virtue is may be shown more by behaviour than by
verbal profession; the bias of his actions and choices may
reveal an underlying policy of life that maybe has never
received explicit, conscious formulation. Butler puts a
question-mark now against one such identification of virtue,
now against another. His 'greatness as a moral psychologist'
is here.

But more than that, and here we pass to the contribution
he makes to perplexities at another level, his reminders are
always in the name of our proper human nature. The complexity he bids us recognise is one in our actual nature; it is
not a complexity implied by the intuitively recognised diversity of the terms entering the 'axioms of moral space'. Butler
is certainly not a thorough-going utilitarian; he is a *Gesinnungsethiker*; but he has a certain amount of sympathy with
the impulse which pushes man to accept some kind of vague
utilitarianism, in that he will allow that our various duties
must somehow 'make sense'. Their claim upon us has some-

thing to do with the stuff of which we are made; sometimes he writes as if in the end we will know their fulfilment to advantage us; at other times he is more tentative, as if the word 'advantage' in such a context were misleading, and as if his deepest view was that if we were patient we should see where our duties belonged in our lives as a whole, *how* they fitted in, what they contributed, what damage followed their neglect; and here his attitude is subtly different from that of any sort of utilitarian. But it is still, for Butler, not the least of Wollaston's faults that he makes impossible the fulfilment of that which for him is certainly valid in the utilitarians' demand: namely, that our duties be related to our actual nature. Butler is obviously hostile to any suggestion that morality stands unsupported in the air, if sometimes he writes like an intuitionist. He is wholly unwilling to accept any view that altogether severs 'ought' from 'is'; these two cannot fall apart and there is a sense in which Butler's whole doctrine embodies a subtle and continuous attempt to establish their proper relation. Butler certainly did not acknowledge the sovereignty of 'fact' as the Benthamites understood 'fact'; at times he certainly wrote as if conscience were intuitive; but at others he appealed to the world as we knew it around us, always allowing that we were able (and this, for him, is a crucial manifestation of characteristically moral consciousness) to read its lessons and to decipher its warnings.

C. BUTLER AND THEORETICAL PERPLEXITY

How is the 'ought' related to the 'is'? It is with this question that Butler, as much as any of the previous moralists we have considered, is concerned; and it is tempting to say that his answer has in it something of the temper of Kant, and something of that of the utilitarians.

1. (*a*) Thus in the concluding part of the previous section of this chapter his kinship with the utilitarians has been stressed and partly interpreted; stressed because it is certainly an ingredient in his presentation of the issues of human living,

but interpreted because the elements of utilitarianism in his doctrine have been presented as subordinate to his continual emphasis on the complex unity of our actual human nature. Certainly Butler recognises how important the appeal to enlightened self-interest is; a man may be restrained from evil-doing when he sees how destructive its consequences are likely to be; a proper self-regard may effectively dissuade a man from violence and cruelty. Of course this self-regard must be a proper self-regard; here as always we must take stock of the stuff of which we are made. Yet Butler certainly sometimes writes as if this stock-taking involved no more than the proper balancing of our own considered needs with those of our neighbours, and as if it was enough for us in fact to ask where our happiness most surely may be found. His readers can hardly sometimes escape the impression of a vague, comfortable doctrine according to which there is so certainly prearranged a harmony between virtue and happiness that *in the end* prudence is sufficient guide and authority for mortal men. Certainly, even in those passages in the Sermons which are most nearly utilitarian, Butler writes as a *Gesinnungsethiker*, stressing motive and disposition rather than act and consequence. Goodness is presented as reasonable because the good man is before all else the prudent man, and no one would contest our right to speak of prudence as reasonable. But what for Butler is prudence? Is it simply a capacity to judge effectively the routes to the largest and most stable human happiness? Or is it the name of a more subtle, complex wisdom? Here Butler is certainly ambiguous, seeming to say now the one thing, now the other.

It is characteristic of the thorough-going utilitarian that in the end, for him, prudence is measured always by the effectiveness of the ways it commends of promoting human happiness, and that where that happiness is concerned we have something which admits of no uncertainty. Whereas with Butler nothing is as clear-cut as this; in the last analysis, for him, it is impossible for us to sever our understanding *either* of prudence *or* of happiness from our understanding of human nature. And our understanding of human nature he presents as something precarious, easily lost, continually menaced.

(*b*) There is much in Butler, of course, that most obviously points in a different direction from the utilitarian, especially perhaps the Fifteenth Sermon, where we have his brilliant *esquisse* of a doctrine of the primacy of practical reason. If one can find in him passages which make him a somewhat long-winded 18th-century apostle of the coincidence of virtue and self-interest, there is in this sermon much that makes him, *at first sight*, the intellectual kinsman of Kant.

In this sermon morality is presented as something self-evident, luminous, categorically imperative; we recognise its authority upon us without being compelled to wait for the solution of this or that cosmological or theological riddle. It is at the level of the categorical imperative of conscience we are brought face to face with that which is ultimate.[1] Here Butler is as impatient as Prichard with the sophistication that the honest man sometimes discerns in the utilitarian argument, and he succeeds in bringing out (more effectively, perhaps, in this sermon than in the Dissertation) something of what it is that the intuitionist is struggling to assert by his insistence on the immediacy of the deliverances of moral consciousness. He shows in a few brief pages the ground of the alliance between ethical absolutism and metaphysical agnosticism we have already remarked in the chapter on Kant; this although there are very important differences between the style of his agnosticism and Kant's. Here again, as always in Butler, we are reminded that we are reckoning with our actual human nature.

2. It is as if in Butler we have to reckon with *three* strands of thought. There is a certain readiness to endorse utilitarianism which is more than the readiness of the pulpit moralist to impress on his hearers that honesty is the best policy. It can

---

[1] It was here that Newman learnt much from Butler. His *University Sermons* are a very valuable commentary on Butler's views.

use the language of an 18th-century Samuel Smiles; it can
commend prudence, even while ironically pointing out that
the need to do so is itself an argument against the psychological egoism of Hobbes; yet all the while we are reminded
that this is only a fragment of the language of ethics, a
moment in the whole process of moral reflection. There is, on
the other hand, the repeated suggestion that morality
possesses a kind of deep self-evidence, a luminously self-
authenticating character. Indeed Butler can be claimed as a
moralist who is prepared to make the evidence of morality a
kind of standard of what we mean by self-evidence, its claim
upon us the paradigm and exemplar of those claims from
which we can acknowledge no escape. But there is also the
third strand, the pervasive insistence that we attend to our
actual nature, which from its first mention in sharp contradistinction from the method of Wollaston is the most certain
note of Butler's ethics.

Now at first sight this 'naturalism' of his, if we may so call
it, seems to rejoin the utilitarian strand of his thought. For
even if the modern utilitarian allows that the 'language of
ethics' (the language of prescription, exhortation, persuasion,
moral tradition and what you will) has, as *language*, its own
texture and laws, yet he does insist that it is *in some sense* a
subordinate language, (even if the logical character of that
subordination is the most exacting problem facing the
moral philosopher); the language of fact has primacy, however sophisticated and complex its range. But the curious
thing is that it is precisely Butler's 'naturalism' which sets
him on edge in the presence of utilitarian *simplisme*. In him,
intuitive and naturalistic elements are not in opposition; it is
in some of his most detailed psychological explorations that
he is most obviously opposed to the utilitarian approach, to
the suggestion, for instance, that in a certain kind of pruden-
tial weighing of consequences and deliberate criticism of
policies of life under its guidance we have a master-key to the
business of human living.

N

The strangeness and significance of this procedure can best be brought out by contrasting Butler here with a modern intuitionist like Sir David Ross. Butler and Ross agree in a certain pluralism; thus the former, in many places in his writings, challenges the suggestion that we know *a priori* that our various '*prima facie* obligations' must form some kind of unity through derivation from a single higher principle. Thus our obligation to keep our promises, to repay our debts, to do our best by our dependents, etc. are binding on us because they are what they are, viz. in one case an obligation to keep promises, in another to repay debts, etc. There is a clear kinship between this insistence of Ross and Butler's repeated emphasis upon the fact that the relations in which we stand to other people are often generically different one from another. On Ross's view we can recognise the claim upon us of one '*prima facie* obligation' without apprehending that of another; for the element in the moral universe is, in each case, distinct, even if equally clear, in principle, to the moral consciousness. For him the mistake of the utilitarian (even of the utilitarian who, like Sidgwick, is prepared to recognise a categorical imperative in morality) is that of supposing that the sole ground of obligatoriness is found in the tendency of action to promote the welfare of mankind as a whole; he is convinced that it is mere prejudice on our part to suppose 'optimificity' (to use his own language) a more ultimate character of an act than, e.g., its being the keeping of a promise or the requital of a benefit received to the benefactor from whose hands we have received it.

Ross's arguments against the thesis that 'optimificity is the sole ground of rightness' are worked out in terms of a very definite conception of what knowledge is, particularly knowledge of synthetic *a priori* connections. Butler's fundamental philosophical style is quite different; it is less rigorous, less self-consciously concerned to develop an apologetic for intuitive apprehension of synthetic *a priori* principles; his style is almost pointillistic, his method exploratory, in his own

special sense empirical. But he is, as much as Ross, a
pluralist. His criticism in the Dissertation of the thesis that
benevolence is the whole of virtue is a *locus classicus* here; it is
the whole of virtue, but only within 'the bounds of justice and
veracity'. To pretend that benevolence is the whole of virtue
unconditionally is *either* to stretch language so that we no
longer know what we are saying by 'benevolence', *or* else to
say something that we can easily invoke, as a principle, to
justify action at once shameful and destructive to which we
are drawn. We have to reckon with ourselves as we are; and
behind the argument of the Dissertation lies the series of
Sermons, in which Butler has explored the varied course and
situations of human life, neglecting neither the government
of the tongue nor the continuing conflict between justice and
mercy.

Butler's pluralism is, in fact, basically psychological; this,
course, is revealed in his criticism, e.g., of Hobbes' suggestion
that sympathy is a concealed form of fear, and is often remarked. But what is not so often noticed is the correspondence between this underlying psychological pluralism and
the pluralism of his views concerning the ground of obligation
and the nature of virtue. While Ross maintains the view that
our obligations form an irreducible plurality as something
evident to thought, Butler somehow grounds the complexity
of the world of moral obligation in the complexity of our
human nature. So it is that it can be said of him, as was said
earlier in this chapter, that it is when we come to terms with
the particularities of our actual nature that we are made most
sharply aware of the transcendent claims of morality. We are
inherently complex in nature; our needs and affections, our
desires, aspirations and terrors are various and different. The
impulse is always strongly there to re-fashion that complexity, e.g. by a half-intentional ignoring of some element
within us with which we must come to terms (it might be
said that that 'must' conveys what for Butler was most surely
the categorical element in morality). Ross, according to

Butler, is quite right in insisting that our obligations form a plurality; but the invocation of a special sort of intuitive awareness (modelled on our supposed grasp of the axioms of Euclidean geometry) is both unnecessary and (even apart from the development of non-Euclidean geometry) mistaken. For there is a sense in which the diverse and complex universe in which conscience constrains us to live is the universe of our actual nature.

3. But how far, in the end, is reference to such a correspondence more than a mere verbal jugglery? Certainly we are so familiar to-day with the idea of the difference of the languages of 'ought' and of 'is', with the recognition that the intuitionist, for all his faults, was right in insisting that the two languages were mutually irreducible, that at first sight this suggestion of an 'ought' somehow imposing itself upon us out of the matter of the actual strikes us as ill-conceived and old-fashioned. Yet we do still admit significance to the utilitarian procedure, in some respects at least a variant on Butler's method; and it might even be suggested that the language of correspondence which we have used in connection with Butler is less exacting in its claim than that of derivation and subordination.

What Butler wants to insist is that taking stock of our nature as we find it, refusing to be distracted from acknowledgment of its actualities, is, where human beings are concerned, necessarily pregnant with moral import. Psychological self-scrutiny is not morally neutral; and if we try to pretend that it is, that is because we have not allowed ourselves properly to conduct it under the authoritative leading of conscience. But if psychological self-scrutiny is thus morally significant, we cannot rest in any conception of morality which sees it concerned with the 'abstract relations of things', or which detaches the supposed moral universe from the ordinary routes of human life. Butler is hostile, in principle, to any ethic which finds the 'justification of experience' in the realisation of highly determinate states of affairs recognised as intrinsically valuable, or which isolates the world of obligation as a special segment of the whole complex universe of human existence. It is because men and women are as they are that they have the duties which they have; and if awareness of obligation bears witness to the fact that they are laws to themselves, capable of reflective judgment upon their conduct, the matter of their obligations in its many-levelled diversity attests the inescapable complexity of their nature and the manifoldness of their relations one with another.

4. Butler is the most untidy of moralists; his Sermons do certainly precede in time the subtly woven texture of the *Analogy of Religion*, and it is tempting to wish that they could have been re-fashioned in the light of that achieved argument. Yet, for all his untidiness, his contribution to the persistent questions concerning the status of the ethical, the relation of 'ought' to 'is', is deeply significant. Perhaps in the light of the foregoing it could best be conveyed in a series of statements, followed by qualifications, modifications, and corrections.

Thus: (*a*) morality consists in following human nature; it makes sense. But this does not imply either that (i) it is all, in the end, a matter of adjusting our interest to that of our neighbour for the good of all; or that (ii) we always do as we ought.

Rather it means that human goodness bears some relation to the stuff of which we are made; it is not a movement through a world in which the familiar promptings of anger and pity, hunger and love, have no place. Rather the image of the saint is something we discern as in the end a human likeness; and it is, in a sense, our perception of what it is to be a man that the saint's life enlarges.

(*b*) Conscience is supremely authoritative. It is a principle of reflection by which we judge ourselves, which in us bears a unique, disposing authority. Do we deny that we have consciences? If we do, we ignore that which makes us men, which even admits us to the drawing of such significant distinctions as that between power and authority itself. It is not that conscience is the name of an esoteric faculty; it is a way of referring to the manner in which human beings comment on their behaviour, and set before themselves the successive tasks and possibilities of their existence. If in the language which we use to characterise it the idiom of restraint is commonly present, it is not of an arbitrary conscience that we speak but of a law that brings us to ourselves.

The authority of conscience, the present, unquestionable dignity of the ways of goodness, whose justification and claim upon us are found in, their description, the primacy of the moral consciousness—all these we must concede as evidence, as indeed so many different characterisations of what is most familiar in human life. But we must not allow this recognition of conscience as uniquely authoritative to tempt us to forget that, as men and women, we belong to the natural world. The mere presentation of virtue as an end in itself must not conceal from us that it is human virtue of which we are speaking. The minute successive scrutiny of the elements of our passional nature forms an inescapable part of the moralist's task. Thus if we concede as valid that element in the intuitionist's view which stresses the immediacy and underivative character of moral principles, we must not forget that morality is the law of human life, of the life of beings who belong to nature. If there is uniqueness in the 'ought' of morality, its content must still embody reference to men's dependence on food and drink, their need for love and friendship, their jealousies and resentments, their manifold, subtle, elusive relations to the natural world, animate and inanimate, to which they belong.

Nor must the unique authority of conscience distract us from a proper acknowledgment of those other principles of reflection, called by Butler 'true self-love' and 'benevolence', whereby men introduce a measure of rational order into their affairs. They are certainly subordinate to conscience, and the reflection present in them is largely exhausted in a proper choosing of means to ends, a cautious discrimination of consequences, weighing of possibilities, enlargement through manipulation of environment, of opportunity open to the agent, etc. The level at which they work is that of 'extrovert rationality'; they are manifested, to use Plato's language, 'in larger letters' in the world of public affairs, where men serve the causes of human welfare in general. However clumsy and misleading Butler's hierarchical imagery may be, he is surely right to insist that in human life we have to reckon with the utilitarian element, at once at the level of personal and of collective life; and he is further right to insist at once on its continuity with, and discontinuity from, the passional elements in human nature which underlie it.

If conscience is concerned to judge between the 'propensions', it also reveals its character as authoritative by passing in review the rival claims upon men of, e.g., the welfare of their society at large, and the particular needs of some one individual to whom they are specially tied. If 'benevolence is not the whole of virtue', that is partly because in certain situations the claims of the more intimate relationships of human life must over-ride concern for the welfare of mankind at large; yet this problem is peculiarly crucial only because such concern is so important and so specially situated an element within the moral life.

5. The empiricist, for Butler, is right; we must eschew any suggestion that we can by deduction from the supposedly *a priori* evident establish the proper ordering of human life. We must obey the principles implicit in Locke's polemic against 'innate ideas', and reckon with men and women as they are. We must not complain if this compels us to reckon with a human nature which is various and diverse. But a proper empiricism will allow that when we come to men and women as they are, we have to reckon with that which is continuous with nature, but also discontinuous from it. We

must not take men and women out of their natural environment; we must take seriously what we are saying about them when indeed we speak of their 'human nature'; we must not cut the linkages which tie them to the universe around them or deny analogy between order in human life and order in the natural world. Yet we must not be 'naturalistic' in the sense of forgetting the uniqueness of human life, the reality of what perhaps can only be called spiritual experience.

All the time (as the *Analogy* makes very clear) Butler is searching for the proper method of representing, e.g., man's relation to the world around him, and drawing on the resources of a very considerable, if partly submerged, philosophical culture in doing so. Where his ethics are concerned, we can say that his problem is, in one sense, that of understanding the relation between the sort of observation on which moral perception rests and that which is involved in natural and social science. When men advance in moral awareness, they are coming to terms with themselves, whether it be through the rough and tumble of actual life, or in the sort of study of the ways of mankind which the Sermons embody, or in responding to the questions which the Sermons put to their hearer. But what can we say of such awareness? Butler would reject the intuitionist's attempted characterisation of it by way of analogy with our supposed knowledge of Euclid's axioms; it is, for him, a more earthy thing than that. Thus David's sudden self-knowledge at the challenge of Nathan is something which hardly fits the intuitionist's paradigm. But what can we say of it? It certainly overlaps the observation on which our ordinary every-day descriptive statements rest; it relates to the same world. So too with the more general perception that 'benevolence is not the whole of virtue'. There too one is passing judgment on the world in which men think and plan their welfare and that of their fellows, duly proportioning means to ends. What is the status of this recognition of such activity as not the whole of virtue?

Butler's answer is curiously hard to pin down; it is strangely indirect, and one is tempted almost to say that for him the true empiricist is the man who reckons with such recognition and such self-judgment as *fact*, who does not rule out as inadmissible what proper loyalty to experience compels him to acknowledge. He will not rule out what he must admit; nor will he prize morality apart from the actual run of human life as something unique, as, e.g., the axioms of geometry were supposed once to be unique. For Butler the way of 'synthetic necessary knowledge' and the way of 'reducing the moral to the non-moral' (after the example of the thorough-going utilitarian or naturalist) are alike ways of escape. We have to reckon with the curious, many-levelled character of experience, or the inevitable overlap and interpenetration of the languages by which we refer to, and bring home to ourselves, the different facets of our condition. It is in the overlap and interpenetration that we present to ourselves the character of our human situation, that we speak as men. Butler in the end would ask his critics (who agree with him in rejecting the methods of Wollaston) whether they had ever asked themselves what it is to be a true empiricist. As was said at the outset of this chapter, he argues from within the English empiricist tradition. But he is one of those for whom empiricism is manifested pre-eminently in a readiness to subordinate general principle to particular illuminations. The temper of his writing is not dogmatic; he will demand that we recast our theoretical construction to make room for unexpected fact; he prefers a kind of tortuous thoroughness to rigour. We know, he argues, that we have not got the human situation straight if we have withdrawn men from nature, cut, as it were, the linkages that tie men to their environment, severed altogether the languages we use in respect, e.g., of human and of plant ecology. But men are not just 'natural objects'; they are men. How then can we capture their uniqueness, which is our uniqueness? How can we do so in such a way as neither to disobey the law of obedience to fact, nor to suppose (after the manner, e.g., of the Benthamites) the form of fact to be definitively and narrowly established?

One cannot, in speaking of Butler, speak easily of his attitude to the problem of the 'possibility of metaphysics'. In a way, he never faced it, certainly not as a problem of somehow justifying an extension of the reach of conceptual thought from the familiar to the unfamiliar.[1] Rather his problem was one of properly esteeming our actual experience, letting it have proper authority over us. It is for this reason that for him, as was remarked above, the peculiarly transcendent character of morality is revealed to men when they attend to the particularities of their actual nature, and resist distraction from them by some artificial or partial model of the proper manner of human life. Obedience to experience is acceptance of the complex as such; it is refusal to be tricked, by the temptation of over-simplification, into denying that men are 'as they are, and not another thing'.

In the end Butler seeks a vantage-point from which the opposition between 'ought' and 'is' is recognised for what it is, as a discontinuity, a jump within the order of a world wherein there is at once plurality and unity, wherein there are certainly many different sorts of entity, but which is yet still in some sense a unity, not a bare aggregate. He seeks such a vantage-point; yet he recognises (in the Fifteenth Sermon) that its actual achievement must be denied him; for if men are not animals, neither are they God. And it is to Butler's concept of God, and to the rôle of God in his ethics and in particular in relation to his empiricism, that we must now pass.

D. THE RÔLE OF GOD IN BUTLER'S ETHICS

How did Butler conceive God? How did he understand the relations of man to God. In particular, how did he conceive the relation of God to the moral laws by which men order

---

[1] This somewhat dogmatic statement would require to be modified in the light of a thorough exploration of his concept of analogy.

their comings and goings? It is to these matters that we must now turn.

Certainly Butler did not conceive morality as obedience to divine command. Men were laws to themselves; the secret of their proper order was in their own nature. Conscience did not mediate to men the oracular communications of the eternal; rather by its authority men were constrained to follow the ways of their own being. Moreover, in some of the situations of human life, conscience could intervene to prevent men from being deflected by, for instance, a supposedly religiously perceptive pity from the zealous pursuit of justice; Butler certainly acknowledged the right of conscience to sit in judgment on supposed religious sensibility. A man could easily mistake a slothful sentimentality for the prompting of true compassion, and could need recalling to sterner, if less obviously religious, policies of life. Again, the fanatical zeal of the persecutor might express a genuine devotion to God and go hand in hand with an austere asceticism of personal life. Yet by his conscience he stands condemned as one who has turned aside from a proper following of human nature; and that conscience is, for Butler, authoritative over the particularities of religious practice and obedience which the persecutor may wish to enforce upon his fellows.

For Butler there is a 'primacy of the practical reason'. How then does he conceive the relation of God to man? Is God simply the guarantor that men do not labour in vain? For Butler his rôle is certainly more pervasive than this. It was remarked above that in Butler the problem of the 'possibility of metaphysics' need not arise; with him the issue was rather one of the proper esteeming of experience, almost of capturing the fundamental character of specifically human experience in its moral aspects. It is his underlying theology which compels him to pose the central theoretical issues of ethics in these terms, almost to move in upon the stuff and structure of our human existence from the viewpoint of assured conviction that the foundations of its being were laid in wonder and honour by God. Nothing is too small or too trivial to be ignored, nothing too slight to merit the attention of a proper estimation. Butler's faith in God is revealed by the intense reverence for human nature that pervades his ethical writings, by his preoccupation with the problem, which he never finally resolves, of a proper and valid conception of experience as at once revealing to us the unsuspected richness and complexity of our existence, and yet compelling us to acknowledge frontiers which we must not pass.

To bring out these points more clearly it may be worth while recalling here in outline some of the differentiating features of metaphysical theism. Thus it has often been remarked by those who have analysed the logical structure of theism that it cannot be conceived either as a form of monism or as a form of pluralism. For the theist the world is sharply distinguished from God; it is something quite other than a phase or moment in his being. Although God alone exists of Himself, enjoys *aseity* (to use the technical word), the world most certainly exists. Yet it does not exist simply as something juxtaposed beside God; it depends wholly on Him, while He in no sense depends upon it. Thus it is perfectly legitimate for Lord Russell to point out the radical incompatibility between theism and any sort of pluralism; and it is equally clear that there is an analogous incompatibility between belief in the existence of God and treatment of the Absolute as a necessarily self-differentiating, all-embracing unity. However difficult it may be to find the means of representing the relations of created to creator, the enterprise is compelled to seek some sort of middle way between monism and pluralism; indeed the historian of philosophy soon realises that the attraction for the mediaeval schoolmen of the Aristotelian doctrine of the categories of being resided in the suggestion, conveyed by that doctrine, that such a middle way could be found.

Now it could surely be said that the reader who comes to

Butler's ethics with some recollection, however vague, of this sort of thinking, finds in them more than a hint of something similar. Thus Butler is determined to lose sight neither of that which makes human life unique, nor of that which makes it continuous with the natural environment on which it depends. Again he sometimes argues as if men could be looked at in isolation from the world to which they belong, as if their lives were transparent to themselves in isolation from their context; and yet at other times he makes it plain that, to read the order of human life aright, we must avoid that sort of detachment and diminution of the human image which would leave us with something less than men in their concrete actuality. We must reckon with human nature as a whole; and yet there is a sense in which the fundamental laws of our being are immediately and certainly known to the honest and unsophisticated.

How can we think men in their self-containedness, and in their dependence on their world? How can we hold together in a single perception the unity and the complexity of human nature? How can we avoid either ignoring men's unique and special dignity or forgetting the richness and variety of their passional nature? How can we acknowledge both these, and yet at the same time duly esteem the 'extrovert rationality manifested at the level of cool self-love and benevolence? For Butler it is in the context of a religious vision of the world that such perception is most easily achieved, and the dangers which threaten it most surely avoided. Certainly in his writings he often conveys this vision by means of teleological imagery forced and artificial in quality. We are bidden look, e.g., for the purpose in human life of this or that passion, and the purpose is often purpose in relation to a crudely utilitarian conception of human society and welfare. But the implication of Butler's argument is more subtle: the man who recalls the creator is, by that recollection, all the time constrained to attend to the detail of the creation. It is as if his sense of the range and diversity of the matter of which conscience must pass judgment is corrected and extended; he is protected against the besetting danger of over-simplification. And yet at the same time his sense of the unity, even the *substantial* character, of that human life he must live under the guidance and authority of conscience is upheld. For if the recollection of the creator guards a man against over-simplification, so also he is by it secured in the sense that the virtues he must cultivate, however intrinsically different the one from another, are yet the dispositions of a single individual, who is 'a law unto himself'.

In the *Analogy of Religion*, Butler makes it clear that for him an elusive notion of correspondence plays a rôle in setting out the relations of man to God akin to that played in the writings of the schoolmen by the notion of analogy; to understand this notion is to understand the work and grasp Butler's vision of his world. The same notion is there in his ethical writings, sometimes, certainly, obscured by the more artificial teleology on which we have commented. He makes no effort to vindicate his use of it; indeed it is hardly explicit. Yet it is there all the time and provides the way in which Butler holds together the continuities and discontinuities of the human existence whose order he is exploring. It belongs to an essentially religious vision of the world which Butler is not concerned systematically to defend, only to realise, now in one way, now in another, in the particular field of human conduct.

As was said above, Butler is concerned that our actual experience shall have proper authority over us, that we shall learn from *experience*; he is concerned in fact to re-define empiricism, to expound the contours of a theistic empiricism. In such a concept there is an element of paradox, even of self-contradiction. For we are familiar with empiricism as the name of that logical programme which seeks to eliminate the appeal to the unobservable. Bentham, for instance, seems to provide us with an obvious paradigm of the application of empiricist principles in ethics. Yet Butler is avowedly an empiricist; there is a real kinship with Locke, an implicit

hostility to rationalist self-confidence, a sceptical unwillingness to delimit *a priori*.

But it is an empiricism that is over-arched by belief in the
reality of God, an acknowledgment of fact that is given a
peculiar quality by being treated as an expression of a characteristically religious reverence. Men must treat their nature
as something given to them; although they are 'laws to
themselves' they must not play tricks with their human
inheritance, which they receive. Men *find* the stuff of which
they are made; they have to learn what it is, painfully maybe,
but the lessons are within their grasp. In Butler, as in Burke's
political theory, there is an acknowledgment of the authority
of moral tradition. His temper, as displayed in his criticism of
Hobbes, is conservative, and he shows, as Burke does, that in
empiricism there is a certain ambivalence. The empiricist is
not necessarily committed to finding wisdom only in the
claims of the radical.

Certainly Butler's doctrine is an elusive one; but it is
elusive only because he is bringing together what we are
familiar with as incompatibles, acknowledgment at once of
the authority of God and of experience, the latter involving
always some reference to conscience or the principles of
reflection. In consequence our concepts of both alike are
transformed. For if experience becomes something looser,
less capable of once-for-all-definition, than in traditional
empiricism, the notion of God becomes less that of a first
cause or a law-giver, and more that of the unknown whose
acknowledgment constrains us properly to reverence ourselves. If He is creator, our concept of creation receives a
renewal of content through being schematised in terms of our
perception of the ways of our own being. Because that being
is rooted in our natural environment, our understanding of it
involves us in the continuing deepening of our comprehension
of that environment; and the latter in its turn plays upon the
way we see ourselves.

Butler's method is far removed from the formalisms alike of

Kantian and of utilitarian. He is tentative, exploratory, always concrete, for all the frequent creaking of his teleological apparatus. And it is impressive to notice how, for all his hierarchical conception of human nature (with its distinctly 18th-century colouring in addition), his understanding of the moral life admits the reality of dialectic. Sometimes the elements in our human nature, as he conceives them, seem to fall neatly into their places; yet he is also aware of opposition between their claims, e.g. opposition between our obligation to promote the welfare of mankind at large and our sense of the more intimate, searchingly personal obligations of our private individual lives, opposition between the claims of justice and of pity. If human nature is the place where we must seek the key to our understanding of the moral life, Butler acknowledges in his writings that men are often estranged from themselves. If he lacks Hegel's overt recognition of the significance of the tragic, yet by his method he displays continual awareness of the presence of tragic contradiction in human life. Thus in the order of this book, this study (if it may be so called) of his doctrine precedes chapters in which we shall be concerned with the relations of ethics and politics and of ethics and religion. It does so because in Butler there is a definite and sustained repudiation of formalism in method. His Fifteenth Sermon expresses an agnosticism which is, in some respects, akin to that of Kant; he seems to subscribe to a doctrine of the primacy of practical reason, and to share Kant's insistence on the validity of quite unsophisticated conviction concerning the reality of human freedom. But these things have their place in a vision which somehow reaches beyond them. The temper of Butler's agnosticism is religious, not philosophical;[1] he seems to reach back beyond the attempts of the schoolmen to anatomise the mysteries of being, to the avowal of a simple reverence in the presence of the unknown, which is yet capable of bearing fruit in resolute acceptance at once of the setting, the circum-

[1] Cf. Chapter VII.

stances and the order of human life. Because he is agnostic, Butler is ready to set out the moral life piecemeal, now letting his attention fall on one set of problems, now on another. It is against the general rubric that his face is set, and it is by an appeal to human nature, wherein unity comprises diverse springs of action, that his procedure is held together.

E. CONCLUSIONS

The importance of Butler's work in ethics lies in the contribution which he makes to the problem of method. The texture of his argument is so loose that this can easily be overlooked; but he does raise, in the most crucial way, the problem of the appeal to experience in conduct, even of the nature of moral experience. He is hard to read because he does insist that we bring together what prevailing forms of philosophical fashion have long encouraged us to separate, now in one way, now in another. It is in human life that the moralist must be interested, human life as it is lived. There are many different kinds of distraction to withdraw us from this healthful concentration, and in a way Butler reviews them all. Thus the attentive reader finds in his sermons criticism of various opposed styles of ethical reflection, formalist, utilitarian, abstractly speculative, naturalist, etc. But he may think that at the end he still lacks a clear conception of what it is that Butler would put in their place, what the appeal to human nature is on which he lays such stress.

There is no escape from this central obscurity in Butler's thought; but at least the reader has his gaze directed aright, that is, to the point of greatest uncertainty. Butler wants to make the final authority in human conduct something that does not give the lie to what we know that conduct actually to be; he does not wish to identify that authority either with a mysterious intuition or with the dictates of prudence and concern for the welfare of mankind at large, somehow imposed on men as authoritative. Still less does he want to identify the authority with the blind will of God.

o

What can we say of the experience which reveals the contours of human goodness to us? In what sense can we speak of it as experience? In a sense we do speak of our standards of moral judgment as the measuring rods which we bring ready with us into our daily lives; but this *a priorist* metaphor is one that we soon find misleading and know we must correct by other and different idioms. This process of correction is, of course, itself part of what we call our moral experience; but what assurance have we, or can we find, that we are allowing ourselves rightly to be taught by, and properly to respond to, what comes to us day by day? It is part of Butler's greatness as a moralist that he was not dissuaded by the complexity of these issues from raising them; no doubt here he was encouraged by his religious vision; but even the reader who finds that vision quite alien must still allow to Butler's ethics remarkable effectiveness in breaking down every sort of cherished artificial division and opposition.

CHAPTER VI

ETHICS AND POLITICS

At first sight the chapter on Butler may seem oddly to interrupt the advance of the argument of this book. At the end of the discussion of moral freedom in the fourth chapter the ground seemed prepared for a discussion of the relationship of ethical to political conceptions, for instance of the relation of the notions of moral and political freedom. The study of Butler's ethics may seem to some a mere break in the argument; but against this criticism two points might be made.

Firstly, although Butler is very largely preoccupied by questions of personal morality, anyone who reads his text closely may discern in him something akin to an elementary phenomenology of the moral life, with that sort of concern for public welfare which expresses itself most naturally in political action duly recognised. It has its place in human life; its exercise is not the whole of virtue, but still it is a very important part thereof. Moreover Butler clearly sees how complex and typical the questions are concerning the relationship of this sort of concern for our fellows to other kinds of moral obligation.

Secondly, the notion of experience, acknowledged to be central, for all its elusiveness, in Butler's view concerning our knowledge of human nature, is one which may prove significant in discussion of the relations of the ethical to the political in the concrete.

1. There are two sorts of writing which would to-day naturally be classified as belonging to political philosophy; and the former of these would be denied its right to the title 'philosophy' by many contemporary philosophers.

Thus the uninitiated would be tempted to treat as an essay in political philosophy any attempt to draw up a new table of the 'rights of man'; for, after all, works in which such tables have found their place in the past have been regarded as classics in the history of the subject. On such a view the political philosopher is a man actively engaged in a political struggle, and his writing will often therefore be more of the nature of a pamphlet than a treatise. In such a pamphlet principles will be worked out or enunciated with a new relevance and clarity; but the work will be, in some measure at least, a response to the needs of the hour of its writing. No doubt the situation which provoked it may be changed by its appearance; it may enable men to discern with a new sharpness of insight principles involved in the issues of their day which they had not previously seen clearly to be at stake in those issues.

Of course the style of such writing may vary enormously; thus it may be more or less abstract, more or less detached from the immediate practical needs of a political society. It may be more or less academic, more or less historically informed, more or less influenced by this or that general conception of human origin and destiny. But it will be written with an eye to the enlightenment of its readers, even to persuade and to inspire them.

Now it is certainly true that many contemporary philosophers would deny the right of such work to the name 'philosophy'. Certainly they would protest hotly against the suggestion that this is the kind of thing that philosophers, as philosophers, ought to write; if they do, then in so far as they do they are not writing as philosophers, but as men disturbed and moved to action by the plight of their society, or by this or that episode of contemporary history—say, the Spanish Civil War. Of course the philosopher *quâ* philosopher is interested in this first sort of writing, to which men have given the name of political philosophy; it is in fact part of what the political philosopher is philosophising about, an important chapter of political action, indeed that kind of political action with which the political philosopher is most obviously concerned. For no one would dispute the duty of the political philosopher to disentangle the language in which political arguments are carried on, to plot its peculiar logic, to lay bare the relations between what we call 'political theory' and the theories propounded by social scientists, etc. But the political philosopher must remember that he is a philosopher and not a prophet, that he wears a gown and not the mantle of Elijah.

Now these distinctions should certainly recall distinctions drawn at the outset of this book between the levels at which moral philosophers speak, the conversations which they interrupt, etc. It might be thought that the implications of what is here said about the task of the political philosopher in effect prohibits him from speaking at all to the perplexities and uncertainties of ordinary people; it seems suggested at least that if they want enlightenment concerning the principles of politics they must look elsewhere; or if they do look to philosophers, they must look to those philosophers in their off moments! But if the earlier chapters of this book have conveyed anything to the reader at all, they may have suggested to him how extremely hard it is to constrain actual philosophical work into a precisely divided, logical scheme. Thus if we ask ourselves what is needed if a man is to say something significant concerning the language of political theory, its significance and its logic, we must surely allow as necessary that he is concerned with the affairs of that world to which the language belongs. It is easy to say that there are in fact two activities, namely thinking about the State and thinking about thought about the State, or, if it is preferred, talking about the State and talking about talk about the State. But if one is to think seriously about thought about the State, one must understand something of what the thought one is thinking about has tried to achieve; one must be in tune with the enterprise concerning which one is thinking. Further, one must see that there belongs inescapably to the thinking about which one is thinking the duty of coming to a decision. When one thinks about the 'social contract', the 'general will' and the rest, one is thinking about notions in whose name, however the fact was concealed, men have been prepared to shed blood. The issues of political theory are grave and serious, and the mistakes which men have made in these fields have been paid for by the suffering of the innocent.

Whatever philosophers may say, men will continue to think about government and its justification, power and its necessary limitation, etc. They will still by their efforts provide philosophers with matter for commentary and discussion, criticism and analysis. It must be recognised that the philosopher will only do his work properly in respect of political thought if he has some knowledge of the issues at stake, some sense of their history and gravity. Of course a mere combination of historical knowledge and seriousness of purpose will not by themselves avail to make a philosopher do his work properly in this field; but at least they will guard him against writing off too lightly particular manifestations of the human spirit as mere muddle and confusion, sound and fury, signifying in the last analysis nothing. Thus, in discussing such a proposition as 'Will, not force, is the basis of the State', the political philosopher will want to be sure that he has really taken stock of the actual use of the expression in the context in which it was first formulated and in other contexts in which it can be used. He will ask what precisely the power of the expression is, what sort of moves, in practice as well as theory, can be made by its means. He will not treat it as an atomic unit to be scrutinised under a microscope, but rather as a piece in a game whose significance is a function of the rules which govern its use. It is surely obvious that if he is to do this at all adequately he must have some feeling for the game, some interest in it, some sense of the worth of those manifestations of the human spirit disclosed in its playing.

2. It would, however, be a great mistake to suppose that,

even as a starting point in discussion of the nature of political philosophy, this separation of levels should be taken too seriously. Where moral philosophy was concerned, we saw in discussing the ethics of Kant that for him the establishment of the autonomy of ethical discourse was something much more than a mere logical clarification; rather for him the autonomy of ethical discourse was inseparably one with his view of morality as commerce with the unconditioned. His formalism had an unmistakable bearing on his conception of the very nature of morality as something universal and absolute; it enabled him to establish the moral as such in sovereign authority, and at the same time in an abstract purity unaffected by any contingent circumstance. Kant's view of moral discourse as autonomous was for him simply an aspect, although a very important one, of his vindication of the transcendent import of the moral as such. Now this crucial argument of Kant's cannot be regarded as belonging to one or other of the levels distinguished in the first chapter, as breaking in on one or other of the conversations distinguished there; his articulation of the moral as such belongs to both together simultaneously.

Now in political philosophy to-day we have in the writings of men like Mr. Isaiah Berlin (to which reference has already been made) a clear invocation of the Kantian conception of the moral as such in the formulation and defence of liberal principles. What can easily be misconstrued simply as the proper logical placing of a particular sort of discourse here comes into its own as a vindication of the dignity of the individual moral person. It is no longer a matter simply of logical analysis; the status of the moral as such is presented as an issue of belief. To affirm the reality of the moral in the Kantian sense is to be committed to the taking of sides in the world of politics. If this is so, then inevitably the implications of what Kant has done, or tried to do, are clarified, his formalism distinguished from that of contemporary analysts, etc. Moreover we are furnished with a remarkable example

of the way in which political philosophy may in effect be
shaped by taking into itself, reflectively and self-consciously,
ideas that, superficially at least, belong to much more
abstract styles of discussion, but which themselves receive a
new force and bite by the use made of them in reference to
politics.

No doubt, in terms of the classification made in the first
section of this chapter, Mr. Berlin would have to be classed
with the former rather than the latter group there distinguished; but such a paper as his August Comte lecture
does more than adorn liberal prophesying with a garment of
wide philosophical culture. It succeeds in bringing out
something very important, and easily lost sight of, in the
distinctly philosophical work of men like Kant. Thus it lays
hold of a highly technical element in Kant's doctrine and
incorporates it into the living tissue of a vehement political
protestation. Of course Kant's doctrines alike of freedom and
of the autonomy of the ethical look different, when thus
invoked and used by Berlin, from what they appear in the
context of formal exposition; yet it cannot be denied that we
win a sort of insight into their inwardness, otherwise withheld
from us, by studying the use Berlin has made of them, even,
to return to a previously used metaphor, the moves they have
enabled him to make.

There is a fluidity in philosophical insights, an 'openness of
texture' in their sense; it is not enough to say, of such an
elaborately argued and painfully won thesis as Kant's
defence of the autonomy of the moral, that it is simply a
matter of logic. Certainly it is worked out by means of the
radical separation of two sorts of discourse; but such a
separation is something which, as was suggested in previous
chapters, may touch the way in which men see human life.

At first sight this further reference to Berlin's work may
seem to break the continuity of this chapter; but it is introduced in order to indicate the sort of perilous over-simplification which may follow rigid adherence to the division

indicated in the first part of the chapter. Of course philosophical discovery often does take the shape of deepened understanding concerning the intimate relations of different conceptual systems, different languages, etc. But such a philosopher as Kant goes further than this and claims that a certain language, namely the language of categorical imperative, touches the unconditioned as no other language whatsoever can do; as was suggested earlier in this book, his whole philosophical work, including his criticism of metaphysics, is bent to this end. He is concerned to analyse and discriminate, but he also hopes to prove and establish.

Now in writing about political philosophy Berlin takes Kant's argument to some extent for granted. He criticises certain relevant political idioms, and his criticism can certainly be described as a logical critique of the language of politics. He seeks to throw light on the logical sins committed by those who have written glibly of historical development and direction, on the abuse of language of which they are certainly guilty. But in this task he is guided not simply by a sense of the way in which different languages are properly related, but by a conviction concerning the sort of language which is fundamental. He does not write as a detached and critical spectator, but one who is committed to challenge those whom he is criticising, in the name of deeply held convictions.

In the third and fourth chapters of this book certain concepts central to Kant's philosophy were examined and discussed; they included such various notions as metaphysical agnosticism and moral freedom. It was suggested, among other things, that the metaphysically agnostic posture which Kant deemed proper to men was in fact the setting in which alone the quality and dignity of their freedom could be discerned for what it was. Such a writer as Berlin enables one to see what becomes of this sort of conviction when it is set in a context of social and political, as distinct from private and personal, perplexity; when the metaphysical doctrines to which it is opposed concern the supposed necessary order of human history. What we are offered is, in fact, an account of the relations of ethical and political language, an indication of the proper subordination of the latter; for it is only through the use of the former that a man comes to himself. But the exhibition of the relation of moral to political language helps us to see something about the former that was less easily noticed when the contrast with which he was concerned was simply that between ethical and factual language in general. All this, of course, has been more than touched on in earlier chapters of this book, but it is important to recall it now because something at least of the present confused state of moral philosophy in this country is due to a failure to be sufficiently self-conscious concerning the interplay, not of ethical and factual language, but of ethical and political. It is part of the great value of Mr. Berlin's work that he has succeeded in throwing this problem into clear relief, and doing so by means of the invocation and use of a classical piece of moral *philosophising*.

It would be no exaggeration to say that when Mr. Berlin takes hold of Kant's views and thrusts them into a political context, they begin to vibrate anew with some of their searching and illuminating power. We are no longer able to conceal from ourselves their implications by pretending that their yield is simply an increase of logical insight, their value exhausted in the discriminations they make possible. Morality, for Kant, is concerned with the unconditioned; as was argued in the third chapter, there is a sense in which he takes existence of such concern for granted and faces the question whether it belongs more properly to the theoretical or to the practical aspects of human consciousness. It is his view that it is at the level of the *Sollen* of morality that we are related to what is absolute; this conception provides, in one sense, the setting of his metaphysical agnosticism, while, in another, that agnosticism is the context within which we take the measure of the peculiar absoluteness of morality. If this language seems unhealthily Hegelian, it can only be pleaded that something of the sort is required in order to bring out the reciprocal interplay of Kant's moralism and his agnosticism. In Berlin's writings we receive new illumination concerning the content and force of these views through being compelled to set them in a determinately political context, we might even say to schematise them in terms of human society. Set in such a context, Kant's emphasis on personal integrity and the self-scrutiny which alone begins to guarantee it becomes a powerful justification of the right, even of the duty, of protest and revolt. Men as rational beings are bearers of the moral law which alone constrains them unconditionally; there is an authority *within* them which provides the measure and standard by which all externally imposed policies must be judged, especially when those policies try to sell themselves through assuming the trappings of metaphysical necessity. It is no accident that for Kant, as we saw, the criticism of metaphysics is in fact the criticism of the claims upon us of all those spurious absolutes which would rob us of our freedom as rational beings, in which our ultimate dignity is found. Berlin helps us to see the inwardness of this conviction by interpreting it in terms of the relation of the individual to the State, making that interpretation the more effective by insisting that we remember for how many the State is, in fact, the monolithic totalitarian power of the 20th century.

3. The argument in the second section of this chapter has two purposes. It is concerned partly to free the reader from illusions which may be encouraged by the suggestion that the task of the political philosopher is limited to the detached study of the language of political theory. In fact there can be no effective study of the language of political theory apart from the understanding that comes through using it, both receiving the language of one's predecessors and extending it. Of course this does not mean that the criticism of the language which one is using is not a very important part of the effective use made of it. If by the study of the language of

political theory one means the achievement of a proper linguistic self-consciousness concerning its origin, import and powers, then such study is an inseparable part of the disciplined use of such language. Whether one treats Mr. Berlin's writings as political philosophy or as political prophesying, their text does supply abundant illustration of the interpenetration of what one may be tempted to distinguish too rigidly; they help to break up the supposedly obvious view of what the yield of philosophical reflection can be. Berlin quarries in the technical writings of most certainly professional philosophers, and finds in them ideas, forms of language, categories, what you will, admirably suited to convey the points he is trying to make; indeed they help him make those points so well that one is tempted to say, however shocking the philosophical scholars may find the suggestion, that this in fact is what, e.g., Kant is 'really saying'! It is perhaps worth noticing that one does not speak here of Kant's conceptions being 'tailor-made' to fit what Berlin wants to bring out; rather one would prefer to speak of a tradition of thought suddenly revivified through effective and informed use.

But the argument in the second section has another purpose as well. If the present state of moral philosophy in these islands is deplored by many, still more lament the decay of political philosophy, of work of the order of T. H. Green's *Principles of Political Obligation*. No doubt these complaints are confused and unfair; and no doubt their causes, when they are properly disentangled, may be recognised as many and various. Thus mention might be made of the significance in this respect of the premature eclipse of the work of the political pluralists of the first decade of this century, who at least had the merit of focussing attention on the problems created by so-called subordinate associations in the State and their claims upon the individual. Others might remark too the considerable ignorance displayed by writers in this field concerning economic organisation, the efforts, however piecemeal and frustrated of accomplishment in many respects, to establish effective international institutions, elementary principles of sociology, and much else. In any study concerning the state of political philosophy to-day such matters would require attention; but within the design of this book attention may properly be directed to one group of questions, namely issues indicated by the word relativity.

Berlin's work has the effect of raising these issues in a peculiarly acute form; for he rivets our attention on the notion of agnosticism, a notion closely allied to the denial of the possibility of metaphysics. In the chapter on Kant it was insisted that for him the denial of the possibility of metaphysics was intimately tied up with what for want of a better phrase must be called his vindication of humanism. Men were driven to a proper appraisal of the moral law within them by which they disciplined and scrutinised the springs of their conduct, by an acknowledgment of those conditions which made for them the speculative embrace of the absolute an achievement impossible of realisation. Agnosticism, freedom, humanism—for Kant these three are woven together into a tightly composed unity. Berlin suggests to us that men can challenge the right of the dictator to order all things in heaven and earth in accordance with his concept of what is, in the name of such a triad, with due emphasis laid upon its first member. This agnosticism is that of Kant rather than the self-confident repudiation of assertion concerning the transcendent which one finds in Bentham and his epigoni; it has a certain kinship with the self-critical inconsistency of John Stuart Mill and perhaps, for all the differences in style, with the mood of Butler; but it is Kant who is most certainly the intellectual inspiration of this style of liberalism.

In previous chapters of this book reference has been made to the ambivalence, the manifold ambiguity, of the 'denial of the possibility of metaphysics'. This 'denial' is not the name of some one thing; there is not one enterprise which is being abandoned, but a whole number of different varieties of intellectual style, misleadingly grouped together under this single label. The Kantian 'denial', set in the context of political theory, is easily schematised as a confession of the profound, rationally based dignity of man; its inwardness is quite other from that of the utilitarian refusal to admit the criticism of satisfactions as a valid intellectual enterprise on the ground that we can provide no method for satisfactorily carrying it through. But there is a sense in which this schematisation transformed what is schematised, or rather somehow redistributed its emphasis. The Thomist critic of Kant's agnosticism sees that philosopher as a man trying to find the means to extrapolate concepts which he has deliberately confined within the limits of experience, beyond its frontiers; and he seems to find the answer to Kant's predicament in the doctrine of an analogically participated being, derived certainly from Aristotle but given a new force and power. But the Thomist finds it natural to speak of Kant's *predicament*, and indeed the philosopher's own language gives him real excuse for doing so. There is a reaching after the unattainable which seems to withdraw, or to lose its character, as soon as we try to capture it within the network of our concepts; there is the attempt to take flight in an air which will not support the wings of our thought. The background imagery is that of flight, of ascent from the conditioned to the unconditioned, from the relative to the absolute. In his first Critique, Kant certainly thinks of the movement from the relative to the absolute in terms of such imagery of vertical ascent, of upward stretching; of course his perception of the nature of our intellectual activity and dispositions is too subtle for him long to be misled by this irrelevant spatial imagery. But its besetting power is there all the same, still more perhaps in the minds of his readers for whom the temptation to represent the relation of relative to absolute in terms of a vertical line may prove too strong for conscious criticism to expel it from their imaginations. Paradoxical though it may seem, the denial of the possibility of metaphysics may itself acquire the force of an escape from the relative.

This has indeed been already admitted where Kant is concerned; for him, at the level of practical reason men have commerce with the unconditioned and the task of the critical philosopher is to free them from those confusions which may hinder them from accepting their commerce for what it is. In such a writer as Berlin this whole movement of thought assumes something of the fixity and finality of a metaphysical insight; it is visibly clothed with the immunity from criticism which is the supposed prerogative of such insight. It is in fact the categorical denial of the relevance of any sort of relativist criticism.

It is a curious freak of intellectual history that those who are most concerned to stress the importance of understanding the relations of one form of language to another should also be, for the most part, most deliberately hostile to the kind of probing of such relationships that has been carried on, however confusedly and even disastrously, under the guidance of relativist ideas, deriving in the first instance from Hegel, but capable of very different interpretations and use from that which he gave them. It may sound startling and even fantastic to suggest that Hegel's dialectic is from one point of view a method of the criticism of metaphysics. But that in fact is what it most certainly is; by its employment we are prevented from the familiar metaphysical move of erecting relatives into absolutes, and this particularly when the move takes the specific form of isolating what we want to treat as an absolute from that to which it is necessarily related on the plane of the horizontal. Metaphysics may proceed by launching out into an air in which the wings of our thought are unsupported; but it may also begin and advance by deliberately ignoring the *Sitz im Leben* of what is proposed as an absolute. In fact it might be suggested (indeed it was suggested by Hegel) that this was precisely what those meta-physically-minded philosophers had done whose interest and concern were primarily with the principles of moral and political behaviour. Thus in one way or another they took hold of relative principles—say, the rights of Englishmen in common law—and converted them into absolutes—say, the intuitively evident rights of man. One could say (and here, of course, Hegel and Burke are in fundamental agreement with the utilitarians) that the intuition was tailor-made to disclose the law behind the laws, the rights behind the rights. It is odd but true that this style of criticism, received as a liberation in its use by the utilitarians, becomes on the lips of the relativists something terrifying and needing every sort of resistance.

In part at least the present state of confusion in political philosophy is tied up with the failure to measure up to the challenge of relativity; and it is the aim of this chapter to bring out some neglected aspects of the relation of that challenge to the problem of the possibility of metaphysics. It has indeed been argued in the previous paragraphs that to rehearse the Kantian criticism of metaphysics in the context of political theory to-day is to deny the need to take relativism seriously. It is, in Kant's own language, a move from the critical to the dogmatic plane. This is only seen when one realises that what the critic of metaphysics may have to criticise is something quite different from the groping efforts to capture the lineaments of the transcendent by means of conceptual thought. As was made clear in Chapter IV, by intention if not by achievement, the individual will often make the effort, whether in Kant's style or in very different style, to lay hold on his own spiritual life as in fact a terri-tory in which he is metaphysically secure. But the relativist points out to him, now in one way, now in another, how unreal and vulnerable that security is. It may be that *one* of the immediate tasks facing the political philosopher is to formulate in a significant and relevant way the sort of criticism of metaphysics which touches most sharply our political and social ideas. It may be that our exposition of those ideas must flag and lack conviction till we have brought out into the open the sort of criticism of metaphysics that touches them most sharply. It is not the least value of Berlin's work that he provides to those who think that they must part company from him the stimulus they need to frame the grounds on which they must do so.

4. *Hierarchy and Dialectic*. We have met with the notion of dialectic in two places, in earlier chapters in this book. In one case, the use of the notion was relatively precise and restricted; in the other, it was encountered less precisely, but more pervasively, in connection with the whole of the opposition between *Erfolgsethik* and *Gesinnungsethik*. If the latter reference is less restricted, this is partly due to the fact that the study of this opposition, or of some of its aspects and ramifications, is a central object of this book.

The more precise and restricted reference to the notion occurred in the chapter on Butler, in particular in the discussion of his criticism of Shaftesbury's views. Butler would not allow benevolence to be the whole of virtue; it could only be allowed to be so within the limits of justice and veracity. Thus he commits himself to a view of our *prima facie* duties as forming a plurality; he does not try to subordinate the more intimate and searching obligations of personal integrity and fair dealing to the more impersonal principle of the promotion of human welfare as a whole. Both alike are acknowledged, and Butler displays a characteristic reserve where the resolution of possible conflicts between them is concerned. All the time he writes from the standpoint of a *Gesinnungsethiker* who is yet concerned, now in one way, now in another, to do justice to the fundamental utilitarian emphases. He acknowledges the possibility of deep division in respect of the principles acknowledged by the good man; his conception of human nature was, as we saw in the last chapter, hierarchical, and he acknowledged both continuity and discontinuity betwixt the several springs of our conduct. But implicit in his argument, although in his more optimistic moments he would wish to retreat from admitting it, is a

P

sense that men are sometimes not only estranged from their own proper nature, but in a sense divided against themselves.

It is, of course, from the admission of this division of men against themselves that the Hegelian dialectic begins. Thus if contemporary philosophers in this country and in America find in Hegel little but a farrago of elaborate speculative nonsense to justify acquiescence in things as they are, the distinguished American literary critic Mr. Lionel Trilling can preface his recent volume of essays, *The Opposing Self*,[1] with a tribute to the depth of Hegel's insight into the predicament of the individual in modern society and the way in which acceptance of its institutions and order necessarily, in one way or another, estranges a man from himself, divides him against himself. There is continuity here with the sort of moral reflection implicit in Butler's Sermons and Dissertation; there is the same recognition that loyalty to one sort of principle, one sort of policy of life, may get in the way of loyalty to another. But there is also deeper and more tragically searching insight; for while Butler and Hegel share the standpoint of *Gesinnungsethik*, the latter has a more profound sense than the former of the levels at which a man's thinking and choosing are bound up with the ways of the society to which he belongs; and he is not able, in the manner of the 18th-century Bishop of Durham, to appeal to a hierarchically ordered human nature as a sort of fixed constant. To this point we shall return later.

It is time, however, now to turn to the more pervasive instance of dialectical opposition in the argument of this book, namely the opposition of 'ethics of consequence' to 'ethics of motive'. It should be clear from the foregoing discussion that this opposition is a manifold and complex thing. We come up against it whenever we begin to think seriously about the principles of morality, of their status, significance and import. A man's whole understanding of what goodness

[1] Secker and Warburg (1955).

is must be affected by his choice of standpoint here. This has been worked out in part in discussion of the opposition between the Kantian and utilitarian approaches to the problems of ethics, even in terms of the related opposition between Kantian and the utilitarian denials of the possibility of metaphysics. If we think again of the notion of agnosticism, which has often been mentioned in the foregoing pages, we recall that for the utilitarian the criticism of metaphysics is almost something to get over and done with in order the better to advance the cause of human happiness; whereas for the Kantian agnosticism is rather the name of a habit of mind to be cultivated, akin to, if subtly different from, that of which Butler wrote in his sermon on the ignorance of man. It was suggested indeed that, in the end, the conflict between two standpoints touched the status to be assigned to what can only be called the spiritual life of the individual. It was insisted moreover that if in the end the standpoint of the *Gesinnungsethiker* was adopted, this could only be after due attention had been paid to the criticism of that standpoint by the utilitarian; and this not as something done once for all but as requiring to be done continually anew, now in one way, now in another. If there is a sense in which (to borrow the language of religion) the fundamental question in ethics is still conveyed by the formula 'What shall it profit a man if he gain the whole world and lose his soul', it is also true that he can only put that question to himself when he has seen how far removed from egoism is the gaining of the world which is there mentioned.

Here, then, is certainly a classical instance of dialectical opposition, whether we think of it as the level of practical choice, or at the more detached level at which we survey and evaluate the principles on which we choose. But so far that opposition is presented abstractly as it touches the individual in isolation from the society, from the world to which he belongs. There is no attempt imaginatively to lay hold of the concrete circumstances in which such a choice is actually presented to individual men and women; rather the language which has been used may have created an altogether illusory sense of the sudden presentation of alternatives between which choice can be made out of the blue. It was part of Hegel's genius that he saw the sheerly misleading character of such an abstract presentation of the opposition. Thus he saw, for instance, that a man's choice of personal integrity as alone self-justifying might be made at the cost of others making a totally different choice, or even having to forgo the very possibility of choice at all, in any intelligible sense of the word; the so-called 'dialectic of master and slave' brings out in a sharp and searching way the extent to which our emphasis on personal integrity, our humanist or religious sensibility, may be bound up with social conditions that make the very reference to such things altogether insignificant to those who have to live under them. There may be contradiction in the very conception of our policy of life. Of course Hegel wrote from the standpoint of the *Gesinnungsethiker*; he was notoriously an idealist, and one concerned, as he was, to cast subject for the rôle played in traditional metaphysics by the notion of substance was not likely to be troubled by contemporary scruples concerning the status of introspection. But for all that, on his view dialectical opposition was something bedded deep in the existing world in which men lived and moved and had their being. There was a sense in which the dialectical opposition of principles of conduct and policies of life was but the reflection of a deeper tragic opposition in which men were involved at the level of their personal and collective existence. It is a commonplace to point out the extent to which Hegel's dialectic is an expression of his perception of the tragic element in human life, of the way in which men's efforts seemed somehow fated to achieve only the very opposite of what they actually intended. Of course he was, throughout his ethical and metaphysical writings, at once attracted and sustained by a continually beckoning image of reconciliation;

and it was certainly his fundamental fault that he tried to construe the whole of human history as if it were the gradual working out of a universal reconciliation.

But we may judge him at his profoundest when he searches out the unadmitted ambivalences and ambiguities of our supposed ideals, when he asks us to consider not their apparent self-evidence but the actual circumstance and cost of our adoption of them. He puts a question-mark against any and every supposed self-guaranteeing, immediately evident principle; he takes away our every supposed ethical resting place, whether we give to it the name of natural law, principle of utility, categorical imperative, what you will. He is able to criticise one and all, showing the unacknowledged metaphysical confidence present in our acceptance of any one of them; and he relates such confidence with devastating insight to the very 'lie in the soul' by whose means we would conceal from ourselves the contradiction of our existence. 'Here we have no continuing city'—that phrase might convey the most inward principle of Hegel's criticism of metaphysics and metaphysically-guaranteed ethics.

If reference to the notion of dialectic by name has been confined to the two places mentioned at the outset of this section, it must not be forgotten that the idea was actually mentioned at the very outset of the book, when the moral philosopher was spoken of as improving upon conversations conducted at different levels; dialectic is essentially as well as etymologically conversation, whether with oneself or with another. If we think back to the sort of conversations there mentioned, and review them in the light of what has more recently been said explicitly on the subject of dialectic, some things at least concerning the design and purpose of this book may begin to become clearer. Thus in the first chapter it was suggested that Prichard contributed powerfully to the practical question whether or not there was a single ground of duty; he emphatically denied that there was, and this from the standpoint of a rigorous ethical objectivism. It is perfectly legitimate to separate Prichard's attempt to derive from a single ground our several moral obligations, from his views concerning the status of moral principles in general, his answer to questions concerning the status of the ethical, etc. His atomistic conception of the objects of knowledge made such procedure inevitable, but students of his writing, less in bondage to an impossible theory of knowledge, may make bold to trace correspondences between his pluralism in respect of the grounds of obligation and a view concerning the status of the ethical which, if in some respects sharply different from his own, is none the less in others akin to it, viz. in stressing somehow both the uniqueness and the untidiness of the ethical. If the student illuminates Prichard by Butler, and Butler by Prichard, and both alike by Kant, the correspondence between the pluralist theory of moral obligation and some of the characteristic emphases of a *Gesinnungsethik* begins to emerge. Both alike stress the manifold character of the relationships which engage the individual; he is unable to find any single formula less complex than his actual nature, to reduce that plurality to unity, or to obliterate the distinctions between them. Thus to discern correspondence throws the familiar debate between the thorough-going utilitarian and the intuitionist into a new light; the former traditionally, as was seen in the second chapter, seeks somehow to derive the 'ought' from the 'is', while the latter insists that we rest in the 'ought' as something irreducible and immediate. We can see now how nearly, in one sense, the intuitionist's position is reduced to a mere attempt to express in epistemological language the characteristic tenets of a pluralist theory of obligation, even to deliver them, by a form of words, from the scandalously subjectivist nuances of a *Gesinnungsethik*. By something closely akin to a verbal sleight-of-hand moral principles are endowed with a supposed reality; it is characteristic of the intuitionist that he uses the device of a special kind of awareness in order to assign to morality a special status in being which somehow does justice to his own decision in favour of its unique significance. Of the moralists who might be called intuitionists, Butler comes nearest to avoiding the impossible consequences of that argument; and this he does by invoking the resources of an inherited conception of human nature as a hierarchically ordered unity of parts.

The intuitionist stress on the uniqueness of morality as something immutable, sacrosanct and immediate, even if finding its proper place of realisation in the ultimate *arcana* of the self, is obviously vulnerable to the Hegelian query concerning the authority by which one justifies this tearing out of some one element from the whole of human experience and conferring on it absolute significance. One does not successfully defend the claim of the experience of conscientious decision to be uniquely declaratory of the nature of what is, by treating it as a supposed insight into the necessary principles of ethical 'space'. That experience is what it is, only in the context to which it belongs; it draws its life, as we have seen, from that which contradicted. But Butler's defences are also called in question once one acknowledges the significance of dialectical interrogation; for the elements which Butler constructs into a hierarchically ordered unity suddenly seem to fall apart and to become moments in a dialectical conflict, even occasions for necessarily incomplete choice.

But for all that, Hegel's standpoint remains that of a *Gesinnungsethik*. His idealism is disclosed in the extent to which he makes dialectical self-questioning an end in itself, even the proper self-development of a spiritual life conceived initially in Kantian terms, as it moves towards full internal self-consistency. It is true that if one wishes to do justice to Hegel's insights, one can do so most easily by reflecting on the implications of the dialectic of master and slave, on the extent to which the circumstances of collective human existence call in question the supposedly evident spiritual life of the individual; it is true that there is a definite correspondence between the matter of this reflection and the terms of the opposition between *Gesinnungsethik* and *Erfolgsethik*, between the introspective style of the former and the extroverted style of the latter. But the reflection, the questioning, remains a moment in the spiritual life of the individual; it is no accident that it is a critic like Trilling, familiar with the imaginative literature of the 19th and 20th centuries, who corrects the usual Anglo-Saxon philosophical estimate of Hegel. For Trilling finds in Hegel's account of the individual's situation in society something which he can describe as the raising to the level of self-conscious statement of what he has already met in poets and novelists. The appeal of Hegel's work may well be in the first instance to those who are concerned with the impact of social and political actualities on the spiritual life of the individual, with the kind of metaphysical question which they induce. The perceptions which underlie his work may well belong less to the field of political theory in the narrow sense than to a kind of no-man's land in which an individual finds himself, in taking stock of his situation, almost compelled to define the historical actualities of society as something external to himself to which his existence as an individual is somehow given in pawn.

One may refuse to take seriously such experience; or one may admit it and deny its relevance to and significance for political theory. With both these criticisms we shall be concerned in the concluding section of this chapter. For the time being it must be enough to repeat the point already made, that it is here pre-eminently that one seems to touch the sense of the problem of the possibility of metaphysics that is peculiarly relevant to the domain of social and political theory. It is paradoxical, but intelligible if one has mastered the peculiar criss-cross of dialectical thinking in these fields, to remark that the fashionable refurbishing of utilitarian styles in social and political thinking may be, in a sense, a deliberate retreat from facing the problem of the possibility of metaphysics as it is raised at this point. If there is anything at all in the immediately preceding lines of

thought, it is that the problem of the possibility of metaphysics is raised at the level of social and political realities,
primarily for those whose concern with those realities is
suffused with an almost painfully introspective quality. The
problem comes alive poignantly for those for whom participation in the life of their society, even presence to its institutions, is a crucial part of their moral and spiritual life as
individuals. In a way it is an experience quite removed from
the workaday realities of politics, even though it furnishes a
kind of half-acknowledged background to them. To return to
utilitarian styles of thought is to come back to earth; it is
deliberately to turn one's back on these painful and maybe
sterile self-questionings. It is to deny less the possibility than
the worth-whileness of metaphysics, and to deny that worth-
whileness with sense of what one is doing enlarged by one's
perception of the practical futility of the alternative. But
questions once aroused are hardly dismissed without some
kind of an answer; and even though the man who is most
painfully aware of the experience to which Hegel calls
attention must admit the significance and the validity of
the utilitarian challenge to him, he cannot simply let the
matter rest by accepting that criticism as effectively denying
all significance to his perplexities. Certainly the return, at
this level of reflection, of a challenge from utilitarian styles
of thought is both salutary in itself and a reminder of the
pervasiveness of the opposition between 'ethic of consequence' and 'ethic of motive'. That opposition is with us all
the time; it is perhaps one of the most deeply pervasive of all
oppositions in the moral and spiritual life of men. We cannot
treat a search for some kind of understanding of our situation
in being, for some sort of internal reconciliation between those
elements of our nature and attachments of our individuality,
as if it were an end in itself and 'the whole duty of man'. Even
the effort to enter more deeply into understanding what it is
to be an individual, and to accept it, is only a part of the
matter. For there is still that level of the practical, of the tasks

and projects immediately to our hand in bettering the lot of mankind, which engages us of obligation and from which we must not turn aside. In the concluding section of this chapter an attempt will be made to show how, in actual presence to the political circumstances of the age in which we live, the two attitudes are involved in complementarity one of the other all along the line. It will be suggested that *one* of the tasks facing the political theorist to-day is to bring this out in all its ramifications.

5. *Politics and Metaphysics.* It may seem strange that the part of this book devoted to politics should be as remotely abstract as any. But it is at least arguable that it is its very ultimacy of the issues raised by political theory in the modern world which drives men away from its serious study; this, coupled with the healthy perception implicit in the reference to utilitarianism at the end of the preceding section, that such reflection *may* distract men from actual attack on concrete problems piecemeal and undogmatically, and so prove sterile and destructive.

Yet if one begins to think political issues true, one does seem to come up against the whole intractable issue of relativity; and even if one turns aside from the sort of questions it raises, and almost in the style of John Stuart Mill allows a sense of practical urgency to subdue one's speculative hesitations, yet one's attention to practical tasks cannot remain unaffected by the sense of unanswered theoretical questions one has recognised in the background. No man's actions can possibly remain immune from uncertainties concerning their validity, once the dependence of that validity on total context has been acknowledged.

Thus certainly it was with pacifist opinion in this country in the years before the war. At their best, adherents of the pacifist movement were overwhelmingly conscious of the 'problem of means', of the moral intractability of the methods of total warfare. No doubt their propaganda was glib; but they did discern the threat to the moral integrity of the individual contained in his acceptance of such methods. Their protest had justification; it was an intelligible moral act. Yet their sense of the menace to personal integrity conveyed by total war in fact become overwhelming and obsessive; they were so turned in upon themselves, upon the personal life of the individual, that their attention was deflected from the external menace making inevitable that state of affairs against which they so strongly reacted. It must be admitted that the charge of 'blood upon their hands' brought against the British pacifists of the 'twenties and 'thirties does lie; they cannot deny their measure of responsibility for the terrible suffering which came upon the world in the late 'thirties. They so fell in love with an abstract image of purity of intention that they forgot the realities of the world in which that intention had to be realised in concrete.

The case against them can, of course, be stated in utilitarian terms, whether the accents of the statement be those of Mill or of Burke. Their concentration on personal integrity can be criticised as a false Stoicism, or as the manifestation of a peculiarly destructive egoism. Their attitude stands condemned by its fruits; in the world they helped to make, the road was clear for the accomplishment of Hitler's merciless purpose of aggression. But if one can criticise their position by appeal to principles of utility, one may need the language of poetic irony, or even tragedy, to disclose the inner contradiction of their attitude; and in tragedy, one remembers, lie some of the roots of what in this chapter has been called dialectic. Deep concern with the things of peace, more profoundly a sense of the infinite preciousness and possibilities of the spiritual life of the individual, seems fated either in the end to turn into the effective promotion of its opposite, or else to reduce to a mere acceptance of things as they are, regarded as somehow indifferent to the esoteric levels of individual self-containedness. For the *Gesinnungsethiker* it is purity of intention that matters; in the pre-war world it seemed sometimes as if this doctrine achieved its *reductio ad absurdum*. For either it flirted with the destructive policies of pacifism, in the effort to clothe itself with the external dress of a practical policy of action; or else it seemed to disappear (in the way Bentham said it always must), and to become not a bubble on the surface of things but rather a scarcely audible gurgling in their irrelevant depths! These things are a parable of what to-day seems sometimes near achieving statement in more drastic terms. Few to-day would defend the pacifism of pre-war; most would recognise its contradiction, even the guilt of its adherence in blindly ignoring that contradiction. All this could be stated either in strict utilitarian terms, or else more fashionably by means of a fusion of utilitarian language with the acknowledgment as authoritative of certain values supposed incorporate in the fabric of our society. It would be wrong to deny to these values their claim intimately to touch the spiritual lives of men. No doubt the bias of their statement would be affected by the extent to which their champion was conservative or liberal in his sympathies, traditionalist or radical in his approach. Thus one would find congenial the language of Burke, with his disciplined insistence on the strength of a healthy national tradition embodying in its institutions a genuine rule of law, as a means of disciplining the pretensions of tyrants who conceal from their own eyes the piercing and destructive quality of their cruelty by the deceptive imagery of sup-posed reform. The conservative will always emphasise the superiority, as a political value, of the rule of law to effective consultation of the wishes of majorities. He will see demo-cratic institutions as requiring to be grafted into an existing fabric wherein, constitutionally, already power has been brought under law. The radical will stress, on the other hand, the importance of making possible genuine appeals against the entrenched privileges of traditional élites; he will insist with Rousseau that political power is too comprehensive and decisive an instrument to reside, *in the last resort*, in any other hands than those of the sovereign people. He will be prepared, if he is wise, to face the problem of giving significant content to the latter expression.

But both conservative and radical agree in insisting that the hard practical problems of political existence touch in the end the relations of power to law; they will agree that power has only been transformed into authority when somehow it is revealed as the servant, and not the source, of law. This language is abstract, summary and allusive; but few will deny the extent to which it is these values and these general principles of their realisation that are most emphasised, now in one way, now in another, in traditional Western political thought.

The dignity and the fascination of the political process resides, in part at least, for those who study it, in the manner in which students can see such values and such principles being given shape during its course. Whether such students be religious or sceptical in mind, whether their temper be aristocratic or radical, it is such values as these which at once direct their attention and sustain their critical judgment. It was emphasised in earlier chapters of this book that the liberal agnostic of the temper of John Stuart Mill most certainly lives out something which must be called a spiritual life; one does not need a document of the deep personal self-consciousness of Mill's *Autobiography* to justify such a claim. It is there all the time, and not least when the man is as closely concerned with political and social realities as Mill was. In a way, one would be justified in speaking of such a life as a profound manifestation of that frankly metaphysical reality of freedom of which Mill wrote so well.

Certainly we are now speaking of something very different from the artificial even hypertrophied moral self-consciousness of the pacifist. The liberal will always have something of the utilitarian in his make-up; thus Mill himself in his masterly essays on Bentham and Coleridge shows that, in him, acknowledgment of utility, and of very different, less tangible principles of morality and value, were held in some sort of dialectical balance one with the other. He could not, at least when he wrote these essays, rest in either alone. But still a man like Mill did not treat his intellectual pilgrimage lightly any more than, for instance, George Eliot did. Such a pilgrimage belonged to what was most significant in the life of any society; and this judgment must not be dismissed lightly as expressive simply of the pride of a self-conscious intellectual aristocracy. One may prefer certainly the accents of Burke to those of Mill; but when the former spoke of 'a child, a common soldier, a girl at the door of an inn' as 'changing the face of history and almost of nature', we must acknowledge a continuity in sentiment, even if we rate higher the reach of Burke's imagination. Both liberal and traditionalist alike agree in regarding as profoundly significant what belongs, in some sense, only to the reach of introspection and to those forms of description which embody it.

Such an outlook inevitably thrusts the problem of freedom, in its manifold significance, into the very foreground of the political theorists' concern. But in our present situation it remains peculiarly vulnerable to the sort of criticism which can be brought against it in the name of the Leninist monolithic revolutionary State, presented as an instrument of effective industrial and social revolution, by political means. The outlooks of men like Mill and Burke, with their hesitant, sceptical spirituality, seem necessarily, to those who knew them from afar, the prerogative of a privileged minority; their self-consciousness is easily dismissed as the prerogative of an aristocratic élite, who could enjoy the benefits of the industrial revolution in the West while spared the pain of close contact with its circumstances and accompaniments. They could look at industrialisation from afar, as men who lived reasonably well before its advent and would not themselves have to pay the admittedly bitter price of its achievement. Their attitude and preoccupation alike seem not at all to touch the needs of those who, scratching bare subsistence from the surface of the world, are prepared to pay the price of plenty for their children to those who proclaim such plenty to be possible and have themselves devised the political means of its preparation.

So a question-mark is set, in practice and in theory alike, against the premises as well as the inconsistencies of liberalism. So a question-mark is set against the near-metaphysical reality we speak of by the name of freedom; and the need for its most searching exploration is made plain. It is part of Hegel's prophetic power that he glimpsed at once the gravity and the importance of this exploration, and by doing so, in spite of his unfortunate readiness to accept the actual as somehow furnishing its own justification, he showed how the searching-out of the spiritual depths of human freedom could and must be taken beyond Kant.

But it is easy, and indeed pardonable, to turn away from these things, to refuse the cost of bearing in one's mind and imagination a sense of the historical context to which our values belong and to which they owe their relativity; it is a frightening thing to be reminded that if one examines in global terms the foundations of the freedom we esteem, we see in it a contradiction analogous to that in the attitude of the pacifist; we do not like to be reminded that we purchase it, and have purchased it, at the cost of other men's slavery.

It is, of course, important to recall here three points which have already been made. It is true that the experience of this contradiction at a self-conscious level is something that is peculiar to the exaggeratedly introspective awareness of the writer, the intellectual, etc. If one is justified in discerning a genuine kinship between the ethical style described in the second chapter of this book as utilitarian and that of Leninism, this kinship must not be exaggerated; the ethics of Butler, as well as the writings of John Stuart Mill, serve to remind the student how, in very different ways, acknow-ledgment of the importance of the utilitarian level or dimension in human life can yet be reconciled with admission of the authority of very different sorts of experience and awareness. This reconciliation may set us every sort of theoretical and practical problem; it may drive some to contrive curious essays in epistemology, while others may come to recognise a new wisdom for practical life, as well as for theory, in the untidy empiricism of Butler's ethics. Further the *Gesinnungsethiker* will always be aware of the relativity of his own standpoint, even when that standpoint is partly determined, in respect of its peculiar feeling-tone, by his determination to do justice to such a general challenge to its perspectives as Leninism conveys. He will remember that there is a sense in which a deep self-consciousness concerning the problem of freedom does not necessarily open the doors to any sort of solution, even to an understanding of what form such a solution must take. It is certainly the weakness of the *Gesinnungsethiker* to be more at home with problems than with their solution; almost it could be said of him that he has a vested interest in such problems as that of the conflict of duties!

Yet it does remain true that it is from his standpoint that certain questions are most sharply, even most poignantly, asked. One can dismiss these questions as nonsensical in the name of a particular denial of the possibility of metaphysics. But when one does so, one has to recall the ironic fact that it is another form of the same denial which has set the *Gesinnungsethiker* the problems with which we have been concerned here, and given his reflection on the nature of freedom something at least of the peculiar temper this chapter has tried to bring out.

CHAPTER VII

ETHICS, METAPHYSICS AND RELIGION

A. INTRODUCTORY

IN approaching the problem of the relations of ethics to religion, one is immediately reminded again of the besetting background-perplexity of this book, namely, the issue which has come up, now in one way, now in another, of the possibility of metaphysics. Clearly it is going to be with us again in any serious discussion of the relation of ethics and religion; in order to concentrate and restrict the enquiry, we may best begin by referring to certain places in earlier parts of this book where questions concerning the relations of ethics and religion have been before us. Thus the first section of this chapter will inevitably have something of the character of a recapitulation.

1. It seems clear that the thorough-going utilitarian position rules out any sympathy with what could be called religious attitudes. Thus the denial of the possibility of metaphysics, which is fundamental to its epistemology, leads inevitably to the repudiation of any sort of religious language whether of immanence or of transcendence. Yet at this point two qualifications have to be recalled. Firstly, there is the formalism which it was suggested the thorough-going utilitarian needed to invoke in stating his position: it was insisted that although this formalism was peculiar to himself, in certain respects it revealed an unsuspected kinship between the thorough-going utilitarian and Kant. (In the second and third chapters of this book something was said about the relations between their respective humanisms.) Moreover it was remarked that the most thorough-going utilitarian doctrine was received, and indeed preached, as a liberation.

The language of liberation, of deliverance, of redemption, is religious rather than metaphysical; and there is no doubt that it was the use of this kind of language about it that gave thorough-going utilitarians some of its peculiar force. This does not imply, of course, that language can as it were create doctrine, or that slogans are more significant than the appeal to truth, or to the superiority of exact scientific method over undisciplined appeal to feeling and imagination; nor is it to ignore the context in political and social history to which 'philosophical radicalism' belongs. It is simply to point out that a thorough-going utilitarianism was accepted by some at least as an instrument whereby the citadels of the powers of darkness could be breached and the authority of superstition broken. If we are to understand aright the 'material ethics'[1] of the early Moore and Russell, and their impact on the late Lord Keynes and his circle, one has to see in them a means whereby the intellectual inheritors of the 'radicals' were delivered from the different sort of darkness their masters had in turn created, without being plunged back into the attitudes which the men of the Enlightenment had overthrown. It is an impressive index of the tenacity of a certain form of religious language, language of bondage and deliverance, darkness and light, etc., that it weaved its way almost unnoticed into speech and writing concerned to expose the nonsensical pretensions of supposedly religious authority.

2. Kant had his likenesses to the utilitarians; but he also achieved a measure of intellectual sophistication and subtlety as well as of introspective concentration, which they lacked. In the third chapter of the book we saw how his criticism of the possibility of metaphysics was tied to his resolve to give unimpaired and unchallengeable authority to the *Sollen* of morality; references were also made to his views concerning the rigorous subordination of religion to ethics. It was also remarked that this very subordination itself owed something to the mediaeval treatment of law as the expression of reason,

---

[1] 'Material' in contradistinction from formal.

and not of blind arbitrary will and of the whole repudiation of voluntaristic styles in theology to which it belonged. Behind the discussions concerning the nature of law and of goodness in the schoolmen there lay earlier patristic reflection on the creative Logos, according to which the ground of the order of the world was identified with the eternally begotten Son of God, and rational activity was in consequence seen as suffused with something of the quality of religious worship. Kant had little use for the arts and language of the religious imagination except in so far as they served the cause of a rational morality of which men were the bearers. But his sense of what men were set to achieve by the painful self-discipline of their ethical obedience owed something to the religious vision of order introduced into chaos by the Logos. The order we realise, under the authority of the categorical imperative, whether in ourselves or in the world around us, is a rational order. If it is superior to any religious particularism, in the universality of its scope, that superiority invests it with a kind of religious dignity.

For Kant in his way as much as for the utilitarians in theirs, religious authorities are rejected because they menace men with a dark imprisonment. Certainly he conceives the prison differently; his ethic is always one of 'motive', and not of 'consequence'. He rejects the pretensions of religious authorities because they menace the purity of men's intention, bidding them substitute fear of punishment or hope of reward for the proper motive of respect for law for its own sake. If St. Bernard bade men love God for His own sake, Kant would set them free to acknowledge for its own sake the authority over them, in their inmost being, of that moral law of which they were the bearers. It is therefore by Kant that the contradiction between the ethical and the religious standpoint seems sometimes to have been most sharply brought out. The thorough-going utilitarian is overtly anti-religious as he is overtly antimetaphysical; for Kant the moral universe is the universe with which the transcendent metaphysician, if he understands his job aright,[1] is really concerned; and it is his view that men require rescue from the bondage of false conception alike religious and metaphysical, in order that they may perceive both the dignity and the gravity of their human situation aright.

Thus Kant shows himself, in a sense, the intellectual master of those who, like Mill in his posthumous essays on religion, will refuse to allow God to 'get away with it'; as if the bare fact of His omnipotence can somehow 'cover' in Him what in man would be denounced as stupidity, cruelty, malevolence and the like. We can never abdicate the standpoint to which, in our personal lives, the authority of the categorical imperative holds us fast. For Kant some of those things which the religious man would tend to call blasphemy would be no more than honest expression of genuine moral insight; expression moreover endowed with special dignity in virtue of the peculiar rigour of its acknowledgment of the authority of the moral law.

3. With Butler it is different. His ethics are religious, and the temper of his agnosticism therefore differs from that of Kant. But it is no accident that he gives a quite peculiar place to persecution among the things men might be tempted to justify too easily, if they supposed benevolence to be the whole of virtue. He shared to the full the 18th-century awareness of the peculiar corruption of the religious temper which is manifested in readiness to use methods of coercion and of violence to secure acceptance of characteristically religious authority. If his agnosticism has a genuinely religious root, if it is naturally expressed as a reminder to men that they are men and not God, its fruit is a sense of the dignity and the mystery of human freedom akin to what we find in Kant and Mill. He shares their sense of religious particularism as something threatening; he is aware that, for all the asceticism of his personal life, the inquisitor, the Merry del Val (to mention a significant recent instance of the breed), is wanting in

---

[1] And to understand that job aright is to recognise its impossibility.

a fundamental sense of the honour and dignity of man. It is
characteristic of Butler that he uses strongly and openly
religious language to characterise this lack and its fruits. Thus
for him the separation of ethics from religion, even the
acknowledgment of the supreme authority of conscience, is
something grounded in, founded on, and expressive of,
profound religious belief.

4. With Hegel, matters are much more complicated. He
belongs to so many worlds at once; and this appears even in
those aspects of his work on which we have touched. Thus it
was insisted that his approach to the problems of the individual in society could not be understood apart from the
underlying kinship between his dialectic and the tragic
element in human life as he understood it. Thus we may
quarrel with his interpretation of Sophocles' *Antigone*, and
insist that he converts the characters in the drama into so
many mouthpieces of his own ideas. But, for all that, we must
admire the insight he displays into the extent to which men
are caught and destroyed not by their weakness, but by their
achievement. Thus Antigone is, in a measure, corrupted by
the depth of her affection for her brother and her loyalty
to the intimate and personal values of which she makes herself the champion; whereas Creon owes his downfall to the
extent to which he has identified himself, in genuine disregard of self, with the welfare of his city. One can see this
principle at work in many places: thus the pacifist, whose
concern for purity of intention we emphasised and whose
sense of the menace of war to personal integrity provides its
own underlying justification of his policy, is easily assailed in
that integrity itself, becoming not only indifferent to the
claims of justice, but querulous and bigoted, sanctimonious
and arrogant in his profession of pity and compassion. Again
on the canvas of world-politics to-day, the realistic defender
of the rule of law, and of those liberal values in some way
perceived to be bound up with it, becomes very easily,
almost unnoticed, the champion of a view which makes, or

seems to make, historical accident in the distribution of the crucial forms of power in the modern world a kind of moral justification for their use. Of course in facing those attracted by the promise seemingly conveyed effectively by the Leninist State, the liberal will be careful to conceal the extent to which his accents are those of Thrasymachus and of the 'Melian Dialogue'; he will disguise the extent to which his confidence is in the end more in the superiority of the resources he commands, whether of materials or of technical skill, than in the principles of human order for which he stands; but some of those who listen will claim that they catch the underlying realities beneath the words.

Of course, the way in which both of these illustrations have been developed has something of the revealing harshness of caricature; granted however that caricature is harsh, it must be allowed its own sort of logic, its special style of truth. Few can deny that their self-knowledge is somehow advanced by this sort of presentation of the conflicts in which they are involved, this kind of bitter irony which discloses the intractable, back-lash element in the world which easily catches and makes something grotesque, even pathetic, out of our devotion to our ideals.

But, of course, the reader may well ask how far tragic perception is necessarily religious; admittedly some Christians would insist that sense of the tragic of the sort described here may be in some sense religious, but it is definitely not Christian. There is a certain kinship between the temper expressed in such a reminder and that remarked in the chapter on Kant, when reference was made to that moral philosopher's likely comment on those who defend blind heroism in the name of something called the 'tragic sense of life'. Granted that what we are speaking of here is something different from what we there referred to as 'tragic sense', yet there is always a temptation, when the tragic element in human life in any sense is brought into the picture, to substitute a certain sort of self-indulgent wallowing in the beastliness of things at the expense of tackling the next job to hand. Sense of the tragic may breed its own particular sort of pride, provide its own sort of barriers against proper exercise of responsibility. But, for all that, we must allow in three different respects a quality of deep religious insight to Hegel's ideas as we have been concerned with them.

(*a*) As the reference to Professor Lionel Trilling's admiration for his awareness of the predicament of men in society to-day makes clear, he had in some ways an extraordinarily vivid perception of the concealed depths present in the most familiar and ordinary things. He wrote about secular politics; indeed, as every elementary student of his writings knows, he was sufficiently blinded by his sense of the standards, capacity and integrity of the Prussian Civil Service to be betrayed into a quite uncritical judgment on the institutions of the Prussian State. But this is, from one point of view, only a singularly unfortunate manifestation of one aspect of his greatness, his sense not of an excessively immanent providence at work in history but rather his awareness of the inescapable spiritual import of the changing life of political institutions in its impact upon the individual, and his on them. He did try, by no means often successfully, to say something of the laws and forms of such interplay without losing sight of the reality of historical change and the unrepeatable individuality of historical occasions. In doing this he certainly drew on the resources of the Christian tradition, and of his own understanding of it.

(*b*) Mention was made of the rôle of the idea of reconciliation in his dialectic; and it was admitted that he far too easily acquiesced in the identification of the history of the world with the justification of the world. But the reconciliation of which he wrote had its roots in the *Versöhnung* of German Protestant theology. One might go further than this and insist, as the text of his philosophy of religion fully justifies us in doing, that the movement of his dialectic owes as much to the Christian rhythm of crucifixion and resurrection as to the insights of the Greek tragedians. One could go further still and point to his references to the fourth Gospel as evidence of the possibility that he had glimpsed in that extraordinary book the way in which the language of characteristically tragic irony could be bent and shaped to new uses in the presentation of the central Christian mystery. One thinks of Caiaphas' words to the Sanhedrin that 'one man must die for the people' and of the discussion between Christ and Pilate concerning order and authority. In both cases the *double entendre* is at once obvious and subtle; the discussions turn on questions of political expediency and of the responsibility of government presented as an abstract function which Pilate exercises under the constitution of the Roman Empire. But in both cases the doors are open on the concealed metaphysical background, which gives its final sense alike to the matter discussed on each occasion (in the one the limits of the appeal to expediency, in the other the end and limits of the power of government in the affairs of men) and to these particular discussions, understood as individual events, which we are in the narrative allowed to overhear. Such episodes one can easily see driving Hegel along the road which led him to his characteristic and most difficult doctrine, of the 'concrete universal', viz. the universal that determined the manner of its own particularisation.

Hegel might be judged by some to be intoxicated by the idea of reconciliation; certainly his Christian critics like Kierkegaard, who admittedly knew his writings more at second than at first hand and who reacted against 'Hegelianism' rather than against Hegel, saw in him someone who trivialised the whole idea of reconciliation by making it the pivot of a speculative system. Reconciliation with God was not something to be spoken of as the 'meaning of the historical process'; it was something to which a man might be brought through an agony of prayer, engaging him at the most intimate personal level. In fact, in the Christian tradition, universal reconciliation as the Hegelians understood it

could be judged an alien notion. Christ's words to Judas, 'the
Son of man goes as it is written of Him; but woe unto that
man by whom he is betrayed; it were good for that man that
he had not been born', leave the problem unresolved; the
Christian is never allowed either to overlook, or somehow
by a sublation to transform or obliterate, the reality of that
hell of which Christ there seems to speak. The issues of human
life and choice are never trivial; and, as a fierce modern critic
of Hegel well reveals in the corpus of his writings (I am referring here to Dr. Karl Popper), there is a kinship here
between what men like Kierkegaard and Barth (whose
understanding of Hegel is incidentally far more profound
than that of Kierkegaard) have written in criticism of the
Hegelian attitude and Kant's remorseless emphasis on the
ultimacy of individual responsibility. Yet the sharpness of
the argument and debate is itself evidence of the depth and
reality of Hegel's concern in his ethical and political thought
with its relation to religion.

(c) There is a further point to be made very closely akin to
what was suggested in 4(a) concerning Hegel's sense of the
spiritual depth of political institutions. But it touches more
directly on the notion of dialectic as such, and on an aspect
of the notion mentioned in the last chapter. It was there
pointed out that, for Kant, metaphysics as a speculative
achievement of the nature of ultimate reality was impossible
through the inadequacy of our concepts to lay hold of the
transcendent, even of the relation in which we stood to it. The
imagery was that of ascent, reflecting, at the level of the intellectual quest, that journey of the soul towards God and union
with Him whose stages are distinguished as the purgative,
illuminative, and unitive ways. One might say that for Kant
only something corresponding to the first stage of the journey
is successfully accomplished; we are certainly well capable of
ridding ourselves of any illusions we may entertain concerning, e.g. the transcendent validity of the notion of cause;
again we certainly forfeit any confidence concerning the

notion of substance which might tempt us to suppose that we could demonstrate the immortality of the soul from its alleged substantial quality. But with due regard paid to the regulative value of the 'Ideas' in the movement forward to explanatory as distinct from merely descriptive science, we stop there, only the more forcefully and effectively to be reminded that, at the level of practical reason, we are in commerce with the unconditioned all the time.

With Hegel we insisted that it was different; his dialectic was an instrument whereby we criticised confidence that we had touched bedrock ultimacy, whether theoretical or practical, by achieving a deepened self-consciousness concerning the context of our supposed final and unchallengable assurance. In a way this method is more easily grasped when it is seen as a moment in a spiritual ἄσκησις than simply as an intellectual operation. Whereas Kant's criticism of the possibility of transcendent metaphysics can very easily be expounded in barely logical terms, there is in Hegel's attack on our supposed resting place, our cherished 'abiding city' (whether in his own style or in the partly derivative idioms of Karl Marx, Plekhanov and Lenin) something which seems to require a more explicitly religious accent to convey its inwardness. One can, of course, dismiss this merely as a manifestation of Hegel's romanticism, suggesting perhaps that by doing so one has offered all the criticism that need be given. But if there is certainly something intellectually corrupt and corrupting in various forms of romanticism, there is also made possible, for those who to some extent share the romantic's feeling for the historically diverse and particular, all sorts of new perceptions concerning the human situation. What matters in Hegel is precisely that insight on which Trilling fastened; surely we can acknowledge this, and further try to learn from the language in which Hegel himself clothed the insight, without expressing approval of the wilder extravagances of the romantic movement, whether manifested by others or by Hegel himself.

There is a problem of the possibility of metaphysics which arises when the dialectical situation of which Hegel wrote is perceived; in fact the perception is itself the raising of the problem, and although Kant is no intuitionist in the sense of Ross or Prichard, we have to allow that his confidence in the isolated dignity of practical reason, as admitting them to immediate commerce with the unconditioned, is assailed. Certainly Kant has brought out much concerning freedom by the way in which he has himself criticised the metaphysical enterprise; but it sometimes seems as if, just as in his theory of knowledge he saw perception of the external world less as something achieved than as something to be won through a proper self-submission to the laws of our understanding and the authority of manifested fact, so Hegel reveals the individuality and freedom which Kant took for granted as something to which men must win their way. One can say that and even praise Hegel for his sense of this as almost an ascetic problem, without endorsing much that he said concerning the method of the ἄσκησις, and of its goal.

5. Some readers may well think that we have loaded the dice against the likelihood of any successful discussion of the relations of ethics to religion, and indeed of ethical to religious language, by failing to pay more attention to the familiar discussions concerning the relations of right and good as ethical concepts. Indeed some may suggest that this whole book suffers from a failure to take seriously enough the notion of the good for man, that form of life which at once beckons and commands him and in which he finds his resting place. It might be pointed out in defence against this charge that in the discussion of Kant's ethics it was made clear that, for him, this tradition provided the mould into which his characteristic defence of the supremacy of moral over all other forms of value was poured. A life in accordance with the moral law within us was indeed, for him, our heart's true home;[1]

---

[1] This remains true however inadequate we judge his understanding of that law to be. Cf. the late Prof. A. E. Taylor's article: *The Right and the Good*, in *Mind 1939*.

earlier in this chapter reference was made to the kinship of his language with that of St. Bernard.

Certainly the notion of the good for man is one of very great importance in ethics, and not least where reference is made to the relation of ethics to religion. But it would be a very serious mistake to suppose that we could simply identify the good for man as such with, e.g., the *unum necessarium* of the spiritual writers. Butler brings this out well in his characteristically untidy way when, perhaps revealing a debt to the Quietists, he discusses the love of God, and then leaves in a curious way unanswered the question of its relation to love of our neighbour and the ordinary rough and tumble of human life; while all the time insisting that no man will easily walk the ways of that life aright whose perceptions of its order and complexity are not sharpened and fortified by his acknowledgment of the Creator.

Certainly the catholic tradition took up what Plato and Aristotle had in their different ways written concerning the relation of contemplation and action; and that tradition made of what it found there what it could. The material was complex, and the principles in accordance with which it was used and interpreted were by no means always themselves clear to those who used them for criticism and interpretation. There is no need to point out how easily the alleged superiority of the contemplative life, as something clear on religious grounds, leads to a quite unwarranted depreciation of every sort of practical activity, whether the raising of a family, the promotion of public health, or what you will. Certainly the suggestion that this is the 'good for man' is as absurd as the identification of morality with obedience to supposed divine command. The good for man can be no narrower than human nature; and it might be thought that one implication of the traditional doctrine of the Body of Christ was that the burden of that nature as a whole was too great for any one man to bear. But we must allow that three important points are being made, however confusedly, by those who speak thus boldly of the contemplative life as the *unum necessarium*, even to the point of identifying it, in a wanton disregard of the obvious, with the 'good for man'.

(*a*) If one examines the structure of theism phenomenologically, one soon sees that the theist stands committed to some sort of realism, that is, to some view which allows (to use traditional language) that some at least of the things which we know are as they are altogether apart from our knowledge of them, and that we know this to be so. We may also realise that there is every sort of inadequacy in the language which we use to convey to ourselves and to others what these things are like; but if we have to choose traditional epistemological language, we shall want to say that our contact with such objects is a finding, or a part finding, or an imperfect apprehension; we shall be on edge in the presence of any language which suggests that it is a construction or a development of the immanent resources of our spiritual nature, or what you will.

It must, of course, be clearly allowed that many philosophers have been realists without being theists. Thus it is perfectly possible to have the most serious objections to a view which treats unperceived physical objects, say, the mountains on the other side of the moon, as 'permanent possibilities of sensation' without believing that God exists. It would be manifestly silly to forget how many realists have been materialists in the metaphysical sense, and how many have been metaphysically agnostic.

Per contra a theist can agree with Berkeley (leaving aside for a moment some of the very serious objections which can be brought against his account of the method and aims of theoretical physics[1]) in arguing that what we are discovering is to be identified in the last analysis with the *modus operandi* of 'God's conative dispositions' (to borrow Professor C. D. Broad's vivid and useful expression), in respect of the total system of percipients and percepts which he has established,

---

[1] Cf. Prof. C. D. Broad's British Academy lecture for 1942:*Berkeley's argument concerning material substance.*

and which he maintains in being. There is a sense in which the Berkeleyan conceives that human knowledge whose principles he is exploring to be a *finding* (in the manner of the realist) and not a making, even while he believes that we can reach a perspective from which we can understand it as a communion between finite spirits and the infinite Spirit.

For the theist, God is there to be found, whatever the nature of the finding. Thus he can readily agree with Professor C. C. J. Webb in insisting that we must withhold the name God from anyone on whose privacies an Actaeon could intrude, and whose secrets a Prometheus could wrest at will. The finding may have to wait on the self-disclosure of its object; but still in its self-disclosure it remains unaffected, however much, in the awareness of the one to whom disclosure is made, that awareness is affected at the deepest level, in ways of which the experient is part-conscious, by his manifold limitations. In such a context truth is always in the end conceived as correspondence.

(*b*) This certainly suggests one line of thought which must encourage the theist to bestow a special significance upon the contemplative life, as if that life were an effectual symbol of the fact that religion must always itself, *humanly regarded*, be a movement towards that which itself, even though in one sense it is the sole originator and sustainer of the movement in question, is also in itself altogether unaffected by the measure to which the movement attains its proper end. If in the life of religion there is an ἄσκησις, that ἄσκησις must surely reflect this quality of otherness in the object of its concern. We have certainly mentioned in this book the sort of self-knowledge that may liberate a man for action, either as in the utilitarians, by revealing to him that his concern with the 'criticism of satisfactions' is concern with a project doomed to failure because nonsensical in its conception, or as in Kant, by revealing to him that it is in his life as a morally responsible agent that he is all the time in direct commerce with the unconditioned, and that commerce is the only one such pos-

sible for him. But with the self-knowledge that belongs to
religion, it is otherwise.

It may be worth while remarking here, almost in paren-
thesis, that there is a curious recognition of something
remotely analogous to this in the writings of men like the
early G. E. Moore. Keynes found in Moore's ethics something
which, as was said above, liberated him both from the crude
materialism of Bentham and from something which men like
the followers of the 'philosophical radicals' seemed to share
with some at least of those who had been affected by Kant;
something which, though its manifestations in the two cases
were different, had this in common in both of them: that it
seemed to make effort, busyness, practical self-discipline, ends
in themselves. Moore provided Keynes and others with a
conception of the sort of thing which might be thought of,
indeed which Moore said could be known, as of worth in
themselves. In such experiences as the contemplation of
beautiful objects and the enjoyment of personal relations men
came to rest, and came to rest in states of affairs whose intrinsic excellence was altogether independent of our acknowledging it, whether in general or in particular. Moore's
theory of moral obligation was formally utilitarian, although
altogether free from any sort of hedonism. But one can see
how, in his presentation of the sort of things known to be good
in themselves, he dexterously employed the resources of a
logic which insisted on the externality of some relations to
their terms, to bring out the peculiar quality, the independence of everything outside themselves of those states of
affairs in which we came to rest as excellent in themselves
and justifying all effort by the measure of our attainment of
them. One might mention also as illustrating a similar temper
the attitude of the late Professor G. H. Hardy to work in the
field of pure mathematics; his sense that he was discovering
immutable and necessary truths concerning numbers that
were dependent of all else, that were practically useless, but
that were yet there to be discovered, made him profoundly

critical not only of the treatment of mathematics by men like John Stuart Mill and the idealists, but made him reject, for instance, some of the characteristic meta-mathematical doctrines of the formalists like Hilbert, as altogether failing to do justice to the element of discovery of something waiting to be discovered fundamental in mathematics as he found it.[1]

Here is a non-religious contemplation; but it reveals analogy with religious contemplation in this, that its temper is uncompromisingly, some would say extravagantly, realist.

(c) It may, of course, be asked how far, in order to bring out at once theoretically and practically something of the peculiar quality of the religious ἄσκησις, one is justified in speaking of contemplation, even of a contemplation which one must allow to be transformed out of recognition by its peculiar object. Something indeed may have been said to throw some light on the grounds which have led to the exaltation of the contemplative life; but there is no doubt that many will still feel unconvinced by the seeming arrogation of one form of life above others as peculiarly orientated upon God. Surely religion must have, if it is at all a valid form of human experience, an 'everywhere-nowhere' character analogous to what Kant believed was characteristic of morality. But here one may do well to look back at some points made in the chapter on Butler concerning the peculiar structure of theistic metaphysics. God is not one among many; yet there is a 'many' which is not simply a moment in His self-development. It is always the problem of metaphysical theism to find a middle way between monism and pluralism. We traced various instances of the refraction of this central metaphysical decision in Butler's ethics; we saw how the very oscillation between his sense of human nature as a unity, and his regard for the small details of its being, issued from a pervading resolve to find always a middle way between offering a mere inventory of different sorts of action and presenting a quite spurious picture of the formal essence of morality. This

[1] Cf. his Rouse Bale lecture on *Mathematical Proof*, published in *Mind* for 1929.

manifests the characteristic style of the theist, and it is no accident that commentators seem unable to make up their mind whether Butler's theology is essentially bound up with his ethics, or whether the latter are logically independent. One could say that Butler was all the time trying to avoid having to answer the question in one way or another, fully conscious that neither of the direct answers could possibly come near the truth.

Butler does devote two sermons to the explicit theme of the love of God. They are not perhaps among his best; yet their very presence in the corpus reveals his sense of one aspect of the whole problem with which this section is concerned. If God exists, then a special dignity must be claimed for any sort of activity which can be shown to be in some way peculiarly and uniquely concerned with Him. In a way, the rôle of this activity must in its relation to other forms of human activity refract the unique relation of God to His creatures; the relation between the activities must be grounded in the relations between their objects, but these relations are such that if as a matter of fact there is anything which can be called a special activity orientated upon God, then this activity must in some sense include other forms of activity, without in any sense robbing those forms of their own dignity or their claim to be for the men who exercise them effectually occasions of communion with the Divine. Butler leaves unresolved the question of the relation between what he calls the love of God and, for instance, the pursuit of justice and the promotion of human welfare as a whole. Yet he leaves his readers with a sense of a problem there. He insists that 'everything is what it is and not another thing'; and yet he will try (systematically in the *Analogy*) to find relations between them which are not in the end examples of mere aggregation.

It may well seem to the reader that this introductory section has gone on too long; yet the relation of religion and ethics is a very complex matter. Religious imagery, as in the case of the utilitarian, may enter into and shape the way in

R

which those may see the problems of human life who are strongly antagonistic to the claims of traditional religious authority. A man may give frankly religious accents to his onslaught on metaphysics, on the appeal to mysterious faculties of intuition in whose name every sort of cruelty has been justified. He may denounce the spirit of reverence for law, invoked sometimes to justify the supposed self-evidence of retributive principles of punishment in the name of respect for fact. We may ask, of course, how deep this language goes, how great its power, whether it has any sort of 'logic'. We must ask what we mean if we say there is sometimes a religious impulse behind the onslaught on metaphysics in the utilitarian style.

Again, we must ask ourselves, where Kant's language is concerned, whether he is justified in speaking of his achievement as 'destroying knowledge to make room for faith'. If the knowledge is a name for transcendent metaphysics, we must ask what justification he has for using the word 'faith' in connection with that exaltation of the *Sollen* by which he wishes to replace it. Certainly, however, we may learn much, not least in respect of the interplay of the languages of ethics, metaphysics and religion, if we go on to discuss the relation between faith as Kant understood it and some aspects of faith as we meet it in a classical document of the Christian life: and to this we now turn.

B. GRACE AND FREEDOM

It was made clear in the chapter on Kant that what Kant called faith was rigorously subordinate to morality; he would never allow that the disinterestedness of the moral man's motive should be tainted by expectation of reward for duty done, or fear of pain for following on its dereliction. Moreover more profoundly, for Kant, a morality which sought to please God or somehow to be in accordance with the nature of things would be a heteronomous morality; in following its dictates, even in the discipline of the inmost springs of their actions, men would not be laws to themselves; they would stand under an authority external to their own practical reason. It was allowed in the chapter on Kant that Kant invested the moral law with a definitely impersonal character; it was through the willing submission to its authority for its own sake that men were admitted, in their relationships one with another, to membership of the realm of ends. In their day-to-day actions, wherein this obedience was particularised, if the spring of those actions were human affection, by acceptance of the authority of Kant's supreme principle that affection ceased to be, in his words, *pathological* and became *practical*; one might say that for him the movement from ἔρως to ἀγάπη was effected through the submission of what belonged to the particular situation and desires to the impersonal, objective, searching judgment of law universal. For Kant, as was more recently mentioned, it was the form of law universal which commanded, even as by its presence within us it alone provided the means of fulfilling, a complete disinterestedness. Only the moral law demanded properly to be sought and affirmed for its own sake alone.

For Kant any form of heteronomy, any concessions to the language of heteronomous ethics, were forbidden. To admit any other authority, any other universally valid principle of action, beside the moral law, or as somehow supporting its unique authority, would be to query the unconditional quality of that authority. This makes Kant the sworn enemy of any form of ethics which will enable us see the place of moral obedience, in a wider context, in being as a whole, to use traditional phraseology; this, of course, as we have seen, does not mean that he has not a great deal to say on the relationship of characteristically moral experience to other forms of language and awareness. But it does mean that his quarrel, for instance, with the utilitarians is not simply on the ground that for them moral obligation is justified only by what is achieved for the welfare of mankind through acceptance of its authority. Certainly such an attitude converts the categorical into the hypothetical imperative; but Kant rejects more profoundly the attempt to derive the 'ought' from the 'is'. Whether he admits it or not, the Benthamite has an ontology; granted that this is brought out much more clearly in the writings of some of the logical atomists, we can still, while admiring their greater subtlety and sophistication, see the same *style* of doctrine among the champions of psychological atomism who preceded them, and even committed the fundamental mistake of supposing that in fact philosophy and psychology were one. The Benthamites believed that one could give an account of the sorts of things that there were; and from this they moved out into the territory of ethical and social science in which they were particularly interested, and in which they were confident that the sorts of things and the sorts of laws they would find would be in no way formally different from the sort of things and the sort of laws Newton had established in nature. For Kant such a method was utterly mistaken; and in the chapter on Kant some of the grounds he offered for this judgment, through his analysis of scientific method, have been considered.

It is far harder to answer the question whether Butler's ethics would also have been judged by Kant heteronomous in respect of their principle. For Butler men are laws to themselves; but that is not the whole of the matter, and one cannot find in Butler anything quite like Kant's separation of the realm of nature from the realm of ends. Certainly Butler insists that men are distinguished from animals by the presence within them of a unique and authoritative principle of reflection; yet he will allow, however inconsistent this may be, that that principle requires illumination, and that it must be trained, or train itself, to let its attention wander over the most easily unnoticed and neglected elements in our human nature. The passional side of human nature must be reckoned with in its detail; and it is an interesting thing to notice how sometimes when Butler is discussing the propensions, he will suddenly interject an

explicit reference to the authority of the religious imagination. Thus when he is discussing how in our nature pity and
resentment complement one another, and is actually preaching on forgiveness, he will ask his hearers to think of a man
on his deathbed, even to consider themselves in that situation.
The reference to death transforms the argument; the
preacher's appeal is now overtly religious. He is not speaking
of the rôle in human life of a pity expressed as mercy in certain situations, which has been purged of corruption through
proper distinction from sentimentality. Rather he is asking his
hearers to think of the human situation in the moment of
death, to ask whether they would wish someone who has in-
jured them to die with no word of forgiveness spoken, or
whether they themselves would be prepared to die with no
such utterance from the lips of any they had themselves offended. Butler is not referring to the penalties which have been
thought by some to await the unforgiving heart; he is rather
appealing to men's sense of the peculiar solitariness of death,
which they all await, the frontier and limit not only of human
language, but of human life. 'A language is a way of life.'

To write in these terms is not to imply that a word whether
of regret or of forgiveness, lightly spoken, is of any significance in respect of the undoing of the past. Whatever Butler's
shortcomings as a moralist, he never supposes seriously that
what has been done can somehow, in a moment, be undone.
He is continually aware how men oscillate between a pity
which compromises with honesty and truth, and an inflexible
insistence that things done shall be recognised for what they
are, which can end by closing the doors on the possibility of
mercy, or even of aspects of a total human situation outwith
its ken. Because we are as we are and not otherwise, because
our nature is inherently complex, we have to accept this being
pulled in two directions, always preparing ourselves to correct whichever impulse is in ourselves the stronger.

We cannot somehow rise to a level in which the conflict
between the claims of justice and of mercy is somehow for us

once for all overcome. If religious faith seems sometimes necessarily engaged on the side of pity, that engagement is only valid when the claims of justice and veracity have been most painfully acknowledged. Our own images of pity and forgiveness are at once trivial and distorted: but if we purify them by recollection of the claims of truth, and of our own facility in self-deceit, they may reveal to us something of the way we should comport ourselves in the presence of those on the threshold of death. It is hard not to find here in Butler an inextricable interweaving of the dimensions of ethics and religion.

Now Kant has much to say concerning immortality, but it is subtly different. He would certainly have suspected Butler's whole approach in the passage we have been referring to, and indeed would have found himself on edge in the presence of the Bishop's empiricism. He would have said that the setting, in the sense in which Butler in his sermons on human nature explores the setting of the moral order, does not matter. If a man goes about the business of moral philosophy as Butler does, even if he makes definite and important concessions to the immediacy of conscience, he is bound in the end to justify morality in the name of the contingencies of our own proper nature; and if he goes on as Butler does in the *Analogy* to trace with great delicacy and subtlety the whole pattern of existence to which these contingencies belong, he is on the way to committing the final fault of resting ethics on ontology, moral awareness on knowledge of what is. His guilt is certainly less than that of some; but Kant might have ventured the ironical comment that it is the intrusion of his religion which, even more than his sympathy with certain forms of utilitarianism, involves Butler in offence.

For Kant such a notion as immortality is a postulate of practical reason; it is in his language a matter of faith, of something men venture when first they have made plain to themselves the categorical and unconditional authority of the moral law. It is, to borrow Matthew Arnold's very useful

expression, a matter of *Aberglaube*; we can certainly not give
to it any content without losing ourselves in the antinomous
exercise of attempting, by means of our categories, to know
things in themselves. For all this, as we saw, there is deep
insight in Kant's approach to the problem of immortality; he
does see how deep, even if we cannot make intelligible to
ourselves the conditions of the fulfilment of such a hope, is our
hope that our labour as moral agents will not be in vain,
suddenly cut short by natural circumstance, such as the
Lisbon earthquake, altogether without our control. If the
realm of nature must be separated from that of ends in order
that the peculiar dignity of the latter shall be established,
we yet need sometimes to invoke the imagery of their reconciliation. And it should be noticed that, even for Kant,
this reconciliation, of which immortality is the sign in terms
of the effectual centre of the life of the individual, is not
something which we desire but for which we *hope*. 'Hope' has
a very different grammar from desire; one can hope for that
which one knows it would be pointless to desire either in the
way a man may desire a drink, or success in an enterprise, or
even the improvement of his character in certain respects.
Yet hope is not mere wishing in the way a man may wish it
had not rained on his birthday, or that it will not rain for his
holiday, or that he may live to see the beginnings of space
travel. A man does hope, of course, to recover from an illness,
or that a friend's marriage may turn out well. We understand
what it is to hope, and we know that, among other things, to
hope is not to demand, to exhort, even to request; what we
hope for we acknowledge by hoping, to be in part outside our
power. There is an element of *receptivity* in hope. Of course
Kant cannot explain the way in which the hope of immortality is related to other sorts of hope we have and are quite
familiar with; the language is wrenched into a new context in
which we do not know what we are saying. And moreover
the matter becomes worse if we use the less personal but more
abstractly metaphysical jargon of the reconciliation of the

realm of nature and the realm of freedom. We simply do not know what we are about in the sudden marriage of incompatibles, of abstract technical terms and of something pathetically familiar to all who, in times of bereavement, have heard the question, 'I wonder if I shall ever see him again?'

Of course for Kant it is in the context of the *Sollen* of morality that supposedly the question receives its proper context; if in such a context we still do not know what we are hoping for, we are at least clear what such hope is not. It is certainly not for something which will suddenly over-ride that situation in which we know the authority of the moral law upon us; it will not be a kind of vision which will enable us to stand, as it were, outside the unconditional authority of the moral law and take the measure of that by which we are ourselves measured and defined. Yet such hope is, for Kant, more than the icing of the human cake; although, in old-fashioned language, it is an accident rather than an essential quality of our manhood, its rôle is singularly important. In a way, Kant comes near here the old-fashioned language of religious eschatological expectation; men await, even if they do not know what they await, and that even to speak of themselves as awaiting is to presume the presence of the form of time which, for Kant, is notoriously only the subjective form of characteristically human awareness, and is barren of significance outside its context.

But we must note that the word 'receptivity' has made its appearance. In the chapter on Kant it was rightly emphasised that, for him, the receptivity which for the religious man may well lie near the heart of his characteristic outlook had no place in morality, except in so far as men were morally bound to scrutinise to the best of their powers, with all the expert help which they could command, the details of the situation in which they had to act; to plunge headstrong and pave a way to hell with one's supposed good intentions was no more morally virtuous for Kant than the spirit of Augustine's

prayer, 'Make me pure, O Lord, but not yet.' Where receptivity enters into morality, there the frontier is passed between
autonomy and heteronomy. Men no longer carry the
moral law within them, as the form which they must impose
upon the manifold circumstances of their lives and the manifold stirrings of their desires; they have to await the deliverances of extraneous insight. Moreover the rôle which the
religious moralist naturally assigns to receptivity seems to
invade and overthrow the citadel of freedom. Just as the
admission of a unique revelation may seem to set a barrier
against the unimpeded movement of an exact thought which
knows only the authority of those laws which it has itself
prescribed and acknowledged, so the suggestion that, where
his actions are concerned, a man is in such a way in the debt
of the divine grace that, when he acts virtuously, he cannot
claim what he does as his own, seems to impugn the sense in
which he is creatively the author of what he does.[1]

If we are to face this problem, we might do worse than turn
to a major classic in the religious literature of the Christian
Church, namely Paul's second Epistle to the Corinthians.
This letter raises acute critical problems; yet it contains both
Paul's *apologia pro vita sua* and some of his most profound
reflections on the theme of grace and nature. Thus he reveals
in his letter much of the inwardness of his spiritual life; and
·yet he describes in a way which might be thought boastful, if
one could not almost see the smile on the writer's face, the
extraordinary physical and psychological endurance which
he can lay to his own credit. He does by the emphasis of his
language certainly claim that these things are his own doing
and suffering; and he invokes them as signs of his apostolate.
This he is certainly concerned to defend against critics and
enemies who had denied its validity; but he spends less time
on circumstantial defence of himself as an individual, than on
laying bare to his readers the sense of apostolate, which

---

[1] I owe much here to unpublished writings of Prof. W. G. Maclagan, of the
University of Glasgow.

indeed he treats as a kind of category determining the way in which he sees his own life. Take away the notion, and in fact you destroy the letter (? letters) as coherent and intelligible.

But what sort of category is the category of apostolate? Can we regard it as an ethical category, as we may regard goodness or moral obligation? It will be remembered that Kant has treated both of these in the context of his underlying conviction that the moral existence of human beings can be revealed as conforming to the pattern of a single form which is the source of its peculiar quality and authority. But no one could read long in the second Epistle to the Corinthians without seeing that for Paul apostolate was something particular and determinate; it is (to borrow again Scheler's useful language) a 'material value' which cannot be reduced to terms of anything except itself, which demands to be expounded in its own terms, and which certainly cannot be brought under some general rubric which finds moral excellence in all its manifestations to be in the end the disciplining of the particular by the universal. For one thing, Paul is emphatic that his apostolate has its source and sense in terms of a particular group of events, some of which all would admit as almost certainly having in some sense happened, others of which might be thought likely by some and possible by others, and others of which, however many would dismiss them as illusory to-day, would have been treated as actual occurrences by Paul. Certainly apostolate cannot be understood apart from these events; yet as Paul expounds the sense of the notion, his language becomes almost extravagantly that of the *Gesinnungsethiker;* he will list his endurances, he will even refer indirectly to his visions; but his style is one of a mercilessly introspective self-scrutiny. Of course he does not forget himself, the particular man with the particular associations, history, weaknesses, peculiarities of experience and quirks of temper; but, remembering all this, he presents himself as judge not by what he has achieved, vivid though his memory of that may be, but by what God has worked in him, his apostolate. It is that which makes his life significant, gives it what validity it has; it is by that that he must measure not simply his failures of nerve and action but inmost springs of that action and his very will. He will even welcome, as matter of boasting, disorder of mind and body as enabling him to enter more clearly upon the inwardness of apostolate, and others, perhaps by the very unattractiveness of the circumstances of their realisation, to see that inwardness more clearly, to respond to Paul as one whose significance is in the One who sent him.

The language is that of a *Gesinnungsethiker*; but it is not formalist. Whatever the roots in Rabbinic tradition of the notion of apostleship, Paul uses the notion here to point the sense of his own life, to illuminate that sense by means of it, and even while he does so to enlarge the frontiers of the notion. Of course the immediate background-use in respect of Peter and the rest is significant; so too is the characteristically subtle and allusive language of John concerning the sending and authorising of the Son by the Father. To mention this immediate background is to stress the materiality of the value Paul rates so high; it also helps to bring out that if we are to lay bare the peculiar quality of Paul's *Gesinnungsethik*, we must attend to that notion which supremely conditions and shapes it, in which is present the peculiar sense of the relation of temporal to eternal that gives to the movement of that ethic its peculiar style. We do not have to go far in our analysis of the notion of apostolate before we see that its discussion involves us in a particular view of the nature of what is; Paul's religious *Gesinnungsethik* has its sense in relation to that which he believes to determine his mission. His ontology may be strangely unlike that of Aristotle or Aquinas, Berkeley or Russell; but it is there all the same. What he believes to have happened is something qualitatively different from anything else which has happened before; and to it he will defer now in one way, now in another. He eschews appeal to any sort of self-evident intuition, whether of what is excellent or what is binding upon him. His style is rather descriptive, as if illustrating by his practice the superiority of 'is' over 'ought'.

Yet he has much of the style and temper of the more familiar sort of *Gesinnungsethiker*; it is not only that he has a certain indifference to success or failure; it is rather that he reveals, by way of what he judges it worth-while to include in his letter, how highly he regards the significance of his own endurance, his own self-discipline, above all, his own self-effacement, so that in him and through him men may see that which alone makes sense of his mission; and this, he makes plain by his procedure, cannot be done unless they are admitted to the dialectical twistings and turnings of his relentless self-scrutiny, the paradox of his acceptance of complete self-abandonment (in a sense like and unlike the self-abandonment present in Kant's acknowledgment of the universal) and yet of his joyousness, his vaunting, his confidence. These words indicate psychological states, picked up, and given new definiteness, by their use here; and the language of 2 Corinthians is in part a deliberate violation of an individual's privacies, as if the mere overt record of his doings were insufficient for the disclosure of that which, he would claim, defined what he was.

The Epistle gives us many examples of religious language. It is, in fact, 'a doing things with words', a self-definition in communication, which is itself a contribution to the fashioning of the self which is defined. Paul is apostle only in such communication, only in such self-scrutiny. To say he is writing about something called 'apostolate' is to say something which in its way is as mistaken as to call the 'I will' of the bridegroom a statement about marriage.

But again what is going on belongs to a particular context, has its sense by reference to a particular definition of his work Paul has received. Kierkegaard wrote a vivid essay on the difference between a genius and an apostle, in which he brings out the extent to which his mission obliterates the individuality of the latter so that we cannot speak of him as creative in the way we speak of the genius. Granted that the creativity of the genius achieving unimagined new possibilities, whether in insight into the fundamental order of physical nature, or in musical composition, or in the visual arts, is different from that of the man who can count his own a victory against besetting temptation; yet still we dwell on a common originality our language allows us to recognise in both. It is not mere metaphor when we speak of the poem which the partners to a successful marriage have written. We are certainly advertising less the discipline and the struggle than the achievement; but we are taking for granted that when men achieve something, whether in literature or in human relations, they have made something themselves of the possibilities open to them.

With the apostle it is different. He does not possess the detachment of the artistic genius which the latter owes in part to his sense of the worth of what he has done; and he cannot easily use the language which suggests that, in virtue of the law within him, he is himself the source of that self-scrutiny through which he lives. He does not allow that his action only requires to pass the universal test of such a formal validity as Kant laid bare. His test is almost one of correspondence: certainly not the correspondence of a photograph, but such a correspondence (not unlike the one we mentioned in connection with Butler) as will enable men to see through him, and himself to deepen his sense of being possessed by that which has laid hold of him.

At first sight, the apostle may seem far removed from the contemplative, and the reader may be tempted to say that the one has as little to do with ordinary human life as the other.

But (i) both apostle and contemplative alike agree in their realism, in their sense of the appropriateness of the language of correspondence; what they try to affirm in conduct, to seek through self-discipline, is there to be affirmed or to be sought.

Both alike within the context of such a realism take up the

standpoint of a *Gesinnungsethiker*. But it is only within the context of such a realism that they do so. There may be differences between the way Paul speaks of his mission and, e.g., the language Bernard uses of the necessity of loving God for His own sake. Yet both alike see the spiral movement of their thought and teaching set in motion by that which is.

(ii) It was remarked in an earlier chapter that the image of the saint is still fashioned after the likeness of our human nature. Paul remains a Pharisee, and also a human being. Butler is emphatically right in saying, in answer to every sort of distraction, that we must reckon with our nature as it is. We are men and women; and if we identify our whole duty with the following of a part of it, then what is neglected will surely somehow catch up with us. We are men and women, and particular men and women at that. Yet one can surely allow that in the understanding of that life we owe something to those who, by a concentration of their affections and will, imaginations and intellect, have disclosed the lines of a very special, even a unique and novel, level of existence. Granted that the revelation will be impoverished in so far as other parts of their whole human nature have been neglected, yet still, if that to which they have given themselves has had a quality of genuine inclusiveness (in the sense indicated above and to be developed later), they have enlarged our sense of what may await our humanity.

We are not many of us likely to be apostles; yet apostolicity, as Paul analysed it, is a value (*Wert* in Scheler's sense) which we can begin to understand in something of its uniqueness if we speak of it as an ethico-religious category. We do justice to the way Paul writes in the Epistle, and at the same time show that, while what he therefore describes is so intimately fused with himself as to give the work the character of *Apologia pro vita sua*, yet still what men have seen realised in him can be fulfilled in other contexts and other relativities. Similarly with what we call contemplation, and especially in respect of that which shares with apostolate. The inexhaustible riches of the transcendent in whose near presence men are still, and in which they rejoice for its own sake, are something by which men are drawn to forsake all else; the end of that quest is obscure, and when one speaks of it as contemplation one is only borrowing a word to take and bend to new and unexampled use. Certainly there must be in true contemplation something of what was certainly in Paul, a disciplined, even a painfully won, submission to something wholly other, so that one's life becomes in the end (the language is metaphorical) so much a disclosure of that other, so much a transparency, however broken, that it almost ceases to be anything else. Thus it is that Paul can rejoice (almost as Kant, in Schiller's verses, coveted the loss of affection the more resolutely to do to his neighbour 'duty for duty's sake') in the very afflictions that are laid upon him, as making him more and more one whose sense is in the One whose Apostle he is. And, of course, our crucial criterion of the reality as distinct from the illusory quality of that to which one has thus given oneself is love. 'One is judged in the end by love', said John of the Cross; and Paul in his letter makes it plain that he is concerned both to communicate and, as it were, take into himself the most intimate distresses and perplexities, faults and shortcomings of those to whom he is writing. He offers the picture of a kind of relatedness to God, hardly won, being won perhaps even as he writes; and as he endures the things which he describes, he makes them serve the cause of a supernaturally disinterested love.

It may be worth adding, almost as an appendix to this section, a further reference to the sort of situations in the lives of ordinary men in which the values affirmed by contemplation and apostle touch their familiar occasions.

(*a*) Thus to return to what we have previously mentioned, if we recall men *in articulo mortis*, in that last solitariness, we may be more ready to forgive if we have been offended. Of course, we must suspect such a readiness at such a time as a kind of sentimental self-indulgence; but even if we dismiss it on such a ground, we still wonder: we may even begin to ask ourselves what we mean by the man's 'life' when we speak of that 'life' as 'over'. What is it for 'life' to be *over*? In a way we know perfectly; but the contours of our language are unstable, and perhaps when we consider the 'pure pastness' of the dead we do wonder a little concerning the unity, even the secrets, of the life which now is ended. There may be 'revelations'; the letters to an unknown mistress may be published, curious, almost pathological quirks of character disclosed, the vanity of years made subject of general laughter. But what can we say of the man now dead? If we allow our imagination to play at all round this notion of a life now finished and done with, we begin to acknowledge a kind of reverence which restrains our judgment and our comment, as if we were aware of a quite other perspective from which this life, now a finished thing (however incomplete), is plain for what it is. But of course this is only possible, as has been said, if the claims of veracity and justice are somehow satisfied.

(*b*) Again, it is very easy to diminish, in imagination, the duties of 'special obligation', and sometimes they have to be over-ridden. A widowed mother may prey on her only son to the virtual destruction of his whole life as well (of course) as of hopes in marriage; he may have, in the name of his public responsibilities, to disregard her complaints in order the better to serve mankind at large, to use his gifts in a way best calculated to promote the interests of his fellows. A man *may* have to sacrifice his capacities for the costly, intimate, necessarily time-consuming obligations of private life in order to give himself to public work; but he must see what he is doing. He must not identify his choice simply as one of the ways to the 'greatest happiness'; he must acknowledge the qualitative difference between the two things he has weighed in the scales against each other.

Here again a recollection of religious perspectives may restrain a man, in the sense of preventing him from seeing his choice as other than it is, as something which leaves many

claims unacknowledged, that indeed leaves him, with problems still to solve, claims however properly disregarded that
he must yet somehow meet.

Of course these examples do little more than illustrate a
supremely difficult practical problem, namely how these
things, apostolate and contemplation, these values affirmed
by the saint, can be extrapolated, can even be made to bear
on the different contexts of mere ordinary work-a-day existence. But these are crucial examples of the sort of values
which must be so extrapolated; they express the sort of
insight which is peculiarly religious. Certainly it may spill
over beckoning us, as Butler saw, particularly when our passions are engaged, whether pity or anger, or when we are prepared to justify some temporary indifference to the special
needs of others in the name of something we call the general
welfare. In both cases, different though they are, the spilling-
over may follow a different course: in the former subduing
either our vindictiveness or our sentimentality by recalling the
solemnity of death, in the latter, more indirectly and less by
the evocation of a strangely compelling imagery, than by suggesting to us that we cannot take liberties with the actual
complex of our nature. Butler's agnosticism, so significant in
his criticism of Shaftesbury's utilitarianism, is grounded in his
receptivity; and that receptivity has its source in religious belief, in the sort of religious belief we see at its flash-point of
self-conscious affirmation in the life of the saint.

If this example (of Paul's *apologia*) is at all genuinely illus-
trative, we need go little further to show how strongly Kant is
contradicted. A perfect level of moral achievement is, it is
suggested, a matter of submission in a special way, of which
apostolate is one illustration. Worse (for the Kantian), the
language which Paul uses makes it plain that he would, as far
as possible, claim nothing for himself, make himself a mere
'vessel' through which someone other than himself could
work. Such an outlook may show, with Kant, the *Gesinnungsethiker's* indifference to material success; it may, rightly

s

in the Kantian view, stress the interior purity of motive; but, in the end, it destroys the very character of moral individu ality. The method of destruction may be more subtle than the now familiar derivations of 'ought' from 'is'; but, in the end, moral excellence is dethroned from its unique and universal position, and something substituted that at once submits the moral individual to heteronomy, and at the same time endows that heteronomous certainty with features which, in a peculiar way, detract from the moral dignity of that individual by seeming to set the moral universal in some sense *below* the contingent and the particular. The *Sollen* of law universal is for the Kantian ultimate.

For Kant and his followers there cannot be moral discovery, in the sense of the revelation of new values. The force of the moral law is universal and inclusive, and whatever commands men morally can be shown as boding forth the form of its unique, universal, and final sovereignty. Certainly the haphazard of the Mediterranean world of the first century is not the place to look for a new category to which in any way we should subordinate the evident supreme principle of morality, or allow as admitting us to a perspective from which we can see our moral obedience as somehow subservient to something transcending it in significance and dignity. Even to speak of a *setting* of our obedience to the moral law, even to mention the resources of illumination we may receive through a recollection of the complexity of our nature mediated through religious perception, is to impugn the single universal authority of that law.

We cannot have it both ways. If 'ought' implies 'can', then morality is independent of anything we can call metaphysics, ontology, religious revelation, what you will, even hostile to them. Morality is that in whose light we see everything else whatever; and the task of the critical philosopher is to enable us to see and measure the consequences of this. The many-levelled model of human nature, of which Butler offers us one example, and Pascal with his triad ('order of charity, order of reason, order of nature') another, belongs to different universes of discourse which, for all differences one from another, agree in a kind of empiricism, and in an admission of the authority of styles of self-discipline, touching intellect, emotion, and imagination, that cannot be admitted by Kant. They cut across his formalism, even though, in ways soon to be suggested, those who think in such terms have a 'form of life' which beckons and commands them in ways analogous to the universal moral order of Kant.

In the chapter on 'Ethics and Politics', and indeed in earlier chapters in this book, it was revealed how deeply the understanding of Kant's argument in ethics was increased when an attempt was made to schematise his doctrine of the free, responsible person in terms of the relations of the individual to the State. Then the doctrine appeared as one which presented the individual as set under a law which was that of his own rational nature, endowed with a power at once to judge policies and his attitude towards them by a standard which was at once authoritative and part of his endowment. No doubt the language of endowment here is a philosophical convention, an echo of the theory of 'innate ideas'[1] with which Kant's theory of categories has some kinship, and of which, from one point of view, it could be regarded as a bold re-interpretation. But Kant's meaning is plain: we do not confront the institutions under which we live as clay to be moulded one way or another. No doubt the mythology of the *tabula rasa* served the 'perfectibilians' well in their polemics against the invocation of the doctrine of original sin to justify the worst kind of absolutism. But that mythology could also provide the means whereby the 'benevolent despot' could be defended as providing the most effective instrument for achieving human happiness; and it requires little imagination to see how Kant's individual, obedient of moral obligation only to that law of which he was himself the author, could stand against any such illusory

[1] His categories are dispositionally innate ideas.

claim. Certainly one could derive from Kant's conception a criterion for judging one form of political constitution superior to another; one might well express this in terms of Whitehead's touchstone for the presence of political progress, the 'gradual substitution, in the settlement of differences and the management of affairs, of methods of persuasion for those of coercive force'. But, for him, the morally responsible individual, in the inextinguishable dignity of his freedom, is the axis of his world-view; and if the schematisation of his life in political terms helps us to grasp its sense, we may be similarly aided by opposing it to the religious attitude we have been exploring.

We are now in a position to notice three points of fundamental opposition:

(a) For Kant, morality requires no beliefs about the nature of what is, whether these beliefs be religious or beliefs of a very different order about the nature of the world. Of course a man must be prudent and show every sort of care and foresight in action, and this will mean that he will have to attend to the detail of the situation in which he must act. There is a wide difference between the man who plunges in ignorance, but whom we call loosely 'well-intentioned', and the man who does try to weigh the whole situation to which he must respond, considering what course of action may prove destructive and what beneficial in the light of that knowledge. Thus when, for instance, a man is suffering himself from an acute neurosis, his good intentions in rushing in where angels fear to tread do not acquit him of responsibility for the damage which may ensue.

But morality in itself is something which is altogether independent of the contingencies and idiosyncrasies of individual character and circumstance. By the form of law universal we are all bound. And therefore Kant cannot allow that a special quality of life is open only to those who have acknowledged the peculiar and unique significance of a way of behaviour grounded in, and expressive of, certain beliefs concerning the way things are.

(*b*) This difficulty occurs especially when the beliefs involved, the beliefs of which Paul's life (in our example) might be judged an effective parable, can hardly be expressed except in terms of a transcendent metaphysic. One may say that Paul's behaviour is something inescapably one with the content of his beliefs; so that (to adopt a line of thought ably developed in Professor R. B. Braithwaite's Eddington Lecture[1]) when he says 'I believe' he means that he will act in a certain way, even that he is so acting. On such a view belief would be identified with a way of life, Paul's beliefs with his way of life. But if one tries to set out this way of life, one has to include in the exposition the speaking of certain sorts of words, the making of certain sounds—the speaking, we must emphasise, of these words, and not others. Of course one can then say that it is only these which have the peculiar incantatory power required to help realise this way of life, and not another. But if one says that, one is in fact in danger of tying the scaling of certain heights of moral and spiritual achievement to the use of certain incantatory symbols, and a strict Kantian would scent an element of heteronomy here, especially if in the peculiar quality of the life there was indicated an effort to catch at anything in experience or circumstance which would lend itself to description in terms of an idiom akin to that employed in the so-called incantation. Thus no reader of 2 Corinthians can doubt how significant for Paul was his sense of the overwhelming importance of the crucifixion and resurrection of Jesus. Though these things were unique, in some of the greatest passages of his letter he is bold to see them at work, as it were a law, in his own life. It is not that he crudely and self-consciously imposes a certain interpretation on his experience, to his own glory; it is rather that he presents himself as beginning to understand the ultimate secret of his own life and, by such understanding, to see more clearly the sense of that by which he understands it. No doubt certain historical and metaphysical questions could be by-passed by saying that the

[1] An Empiricist's Approach to Religious Belief (CUP 1955).

credenda had done their work when they enabled a man to achieve a certain level of life, or to be brought to it; for, in what Paul writes about, receptivity and activity are fused together. But still the *credenda* have not functioned as an *Aberglaube* in the sense of, e.g., Kant's belief in immortality. One has to allow that, *behaviouristically* viewed, they have been constitutive; they do not simply provide men with an image whereby they can keep before their minds the abstract possibility of a reconciliation of the realm of nature and that of freedom.

(*c*) But most crucially freedom is jeopardised. It is not that, for Kant, freedom is an arbitrary, lawless, unpredictable thing. As we saw, it has a quality of primary, initiating causality; but it is not a 'leap in the dark', a blind *Entscheidung*, justified, as Existentialists' *Entscheidungen* sometimes seem to be, by the violence of the agent's rupture with any intelligible ground or justification for what he does.

Yet still a man's freedom is inalienable and imprescriptible; and we have to ask what becomes of his action if he takes the law of that action from outside himself to the extent not only of acknowledging that he receives *ab extra* its principle, but that he must regard its very accomplishment as something which he has received. True, he may point, as Paul does, to the range of his endurance; but is it his own? Is it tolerable for a serious morality to speak of 'our sufficiency as being of God'?

When Kant's standpoint is thus sharply opposed to that of a religious morality, we begin to see in a new way what he is arguing for; and we also begin to see what it is that must happen if we allow such categories as apostolate to enlarge our concept of the good life. We can no longer then be formalists, in the Kantian sense certainly; but if we so rate a kind of receptivity, a kind of openness to the transcendent, a kind of readiness to be broken in pieces if only one can be a conduit of the divine in the manner of the saint, we have also to reckon with the reality of the criticisms brought against such a scale of values from the point of view of a universal morality. If we say (as, for instance, Max Scheler) that the saint is a supremely significant ethico-metaphysical category, and by saying so commit ourselves in some sense to the use of the language of 'material values', what is our attitude in face of the moral criticism of religious institutions and ideals?

We are familiar with the fact that Kant's standpoint has received new force from restatement in the setting of such effective protests as those made by Mr. Isaiah Berlin against degenerate political metaphysics of decayed Hegelian inspiration. The language, the very key-notions such as those of metaphysical agnosticism and autonomy, have received new force. Even those who are sure that Hegel's insight remains significant have had powerful warning. If we find through Hegel deeper understanding of the predicament of men in modern society, if we are enlightened by his brilliant enlargement of the use of such familiar concepts as alienation, we are compelled to see that the opposition of 'ought' and 'is' remains. We are enabled to admire Hegel the moral philosopher, the subtle explorer of the frontiers of the problems of political philosophy, without accepting those interpretations of his idea of 'reconciliation' which would make of it simply a glorified way of vindicating what is going to happen anyhow! Something analogous must surely happen when we pause to set his conception of the way men should live over against that way which somehow regards as supremely significant, the realisation in such a way as to reveal them as constitutive of a life lived, of the values of revealed religion. To this we must now turn.

C. MORAL DISCOVERY

M. Albert Camus, at the end of his very valuable study, *L'Homme Révolté*,[1] presents the picture of certain Spanish Catholics who, remaining convinced of the truth of their faith, refuse the consolations of its practice while serving

[1] Gallimard—1951.

sentences in France's gaols, in protest against the readiness of the Catholic Church to rely on every sort of coercive method to extend and maintain its sway. Such men are in one sense divided against themselves, at war with themselves; committed, at one level, to admitting the supreme significance of a certain institution effectually conveying the ultimate secrets of the divine mercy, and, at another, to following the principles variously articulated by Mill, Dostoevsky, and Kant.

Certainly one may say that they see human life in terms of a many-levelled model. There is faith; and there is freedom. Presumably they are convinced that, in the end, the methods of the Church must be those of Christ, not of the 'Grand Inquisitor' .And in order to affirm this, while still confessing that to which the Church bears witness, they try to incorporate in their lives that which they have learnt from those who, often in protest against religious tyranny, have esteemed most highly the mystery of human freedom. If they have learnt from Kant, they seem to have used the language of 'material values' in order that they may present to themselves his vision of human life as something which they may choose to affirm; even as in Butler's many-levelled model of human nature a man may, in certain circumstances, believe himself justified in postponing his fulfilment of particular, intimate obligations, to the service of the common good.

Are such men ridiculous, or are they significant? Certainly they help one to see in a new way the problem concealed by the familiar phrase, 'the relation of religion and ethics'. Certainly no one who believes, in any sense, as Paul believed can ever be the same again. He cannot discard his peculiar categories; they will always intrude themselves and he will know that he can never quite accept the word of those who tell him that, e.g., they can be seen simply as transcribable into near-universal terms, as Kant may have thought he had distilled the essence of the distinction of ἀγάπη and ἔρως in that of practical and pathological love. In Pascal's term, the 'order of charity' cannot be dissolved in terms of that of 'reason'. The man who has once been religious will always recall the phenomenological uniqueness of his viewpoint, even when the secrets of human life seem elsewhere, or when his experience of the world has outgrown the elementary confidence of early years.

The Spaniards of whom Camus has written have acknowledged in themselves the conflict between the way of faith and the way of conscience, and have therefore illuminated both. They have presented us with an instance of a new style of rebellion: one that is not Promethean, but rather endeavours, at the inmost level, to affirm simultaneously receptivity and autonomy, an autonomy given new sharpness of outline in near-contrast with receptivity. Can such a thing be done, or even said?

We suggested above that it was Kant's weakness that, in seeking to set morality free from any sort of heteronomous bondage through the criticism of metaphysics, he yet drew its frontiers too sharply and defended them with too impenetrable fortifications. This he did even while insisting on the dynamic quality of the form of the moral law. What we saw in one way in attending to Paul's account of that self-slipping in which his charity was rooted, and through which his apostolate was effective, we had seen in another in the references to Hegel's insights. The actual circumstances of human life are too various, the involvements of the individual too complex, for his freedom ever to be the simple, almost intuitively evident thing Kant suggested it. If we have to affirm its simplicity, that affirmation borrows its sense from its context; and therefore it can no longer be regarded as an immediate deliverance.

So too in the field of the relation of ethics and religion, we see from the example with which this section opened that men can make of freedom a value they affirm, while acknowledging a road to holiness through ways established among men by that institution against which they are protesting.

To speak in such terms is to suggest that within the in-

dividual alone can be achieved anything which can conceivably be called a reconciliation of the standpoints of
receptivity and of autonomy. For only within the individual's
life can recognition be given to the paradoxical fact that in
some circumstances the one, and in some the other, represents
the true opening of horizons. Thus a man for whom obedience
to the form of the moral law may seem to confine him within
a perspective that foreshortens the embrace of his compassion
and seems to condemn him to passing a judgment on his neighbour which forecloses altogether the reach of that compassion,
may be enlightened by the sudden revelation of another
point of view whose authority he can affirm by his charity,
however tentatively and incompletely. We all know what it is
to find no alternative to condemning others; to have been
made aware of their shortcomings in such a way that we have
no alternative in integrity but to condemn them. When a
man, for instance, comes to see clearly and almost in spite of
himself the spiritual poverty and brash self-conceit of those
whom in youth he has trusted, he is bound to condemn. Yet
he may hesitate, as if somehow he would grasp the limits of
that judgment. His affection is not dead, and he would, if he
could, draw the sting of the judgment into himself. Such
impulse may be pathological; but it is there in men, and even
suggests the pull upon them of an order of love to which they
cannot themselves attain, but which in moments, which are
often moments of great weakness, they believe themselves to
be raised.[1]

Such experience may even take the shape of a prayer for
the purification of memory, that we remember those to whom
we are indebted for good or ill as they are. We would recall
them not simply so as to repudiate and condemn clearly what
was at fault in them, nor so as to blur by false sentiment a
fault deeply woven in its consequence, into one's own
present. We start with the rough assurance that we see the
situation aright in terms of the objective, impersonal stan-

[1] Cf. the references to Butler's remarks on death.

dard of the moral law through which things are given their right names, and we are no longer able to deceive ourselves, in their respect, without fault. But we seek to move beyond such a viewpoint, to be conveyed to another; and this not simply to enlarge our theoretical understanding, but to admit us to the practice of a new and most intimately personal caring for each as he or she *is*. But what they *are* we can never know; yet we can all of us, perhaps, know when we are set upon the road of such knowing. For Paul this was the conformity to Christ of which he wrote in 2 Corinthians.

Here is something which liberates, even though it is something received. But sometimes men can be so holden to the esteeming of such receptivity that the presentation of the reality of autonomy becomes a liberation, seems to open the doors of the 'open society'. The ethical formalism which presents the reality of self-discipline, under the universal authority of law, as the *essential* dignity of men breaks down barriers, combining effectively a sense of the irrelevance of all material principles, and of men's power to affirm the 'realm of ends' in the most diverse situations. It is a vision of the most obstinate and complex situations, whether individual or collective, as somehow patient of receiving the impress of that rational order to whose affirmation men are bound, which gives to the 'autonomist' the feeling that his language delivers the heart of the human matter from the illusory, quasi-metaphysical side-tracks of 'material ethics'.

To live out both sorts of principle at the same time, to affirm the significance and the '*givenness*' of the way of charity and yet at the same time to admit that men can acknowledge no higher good than obedience to conscience, may seem to some the attempted affirmation of two mutually exclusive sorts of values. Or it may itself embody a practical essay in the reconciliation of the religious temper of receptivity and the characteristically moral temper that insists that freedom is something never to be over-ridden. Certainly history suggests that men in their many-sided, many-levelled nature require always to do justice in some measure to its every aspect, taking notice not least of what it can do even with that which beckons its understanding beyond itself, enabling it, *per speculum in aenigmate*, to discern something of the hidden secrets of human destiny. And the philosopher who is conscious here of a marriage of incompatibles may remember the problem he has already met in Butler's many-levelled model of human nature, with the element of real discontinuity between its elements.

Moral discovery, growth, advance, however one describes it, is a fact; and if one concedes its possibility, one's general view has to make room for its occurrence. If preferred, remembering how much of the business of the world is carried on in words, one may say that one has to leave room for new ways in which the individual may present to himself his conduct that yet establish themselves as valid. Sometimes one will want to describe this as the establishment of a new category, like apostolate; and sometimes one will see that the way to it lies through the attempt to work out in oneself a reconciliation of contrasted attitudes. But if what beckons and directs one lacks the final exactitude of the Kantian form, yet there is in the abiding constant of human nature that context in which what one seeks to affirm receives embodiment, and is put to the test. The saint ever bears a human image. *Securus judicat orbis terrarum.*

D. CONCLUSION

But the question remains. If we speak and write thus, do we speak and write sound and fury signifying nothing? Of course for Kant the denial of the possibility of metaphysics is a cardinal movement in his argument; for Paul too the idols in his mind, including his false views of himself, had to be smashed; Butler was agnostic in his own special way, so subtly different from Kant. But all alike take for granted, as valid, the standpoint of a *Gesinnungsethik*, and speak from within it. If Paul involves his reader in a unique way, in

trying to understand certain metaphysical propositions which
he seems to take for granted, he is still not writing a metaphysical treatise, but a letter, belonging at once to his mission
and to his self-definition; his 'metaphysic' belongs to that
context.[1] Yet he does regard the enterprise of such self-
definition most seriously, even as Kant the pursuit of disinterestedness. Butler too saw that men's actions were, in the
end, compact of outward and inward; and a man could not
dodge judgment, at the latter level, by pointing how good,
at the former, were the consequences of what he had done.

We are left at the end of this study with the question, at
once theoretical and practical, which at so many levels the
utilitarian puts to the *Gesinnungsethiker*. Are such concerns as
the latter makes his own, mirage? Do the ultimates of human
life lie on the level which he has made his special concern? Or is
he weaving patterns out of nothing which share with the
constructions of the speculative metaphysician the vice of
turning men away from the effort to better their lot and that
of their fellows? Certainly if we say that it profits nothing for
a man to gain the whole world and lose his soul, we must
continually see how valuable and significant a thing, at once
for oneself and others, such gaining may be. Butler was surely
wise in his insistence that the rôle in human life of rational
benevolence must be taken very seriously indeed. But is it the
whole of virtue? That question certainly lies close to some of
the most important issues at present bracketed together under
the confusing rubric: 'the possibility of metaphysics.'

---

[1] One might say that something similar was true of Hegel inasmuch as, in the
Jugendschriften at least, his 'metaphysics' grow out of his attempt to establish the
proper way of freedom, the proper manner of the exercise of responsible choice,
the proper way of human life. It is his strength that he sees such an attempt
cannot avert attention from the concretes of human history, his weakness that
he fails to see how he has allowed the highly questionable religious vision of
reconciliation that he finally invokes to assume the character of a general idea,
fusing together universal and particular. He failed properly to appreciate the
ethico-religious context out of which his metaphysics grew, and tried in fact to
find in the latter a means of, as it were, putting the former in its place; although
he understood the meaning of the rubric *fides quaerens intellectum*, he failed to
follow out its consequences.

INDEX OF NAMES

Aquinas, St. Thomas, 102, 112, 259

Aristotle, 1, 14–15, 18, 24, 29, 57, 81, 149, 196, 214, 244, 259

Arnold, Matthew, 5, 101, 174, 179, 254

Augustine, St., 115, 121, 163, 256–7

Ayer, Professor A. J., 28

Barth, Karl, 241

Baumgardt, David, 145 n.

Bentham, Jeremy, 2, 3, 4, 5, 18, 20, 24, 25–6, 28, 32, 35, 36, 37, 45, 48, 58, 85, 111, 112, 114, 145, 151, 170, 182, 194, 198, 213, 228, 229, 247, 252

Berdyaev, N., 46, 97

Berkeley, George, 26, 27, 153, 154, 155, 163, 245, 259

Berlin, Isaiah, 47, 124–5, 126, 128 n., 130, 135, 147, 148, 159, 170, 171, 207, 208–11, 212, 213, 215, 217, 271

Bernard, St., 235, 244, 262

Blake, William, 18

Bradley, F. H., 5, 96

Braithwaite, Professor R. B., 269

Broad, Professor C. D., 179, 245

Büber, Martin, 94

Burke, Edmund, 36, 37, 40, 96, 105, 199, 216, 227, 228, 230

Butler, Bishop Joseph, 2, 3, 10, 64, 85 n., 119, 174–202, 203, 213, 217, 218, 219, 222, 223, 231, 232, 236–7, 244, 248–9, 252–4, 262, 265, 266, 272, 274 n., 276, 277

Campbell, Professor C. A., 128 n., 148, 161–2, 164–70, 171

Camus, Albert, 271–2, 273

Carlyle, Thomas, 83

Cassirer, Professor Ernst, 66, 120

Coleridge, S. T., 45, 47, 58, 151, 229

Collingwood, Professor R. G., 9, 32, 41, 57, 71, 92, 111

de Burgh, Professor W. G., 118

de Gaulle, Charles, 171

Descartes, Rene, 123, 127, 149, 153, 158, 162, 163

Dickens, Charles, 5

Dostoevsky, F., 97, 272

Einstein, Albert, 67, 74

Eliot, George, 87, 95, 108, 111, 230

Erfolgsethik, 50–8, 121, 124, 134, 139, 144, 145, 146, 149, 150, 155, 166, 217, 224

Fichte, Johann G., 144

Forsyth, P. T., 119

Garrigou-Lagrange, R. P. R., 154

Gesinnungsethik, 58, 61, 64, 85, 91, 121, 124, 139, 144, 145, 150, 155, 160, 161, 165, 166, 168, 169, 173, 181, 183, 217, 218, 219, 220, 222, 223, 224, 227, 232, 258, 259, 260, 262, 265, 276, 277

Gilson, E., 158, 163

Green, T. H., 2, 3, 4, 5, 46, 212

Halevy, Elie, 40

Hardy, Professor G. H., 247

Hegel, G. W. F., 7, 48, 70, 104, 119, 126, 147, 168, 200, 211, 215, 216, 218, 220–1, 223, 224, 225, 231, 237–43, 271, 273, 277 n.
Heidegger, M., 270
Hilbert, 248
Hitler, 86, 227
Hobbes, Thomas, 185, 187, 199
Hügel, Baron Friedrich von, 75
Hume, David, 2, 121, 153, 154–5

John of the Cross, St., 263
Jones, Dr. Ernest, 132 n.
Jones, Henry, 4
Joseph, H. W. B., 2, 3, 4, 5, 18, 166

Kant, Immanuel, 2, 3, 4, 17, 23, 61–120, 121–3, 126, 129, 133–4, 135, 143–4, 145, 146, 147, 153–5, 158, 159–60, 164, 166–9, 170–1, 172, 174, 177, 182, 184, 200, 207, 208–11, 212, 213, 215, 216, 219, 222, 223, 231, 233, 234–6, 241, 242, 243, 246, 247, 250–2, 254–6, 258, 260, 261, 263, 265, 266, 267–8, 270, 271, 272, 273, 276, 277
Keats, John, 18, 170
Keynes, Lord, 5, 13, 14, 15, 17, 18, 48, 49, 55, 234, 247
Kierkegaard, S., 7, 104, 240, 241, 260
Koestler, Arthur, 73

Laird, Professor John, 3, 143
Laplace, P. S. de, 77, 78
Lawrence, D. H., 17, 18
Lenin, V., 231–2, 242
Locke, John, 153, 174, 191, 198
Lowes Dickinson, G., 2, 12
Luther, Martin, 105

Maclagan, Professor W. G., 257
Malcolm, Professor Norman, 157 n.

Mannheim, Dr. Karl, 149, 153 n.
Marx, Karl, 7, 48, 147, 168, 242
Mill, James, 33, 34
Mill, John Stuart, 2, 3, 5, 8, 20, 44, 46–7, 48, 50, 54, 56, 58, 62, 92, 93, 95, 97, 130, 151, 165, 170, 213, 226, 227, 229–30, 231, 236, 248, 272
Moore, G. E., 2, 3, 4, 5, 10–11, 12, 13–14, 15, 16, 17, 18, 19, 20, 48, 49, 50, 51, 55, 56, 57, 152, 163, 165, 234, 247
Mussolini, 86
Myers, F. W. H., 87, 111

Newman, John Henry, 184
Newton, Isaac, 33–4, 36, 49, 56, 68, 154
Nowell-Smith, 2

Orwell, George, 133 n.

Pascal, Blaise, 118, 266, 272
Paton, Professor H. J., 64 n.
Paul, St., 172, 257–63, 265, 269–70, 272, 273, 275, 276
Plato, 1, 2, 7, 85, 118, 191, 244
Plekhanov, G. V., 242
Popper, Professor Karl, 67, 74, 83, 106 n., 241
Price, Professor H. H., 2, 63
Prichard, H. A., 2–4, 5–6, 7, 8, 9, 10, 19, 48, 94, 126, 180, 184, 221–2, 243

Richard of St. Victor, 97
Ross, Sir David, 186, 187–8, 243
Rousseau, J.-J., 85, 118, 228
Russell, Bertrand, 196, 234, 259
Ryle, Professor Gilbert, 39, 126, 137 n., 153, 154

Scheler, Max, 2, 129 n., 130 n., 133 n., 258, 262, 271
Schiller, J. C. F. von, 263
Schilpp, Professor P. A., 13

Schlick, Professor Moritz, 109, 154
Shaftesbury, Earl of, 178, 217, 265
Sidgwick, Henry, 32, 63 n., 92 n., 125, 128, 186
Socrates, 7, 47, 50, 54, 58
Solovyev, W. S., 46
Sophocles, 237
Stephen, Fitzjames, 46
Streeter, Dr. B. H., 174

Taylor, Professor A. E., 23, 75, 163, 179, 243 n.
Taylor, Jeremy, 177

Toynbee, Arnold, 147
Trilling, Lionel, 218, 224, 239, 242

von Balthasar, Hans Urs, 103
von Mises, 76 n.

Webb, Professor C. C. J., 246
Wisdom, Professor John, 7, 63n., 127
Wittgenstein, L., 7, 17, 157
Woolaston, W., 175–6, 178, 182, 185, 193
Wordsworth, W., 151